Mable —
Blessings for your
journey!   *Mary*

WINNING
with a Bad Hand

A Story of Love,
Loss,
and Healing

Mary Christopherson

Mary Christopherson

Halli Press, 2005

To Duane Gary Leach

My Knight in Shining Armor

I Love You...Don't Forget

What others are saying about

WINNING
with a Bad Hand

"**What a memorable love story!** I'm sure it will bring deep meaning to the lives of many others who are facing the difficult journey that Mary and Duane took. Their ability to find love and peace was remarkable: a good model for us all."

— **Marilyn Mason**, PhD., LP

"In this book Mary Christopherson looks at the courage and compassion it takes to be with yourself and your loved one as he goes through a terminal illness. Finding that deep vulnerability and grief is what allows healing to be possible. So this story of courage, compassion, and healing is really a story of love."

— **Sandy Tribault**
Healer and Transformational Coach
Founder of Selma's Spirit
www.selmasspirit.com

"I am proud of my little sister and her gift of the word. She has written her difficult story with love, pain, sensitivity and passion–giving hope to others who are suffering in grief, not knowing how to see their angels."

— **Barbara Holmstrom**
Caregiver

Author's Notes

Some of the names of people in this book have been changed to preserve confidentiality.

To preserve the flavor and authenticity of the email messages, they will remain in their original form with only minor editing for clarity.

Bible passages are taken from the New King James Version.

Your Daily Motivation from February 14, 2002 was written by Max Steingart, used by permission. © 2005 by Max Steingart www.maxsteingart.com.

ISBN 0-9769208-0-8

LIBRARY OF CONGRESS CATALOGING —
IN PUBLICATION DATA

Cover design by Cindy Brueck and Mary Christopherson
Cover Photo by Loren Burkel, May 2002
Back Cover Photo by Diana Folkman, Proex Portrait Studio
Typesetting by The Sketch Pad, Cindy and Maxine Brueck
First Printing: June 2005   Lightning Source, Inc.

Halli Press
15050 Cedar Avenue #116-142
Apple Valley, MN 55124
(952) 432-2935
mcchristopherson@msn.com

Table of Contents

Acknowledgements

Writing this book has been a true labor of love. Revisiting the events of the past two years has enabled me to heal in ways I could never have imagined. I am honored to have shared Duane's final journey with him, and I am honored to share our story with you.

Writing a book was not my intent. My original intent was only to send updates regarding Duane's condition via email to friends and family members. Thanks to several of those readers, especially to my classmate Jan Bergman, who encouraged me to share our experience in a book, this account of our journey is now a reality. This undertaking would never have been possible without the help and support of countless others.

Without the care of skilled physicians, especially Drs. John Trusheim and Mary Loken, our story would not have been possible. These dedicated doctors, along with their nurses, Kathy Gilliland and Bonnie Rasmussen, treated us with respect and compassion while enabling us to have not only time, but *quality time* together for as long as possible.

The care given by the staff members of the medical communities—especially the Apple Valley Medical Center and its Snyder's Pharmacy branch, the oncology unit at Fairview Southdale Hospital, the rehab department at Fairview Ridges Hospital, and the staff at Ebenezer Ridges Care Center—made our ordeal not only bearable, but often enjoyable! Thanks to all of you for you kindness and support.

Although I cannot possibly name everyone, I am grateful

to all of you who prayed for and encouraged Duane and me all along our journey. The power of your prayers was revealed as we continually received comfort and strength. What could have been a devastating, lonely experience became a blessing not only to Duane and me, to many others as well. May God bless all of you who readily joined our team — our families; the Loose Ladies; THHS classmates of 1964; members of the Minnesota Valley In-Fisherman Club; our "Duluth friends"; my coaching colleagues; our co-workers, past and present; distant friends and relatives across the country; the congregation and prayer team at Prince of Peace; and others, many of whom are strangers.

Thank you to Prince of Peace for an outpouring of support. A large congregation such as this is often thought to be too big to care. This was not our experience. Thank you to the pastors, staff, and Spiritual Care ministers, especially to Pastor Paul Gauche, Rich Mavis, and Stephanie Schrope, for being the hands and feet of Jesus during our ordeal.

Duane and I have been blessed with loving, supportive families who embraced us both, providing us with strength and encouragement. Thank you to — my mom, Martha Erickson, for her love; my sister, Barb, and brother-in-law, Loren, for providing a safe haven; our children Eric and Kris, Ann and Tom, and David and Christi, for their unwavering support; and to the grandkids — Chase, Payton, Elina, Nadia, Will, and now Max and Dylan- for joy and hope for the future.

It is not easy to walk alongside a grieving person in the depths of despair. I am grateful to have had Dee Bailey, a certified grief coach, as my mentor, trusted friend, and "soul sister" walk with me, showing me that amid the chaos, I was normal. She showed me the path to healing.

I am grateful to have had many talented people help me make this book a reality. Thanks to my editor, Pat Samples, and my publishing coach, Michael Chioti, for their enthusiastic support while working with me on this project; to Jan Pedersen, Sandy Thibault, Marilyn Mason, Ph.D., Jackson Huntley, Ph.D., and my sister, Barb for pre-reading my manuscript and offering encouragement along with valuable suggestions.

Finally, to Duane, thank you for loving me, for believing in me, and granting me permission to tell our story. I love you. Don't forget.

Preface

Love is not a matter of counting the years;
it's making the years count.
– William Smith

—•—

Duane Leach and I were two ordinary, very different people, who came together in mid-life and discovered a deep, unshakable love. Eight years later, I lost him to an insidious, unrelenting disease — gliobastoma multiforme, a grade IV brain tumor.

When Duane and I met, we were both content with our lives and set in our ways. Having lived alone for over fifteen years, Duane was fiercely independent. He didn't welcome change. His entire life revolved around fishing — it was his passion. He was fastidious about the upkeep of his boat and his fishing equipment. The upkeep of his neglected, cluttered bachelor pad, however, was another matter.

My life revolved around my family, my friends, my job, and my church. I lived in a tastefully decorated condo filled with Scandinavian knickknacks, Lake Superior art, and photographs of my passion — my family, especially my toddler grandson, Chase. I ardently claimed to be independent, yet I wanted someone to take care of and someone to take care of me.

Our introduction at a wedding rehearsal changed the course of our lives. The attraction was immediate. Cautiously we built a relationship. Although our personalities and lifestyle differed, they complemented and completed each other's.

Duane was my spouse, but we never married in the eyes of the state. We married in spirit, committing to each other and our relationship. Accepting our differences, we loved each other for who we were, imperfections and all. As the Serenity Prayer suggests, we changed what we could (ourselves), accepted what we could not (each other), and somehow knew the difference.

We were anticipating the best days of our lives when Duane was diagnosed with a deadly brain tumor at the age of fifty-nine. Suddenly we were navigating precariously through uncharted waters. During the first uncertain weeks, I was given a book written by a psychologist whose husband had also been diagnosed with gliobastoma multiforme (a name I was just beginning to pronounce). "Ah, help at last!" I thought as I began reading the account of their journey. Halfway through, I put the book back on my shelf, unable to finish it. This couple had no faith, thus no hope. The man died, as had been predicted, within six months of his diagnosis.

The end of Duane's journey was never in doubt. We would fight the relentless tumor, though we knew it would kill him, just as it had killed the man in the book. Yet our experience was entirely different from that of the other couple. We always had faith. We always had hope, even though we didn't expect a "miraculous cure." Our hope was to be able to play the hand we had been dealt well, to give our best to each day, not just get through it.

"Is this a day to which I gave my best?" In a sermon aimed directly at me, this question was posed by Mike Foss, senior pastor at Prince of Peace, my church in Burnsville, Minnesota. Pastor Mike showed us two decoys. The first was mass-produced. There was nothing wrong with it; it was functional, but it was not unique in any way. He showed us the manufacturer's name stamped on the bottom. Thousands of decoys exactly like it were made that same day. The second decoy was exquisite, hand-carved and hand-painted, detailed, a one-of-a-kind work of art with the artist's name signed on the bottom.

Pastor Mike had said our days are like those decoys. What did we want to create? At the end of the day would we proudly sign our names to what we had created? Or did we just show up and get through it? It was our choice.

Each day is a treasure. It is all we have and it is enough. We need to choose wisely. Pastor Mike reminded us that we have only so much time, talent, and energy. With unlimited possibilities and demands, our choice is rarely "good vs. bad;" more often it is "good vs. best."

Early in Duane's journey we each, in our own way, chose to live every day seeking the "best." In what could have been the most devastating time in our lives, we discovered the magnitude of our love for one another. Our faith in God grew as he sustained us, comforted us, and loved us every day, through every step of the journey. We learned to live in a state of gratitude. We realized the power of prayer and the power of love.

Just weeks before he died, Duane held my hand and looked deep into my eyes with a gaze that to this day makes my knees weak when I remember it. He asked, "Babe, this past year we've had our ups and downs, but it hasn't been so bad, has it?" Bad? Absolutely not! It had been the best year of our life together. Our relationship flourished in ways that we never dreamed imaginable. In the words of my daughter, Ann, "Mom, you and Duane taught each other how to be."

When people asked how we got through it, the answer was simple: We always asked God for help, we always got it, and we always said, "Thank you."

Each of us experiences devastating, life-altering challenges in our lifetime. This is how "best" looked to us and how we lived it. At the end, we gladly, boldly signed our names to our journey.

A Really Bad Hand

Life is learning how to play a bad hand well.
– Rudyard Kipling

━━━◆━━━

She stood before us in the surgical family waiting room looking more like a fresh-faced medical student than a highly skilled neurosurgeon. This tiny woman, still dressed in her blue scrubs, had just operated on my beloved Duane, removing as much as she dared of the tumor in his brain. As she spoke, I felt my heart shatter. "You guys have been dealt a really bad hand," she began. Was she speaking to us? Or was I overhearing life-changing words meant for another family? Her words echoed in my mind, "You guys have been dealt a really bad hand, but within that hand everything has gone right. We bought him some time."

I was numb with shock. In a daze, I walked away seeking solitude in a quiet corner. I thought I was alone, unaware of my friend Carol's hands bracing my trembling shoulders. Looking up towards the heavens, I shook my clenched fist and I angrily called out, "God, why do you keep thinking I am so strong? I'm just this weak little nothing."

A psychic once told me, "Your life has not been an easy one. You have experienced many opportunities for growth." She was right. With all those opportunities, I should have been ten feet tall, not five foot two. My first husband betrayed me, leaving me and our two young children for my best friend. My second marriage was a fraud. It wasn't until I was in my early forties that I met the first man who truly loved me;

1

he turned out to be a paranoid schizophrenic. I had learned and grown from each heart-breaking relationship, starting over time and time again. Now, in my mid-fifties, having at last found the love of my life, I faced losing him to a brain tumor! Didn't I deserve to be happy? Didn't I deserve to be loved?

For seven years Duane and I had enjoyed a loving, secure relationship. He was my soulmate, my knight in shining armor. Now we had "bought him some time." In frustration and anger, I had cried out to God. In my soul I heard his answer, "Who are you to question God? If I say you can do this, you will do this." "Okay,"' I meekly replied, "but you've got to help me." Somehow I knew he would.

He leads me beside the still waters. He restores my soul.
– Psalm 23:2,3

Closing my eyes, I returned to the safest place I had ever known, if only in my mind — the pristine bay on Burntside Lake near Ely and Minnesota's Boundary Waters. This rugged land of ancient granite and towering pine had been my refuge since I was a child of four. I no longer owned the property but in my reverie I could still sit on the end of my dock in the early morning stillness, listening to the sound of waves lapping on the sand beach, the whoosh of the breeze high in the white pines, and the familiar call of the white-throated sparrow to his mate. It was here that I would begin my days at the lake, connecting to God. Now, at least in my mind, I was far from the terror of the hospital, feeling peace and strength surround me again.

I remembered the morning of July 4, 1995. As usual, I had begun my day at the cabin meditating on the end of my dock.

2

At forty-eight, I was satisfied with my life as a whole. My two children, Eric and Ann, were both married, and I was a devoted gramma to Eric's toddler son, Chase. I owned a condo in a Twin Cities suburb and had an adequate job as a mortgage loan processor. My co-workers and I, a group of ten women dubbed the "Loose Ladies" by one of the loan officers, were best friends, in and out of the office.

Though I had recently begun dating again after being unattached for a few years, the results had been disastrous. Not wanting to make any more mistakes, I had made a list of the qualities I was looking for in a man. Topping my list were: 1) he had to have a good job, 2) he had to dress well, 3) he had to be physically fit, and 4) he had to enjoy dancing.

"Is there anyone out there who is right for me?" I asked God that morning. "If not, I can live with that, but would you please take away the need? But if there is someone, could you send me a sign?"

I enjoyed the early morning quite a while longer, then turned to leave, ready to start breakfast for my clan who were still asleep in the cabin. A voice in my head whispered, "Look unto the hills . . . ." As I turned around to look at the lake and the hills on the opposite shore, two loons entered the bay, floating in perfect synchronicity, chatting, laughing, diving, and fishing. Transfixed, I stood watching as they moved within a few feet of the end of the dock, so close I thought I could have reached out to touch them. In forty-four summers at our cabin, I had never witnessed shy loons come so near to our dock.

Two days later I entered the front door of Fort Snelling Chapel with my friend Kay to rehearse for her wedding. I was the soloist. She had been trying to fix me up with a friend of her fiancé, Rich, for months, but having met my second

3

husband on a blind date, I wasn't about to repeat that process. Besides, all I knew about this guy was that he was a fanatic about fishing. Why would I want to go out with someone who was a fanatic about anything, let alone fishing?

Just as we got inside the door, Kay introduced me to Rich's friend. Duane Leach was a big teddy bear of a man, ruggedly handsome with gleaming silver hair and a neatly trimmed beard. "Oh, so this is the guy Kay has wanted me to meet," I thought to myself. "He seems pretty nice."

When I placed my order for walleye at the rehearsal dinner later that evening, I heard Duane's playful voice teasing, "You're ordering walleye in a restaurant?" Had I just committed an unthinkable social blunder? It was then I discovered he was not just a "fanatic" about fishing — he was a pro. Most likely he had a freezer filled with walleye fillets. I did not. His brown eyes danced as he winked at me and flashed his engaging smile. The sound of his hearty laughter filled the room, and my heart opened like a rose kissed by the sun. What Fyodor Dostoevsky once said rang true, "If you like a man's laugh before you know anything of him, you may say with confidence that he is a good man."

"Oh, this could be interesting," I thought, remembering another item on my list—a sense of humor. As far as that list was concerned: 1) he did not have my previously required "good job"—he was a professional walleye fisherman, 2) his wardrobe reflected his career, 3) he was big and cuddly — almost a foot taller and at least 125 pounds heavier than my five foot, two inch, 135-pound frame, and 4) as I discovered at the wedding reception, he hated to dance.

At the wedding reception, my chair at the table with the rest of the Loose Ladies remained empty as Duane and I talked for hours learning about each other. Duane was fifty-two, had one adult son, David, and had been divorced from David's mother for many years. In his late forties he had lost his job as an executive vice president and account manager for a large advertising agency and now devoted his life to fishing. After his divorce he had had a couple of serious relationships, but hadn't dated since then — not in more than ten years. "If I met someone, fine," he told me, "but I didn't meet many women in my boat."

Duane kissed me for the first time in the parking lot as we left the reception together, a gesture that I was later told was not his usual style. During the first weeks of our courtship, he would often look at me and say, "I can't believe how beautiful you are." Me? Beautiful? I saw myself as perky, with wispy graying-blond hair, and a nice smile — cute, but certainly not beautiful. But Duane did see me as beautiful, and he made me feel that way every time he looked at me. Like Renee Zellweger's character said in the movie *Jerry McGuire*, he "had me at hello." Apparently, I had him, too.

Duane fiercely guarded his independence. Early in our relationship he told me, "Look. You've got to understand, I fish. If you can live with that, maybe we should pursue this."

Equally stubborn and independent, I replied, "Do you think I lived under a rock until I met you? I have a very full life, and you have to understand that I spend a lot of time with my family. If you can live with that, then maybe we should pursue this."

We dated exclusively for three years, both of us cautious about making another mistake and getting hurt again. During that time, we gradually let down our protective walls as we grew to trust each other. We learned to respect our differences while we nurtured our common interests. We both loved nature and enjoyed spending time together either at my cabin

5

or fishing together on his boat. I was surprised to learn that, like me, my crusty fisherman loved going to the theater — especially productions like Andrew Lloyd Webber's *Phantom of the Opera*. He enjoyed taking me out to dinner, to the movies, and to concerts. He even danced with me — once a year. Gradually we became integral parts of each other's lives. We enjoyed spending time with each other's friends and families. He was on hand for the births of three more of my grandchildren, and I was at his side when his son was married. We were both best friends and passionate lovers.

After three years of dating, on Valentine's Day, 1998, Duane asked me to share his home and his life, a move neither of us took lightly. With tears in his eyes, he placed a Black Hills gold wedding ring on my finger. Our commitment to each other and to our relationship was as binding as any marriage ceremony.

He wanted our home to be a place I would be proud of. Together we fixed up his townhouse, transforming his bachelor pad to reflect both of our tastes. He parted with his orange corduroy couch and the sixties-style dresser adorned with painted orange flowers, but not with his blue oversized Lazy-Boy recliner. His trophy salmon remained hanging over the fireplace, blending nicely with my Scandinavian and Lake Superior art.

We lived our lives as Kahlil Gibran had advised in *The Prophet*. Like the pillars of the temple, we stood "together yet not too near together." Our relationship was loving and strong because we respected and encouraged our individuality and separateness, just as we cherished being together.

I had asked God for a sign back on that July morning and had received one. Duane was my laughing fisherman and the love of my life. He was not what I thought I was looking for, but he was everything I wanted. For the past seven years, we had been as connected as the loons that had entered my bay that morning, and we looked forward to the best yet to be. And now I had been told, "You guys have been dealt a really bad hand. We bought him some time."

So began our story of hope and fear, courage and faith, and love.

For me, it was also a story of loss and rebirth.

The Diagnosis

We cannot control the wind, but we can adjust the sails.
– Cousin Nina's fortune

Our lives changed forever on Thursday, March 7, 2002. The pain in Duane's head was excruciating. "If I have to put in another day like yesterday, I'll have to be put on suicide watch," Duane emphasized to the receptionist, demanding to be squeezed into his endodontist's already full schedule. On Wednesday morning, his boss had sent him home from the car dealership where he worked as a service driver. He had stopped at a green light, gone through a red light, and was "parking the cars funny in the lot." His co-workers said they knew something was wrong when Duane stood around watching everyone else work. The intensifying pain from the root canal surgery he had had two weeks earlier was now debilitating and making him sick to his stomach. When he called me at work Thursday morning, his speech was slurred and he couldn't figure out how to hang up the phone. Expecting to return to my desk later that afternoon, I left work immediately to get him to a doctor.

An hour later, as we walked across the parking lot to the medical building, I noticed Duane was dragging his left foot. Less than two weeks before, when we were shopping for baby gifts for his new grandson, I could barely keep up with his long stride and quick pace. Now he shuffled into the medical building, dragging his foot. In the examining room, Duane held my hand as he reclined on the black leather chair; I felt

9

an unfamiliar ticking in his left hand. His hand also felt cool and clammy, and his skin had a waxy, yellow tinge. After examining Duane, the doctor said yes, the root canal could be the cause of some of this pain, but not all. He prescribed Penicillin for the infection, scheduled another appointment for Duane the following day, and suggested that Duane see his doctor or stop at Urgent Care on the way home — a suggestion that undoubtedly saved Duane's life.

We immediately went to our medical center in Apple Valley where Duane was examined by Dr. Mary Loken, the doctor on call in Urgent Care. All physical and psychological test results seemed normal. Duane knew that it was Thursday, March 7, that George W. Bush was the President of the United States, and so on. He could remember the words "apple, pencil, and table" in sequence after five minutes or so. Dr. Loken's eyes widened when I told her, "I don't know if this means anything or not, but he is dragging his left foot." After observing Duane walk, Dr. Loken scheduled an MRI as soon as possible, thinking he might have had a small stroke. She also mentioned the possibility of a brain tumor.

That afternoon Duane's condition deteriorated rapidly at home as we waited to leave for his seven o'clock appointment at Fairview Southdale Hospital in Edina, about a half-hour's drive from Apple Valley. The soup I fixed him for supper remained untouched as he shivered in his recliner, wearing his winter jacket and gloves while wrapped in my white Icelandic wool blanket. With the thermostat turned up to seventy-five degrees, I thought of how cold he had been for the last few weeks, even before his root canal. We had thought he had a touch of the flu so prevalent that winter. My apprehension intensified as he became increasingly confused and began staring at me with an eerie look in his eyes. Needing some moral support, I called Duane's son, David, and daughter-in-law, Christi, who lived just two miles away, to alert them to his condition.

As Duane and I left our home for the hospital shortly after six o'clock that evening, the first big drops of freezing rain fell as an ice storm descended on the Twin Cities. With white knuckles and a racing pulse, I drove Duane — still wrapped in my Icelandic blanket — to Edina, inching our way on freshly glazed icy roads.

Sitting in the hospital corridor waiting for the MRI, Duane put his arm around me and said, "I must have been a saint in a past life to have gotten you." Maybe he was relieved that I had insisted that he see a doctor that day. Maybe he was afraid and felt safer with me by his side. I felt safer and less afraid with his strong arm wrapped securely around my narrow shoulders. When the technician led Duane to radiology, I watched in disbelief as he walked away from me; he was no longer just dragging his foot — he was staggering, bumping into the corridor wall.

Waiting alone in the radiology lounge, I tried to fit together the jumbled pieces of the past months. When did this start? After returning from a fishing trip to Canada the previous October, Duane told me that he had taken Excedrin by the handful for frequent headaches and pain in his teeth. He had root canal surgery as soon as he got home. In November, he had a complete physical and was given a clean bill of health. But he had a second root canal surgery on another tooth in December and a third in February, just two weeks ago. At that time Duane was told to expect a considerable amount of pain and was given a prescription for Percocet. Not only did he experience pain, he was tired all the time, and cold.

He hadn't felt well enough to go on a Fishing Club couples'

11

outing at a favorite restaurant in February. On March 2, when we attended a baby shower for his grandson, he spilled his coffee and was unable to unwrap a small gift from Meg, his ex-wife. Monday he asked if I minded driving my car when we went to my sister's house for dinner. Duane had never asked me to drive before, not even after he broke his wrist the night before our vacation driving around Lake Superior. Two days earlier he had been too ill to attend the Republican caucus, something he never missed. Today he had misplaced the stamps and return address labels on the mail, and couldn't figure out how to hang up the phone. So many things. What else did we miss?

David and Christi, with two-week-old Will bundled in his baby carrier, braved the ice storm to join us at the hospital for the MRI. Of course David would be there. Duane had always been a devoted father, and he enjoyed a close, loving relationship with his son. He and Meg had been divorced since David was a child, but they always put David's welfare ahead of their own. Whatever their differences had been, they were first and foremost David's parents. Now that Duane was in trouble, his son was by his side.

My own son, Eric, in the Cities for a business meeting, joined us at the hospital to await the results. Both he and my daughter, Ann, were terribly fond of Duane, not only because of the quality of his character, but also because for the first time they saw their mom in a loving, happy relationship. How supported and loved I felt when he arrived and put his arms around me saying, "It'll be ok, Mom. It'll be ok." If only it were that simple.

When Duane joined us in the lobby to wait as the MRI was being read, he seemed irritated, looking at David and Eric as if to say, "What are you doing here?" The sudden ringing of the lobby phone broke the tension. Duane answered it. With a dazed look on his face he announced, "I have something growing on my brain and it has to come off now." David grabbed the phone from his father's hand to get further instructions. For some unknown reason, we were to go to another hospital, in Saint Paul, where a neurologist would be waiting for us.

In a state of shock we navigated the freeways to St. Paul in a treacherous ice storm. At the hospital we came face to face with our new reality as the neurologist, Dr. Ulysses Fowler, showed us the MRI. The hideous tumor was like a giant spider the size of a hockey puck with legs reaching throughout the brain, causing his brain to swell. Our confidence in this doctor waned as he referred to the mass on the "left side," but David noticed he was looking at the film backward. The tumor was actually on the right side. "Great," I said to myself, "Duane's life is in this man's hands and he doesn't know left from right."

Dr. Wendy Fischer, a neurosurgeon, also examined Duane, and again Duane remembered words like apple-pencil-table in sequence. All I could think of was how young this doctor looked. Did she know what she was doing? We had no choice and no time. Something about her indicated to me that she was indeed very competent — and compassionate — as she explained her findings in language we could all understand.

This situation was critical, but we were also relieved to know that at least she knew which side of the brain the tumor was on. The brain stem was also involved, and a major vein in that area was in danger. Duane's left-handedness also posed a serious problem as the area for speech in a left-handed person can be on either side of the brain. If Duane survived the surgery, it was possible he would lose his ability to speak. Duane acknowledged that he understood what she was telling us and signed his authorization for surgery. She said she would remain in the hospital throughout the night to check on Duane in hopes of putting off surgery till morning light.

While Duane was moved to the Intensive Care Unit to be prepared for emergency surgery, Dr. Fowler told David and me that it was time for us to make some serious decisions. The first was whether or not Duane should be placed on a respirator should his breathing become impaired. We both knew Duane would hate that, but we had to give him a chance to survive long enough to have the surgery. Giving consent, we prayed it would not be necessary.

I collapsed in a chair alone in a darkened hallway, sobbing and screaming, "No, no, nooo!" This couldn't be happening. Not to Duane. Not to us. Not now. We had so many dreams with the best years of our lives ahead of us. He had recently become a grandfather. We were counting the weeks till our vacation to Alaska in June. He was my strength, my rock. Now he lay near death and I was frightened and alone, feeling adrift in a tiny boat on a churning, roiling sea. I felt Christi holding me tight. Christi, this beautiful new mom, was comforting me when she too was heartbroken and afraid.

When we entered the ICU, how bizarre it was to see Duane, always healthy, robust, and seeming larger than life, now lying there with IVs dripping steroids into his veins, wires taped to his body, and monitors recording his vitals as he slept. As the minutes and hours ticked by, Duane's brain continued to swell, and he became harder and harder to rouse. More and more steroids were administered through the IVs in an attempt to reduce the swelling. This was critical; if the swelling continued he would die. A brain swelling inside a skull has nowhere to go; pressure builds on the inside, threatening all bodily functions. I knelt by his bedside and prayed that he would survive.

What would happen if he didn't? We had both taken care of the practical things like writing a will and making our final wishes known to each other and to our families, but we never had talked about death in spiritual terms. I knew Duane was a good man, but he was not religious. Attendance at the Methodist church with his parents was a mandatory part of his upbringing, but now his "church" was in his boat on the lakes and rivers. He considered himself to be a Unitarian, although he mostly attended Prince of Peace with me. I didn't know what he believed, although he had mentioned once, "When you're dead, you're dead — that's it." All I knew was that the man I loved had a brain tumor and might not survive the night. No matter what, our life would never be the same. "God, how can I help him face his death?"

Throughout the long night we waited, trying to rest in the uncomfortable upholstered chairs in the tiny ICU family lounge. My sister, Barb, and my cousin Louise arrived sometime after midnight. Eric brought a few niceties from my house — pillows, a thermos with our untouched soup from supper, and my toothbrush. (His new girlfriend thoughtfully suggested that he also include my scented body lotion.) Checking on Duane throughout the night, I could hear the echo of my footsteps — or was it the pounding of my heart?— as I walked alone down the deserted corridors to the ICU.

The first encouraging news came about four o'clock in the morning — the steroids were effectively reducing the swelling. By half past four, Duane was alert and talking again, mostly complaining about his catheter, threatening to pull it out.

About six o'clock another catheter was inserted into his groin, traveling up a vein to examine the brain stem. He had another MRI. More good news — the tumor was contained and the vein was not involved.

We got another break. A computerized device that would map the exact path for the surgeon was already at the hospital from Rochester for another patient. This morning there would not have been time to request it. The technicians who would read it had arrived safely from Rochester in an unrelenting ice storm. As things continued to go our way, we were beginning to have a glimmer of hope.

All of Dr. Fischer's other surgeries were rescheduled, as Duane had become her highest priority patient. In pre-op, she explained the procedure to us in detail, showing us the tiny saws and drills that would be used in surgery. Green rubber dots were stuck to Duane's head, marking the surgeon's path. Only a small area over his right ear would be shaved, leaving most of his silver hair intact. Duane was upbeat and positive as he held little Will and joked with us before going to surgery. We all knew the risks — he might not wake up. If he did, he might be mute. Duane gave me a "to do" list: Call Willy at the dealership and Dave Nystrom, his fishing partner. Cancel his dentist appointment.

Now it was time for him to go. We held hands, looking intently into each other's eyes. His deep brown eyes seemed to look into my very soul as if to take my essence into the operating room with him. He said, "I love you" more poignantly than ever before. I wondered, would he ever say those words to me again? I answered, "I love you, too," then added, " Don't forget." "I won't," he replied as his stretcher was wheeled out of the small pre-op room at ten o'clock headed for surgery. I watched as his stretcher was wheeled down the hall, then out of sight as it turned the corner to the OR. His life was in the hands of the young lady surgeon— and God. And so was mine. I had walked on a bed of hot coals to find this man in my mid-life — my Duane, my knight in shining armor.

The rest of us settled into the surgical family lounge for the long wait. Per Duane's instructions, I canceled Duane's endodontist appointment, then called Willy at the dealership. I was stunned to hear Willy tell me he too had had a brain tumor, and so had Larry, who also worked in the service department. Larry's had been malignant, Willy's had not. Was there a connection, I wondered? They both seemed to be fine now, back at work and leading normal lives once again. At least that was encouraging.

We sat in silence with our pain, our fears, and our thoughts. I remembered the past Friday when Duane and I had our last "date night." We took turns treating each other to a surprise dinner out at a new restaurant on Friday evenings. When Duane got home from work late that afternoon, he called me at my desk, jiggling his glass of Jack Daniels on the rocks in my ear and indicating it was time for me to call it a day. I had made reservations for us at the fireside table at Toby's on the Lake, a charming English restaurant where we sat that evening in large wing-backed chairs in front of a crackling fire. Enjoying our drinks and dinner at a beautifully set table, we anticipated our dream vacation — the gourmet meals we would have and the adventures that lay ahead in Alaska. We were going to do it all — pan for gold, fish, kayak, walk on glaciers, watch for whales, and dance at the captain's dinner. After dinner at home, when were making love, he said, "You know, anyone can do what we are doing, but with us it is so special." Oh, how I loved him. I wondered whether we would we ever make love again.

Support began pouring in as news of our ordeal spread. Fellow Loose Ladies Kathy and Carol had left work and driven in the storm to be with me. Then Meg was there — beautiful Meg, David's mother and Duane's ex-wife and devoted friend. She held me saying, "Mary, I'm so sorry." We both loved him and shared our anguish. She must have been recalling how Duane's father had suffered a fatal heart attack while building a crib for her unborn son. Would Will be another little boy who would never know his strong and loving grandfather?

Six hours later, Duane was in recovery and Dr. Fischer, still dressed in her blue scrubs, tried to assure those of us holding vigil that the surgery had gone well. She had been able to remove much of the tumor, but not all. The brain stem was affected but could not be touched, nor could the many feelers spread throughout the brain. More aggressive surgery could always be done at a later time if necessary, she said, but taking more now would have risked the quality of his life. Pathology should have the results of the biopsy to us on Wednesday. Her words still echo in my mind. "You guys have been dealt a really bad hand, but within that hand everything has gone right. We bought him some time."

We had been given the gift of time. I asked God for help, for the strength to play this hand to the best of my ability and knew he would not fail me. I had also been given the gift of choice. My sister and I had recently sold our beloved lake property for a considerable amount of money, so at this time in my life I was not dependent on my job. I would resign immediately and devote my life to caring for Duane. Whatever time we had left together would not be spent with my being at work.

While we waited for Duane to come out of recovery, I

18

called Dave Nystrom. Dave and Duane had a connection closer than brothers. For eight years they had fished together, and as Dave said, "spent countless hours in boats, trucks, and motel rooms, never having a cross word" between them. Our refrigerator at home was full of pictures of Dave's and Phyllis's two little girls, Kathleen and Maureen. They were Duane's honorary grandchildren. One of Duane's greatest pleasures in life was to leave anonymous Christmas presents for them on their front porch from "Santa's helper," a gesture he never mentioned to Dave.

Twenty-four hours after his initial MRI, my heart pounded with apprehension and gratitude as I tiptoed in to see Duane in the ICU. With his head wrapped in a white gauze turban, he had never looked more handsome to me. He gave me a sleepy smile and said, "Hi, Babe." I thanked God for another miracle. He not only survived the surgery, he could still speak. "Is it cancer?" I answered honestly that I did not know. Next he asked me if I had called Dave and Willy and canceled his dentist appointment — the things he asked me to do just before surgery. After having had his brain invaded, his personality and memory were still intact. God had answered our prayers. He was still my Duane. We had hope.

It was after eight o'clock Friday evening when we left Duane in the hands of the ICU staff to go home. Even baby Will had been keeping vigil for over twenty-four hours. I hadn't slept at all. As we left the hospital, David was looking out for me on behalf of his father, telling me to be sure to wear my boots. I left my car at the hospital and Louise drove me to Barb's, the sanctuary of my family.

Ice storm or no, my daughter, Ann, drove three hours from Duluth to be with me. She held me in her arms as my tears flowed from the depths of my soul. Even with the love and strength of my family around me, all I felt was the emptiness, alone in a room filled with people. Was it only Monday when Duane was here with us frying walleye? Louise commented that she thought Duane had looked terrible that night and wondered if he was ill. She also mentioned how lovingly we had looked at each other.

How would I get through this? He was my rock, not the other way around. I dreamed of growing old with him. Questions of how, why, what could not be answered. My family was hurting for me, especially because they had seen me truly happy for the first time in years. Now this. Life just wasn't fair.

Ann and I spent the night at Barb's. Even after two endless days and a sleepless night, my daughter had to force me into bed. I could not bear the thought of lying down without Duane beside me. My body tried to sleep, but my heart and mind were at Duane's bedside in the ICU.

In the morning we spent an hour chipping ice from Ann's car to open the doors, then inched our way back to the hospital. As we neared the ICU, we were delighted to hear laughter coming from Duane's room. Dave Nystrom was already visiting, leaning back against the wall, flashing his bright smile as he and Duane swapped stories and shared a good joke. Since it was Saturday morning, naturally a fishing program was on TV.

"I knew something was wrong," Dave told me in the hall. "I woke with a start about two o'clock Friday morning" (the same time Duane's brain was swelling and I was afraid he would die). "I couldn't get back to sleep and was ready to jump out of my skin. I was a mess at work all day yesterday, knowing something was very, very wrong in the universe but I didn't know what it was. Then I heard about Duane."

Throughout the day Duane put everyone at ease with the strength and power of his personality. He warmly greeted visitors with a smile, gratitude, and a laugh. We joked about his looking like an American Taliban with his huge brown eyes, his beard, and his head wrapped in a "turban." If it weren't for that gauze bandage wrapped around his head, it would have been hard to imagine why Duane was hospitalized at all, let alone in the ICU. Concerned friends would call and be surprised to hear his laughter all the way from the phone at the nurses' station. His best medicine was seeing Will and cooing, "Ahh, Sunshine," as his infant grandson was placed in his strong arms. We were well aware of the gravity of the situation, but for now we were enjoying Duane, his marvelous smile, his laugh, his sense of humor, and his positive attitude. After another MRI early in the evening, Duane was released from ICU and transferred to a large private room.

The phone rang at four o'clock on Sunday morning, jolting me from a sound sleep. My heart was pounding as I bolted out of bed, fearing it was the hospital calling. "Oh, were you sleeping?" Duane's cheerful voice innocently greeted me. He had a list of things he wanted me to bring to the hospital for him — earplugs, his little flashlight, his box of thank you notes, and a frame for the new picture of the Nystrom girls in their tiaras.

Sunday the storm was finally over and the sun was shining brightly again. Every branch of the ice-covered trees glistened in the sunlight against a bright blue sky. Duane's gauze turban had been removed, replaced by a soft cotton cap like the ones baby Will was given when he was born. Grandpa and grandson both wore their "Will hats" as Duane, dressed in his hospital gown and robe, sat in a chair for the first time since surgery, holding little Will in his big hands now bruised and covered with tape and IVs.

Now we were able to examine the incision that Duane described as making him look like a "poorly made baseball." The area over his right ear had been shaved and it sported a red horseshoe-shaped cut about two and a half inches high and one and a half inches wide, held together with about thirty-five tiny staples. The yellow stain from the antiseptic ointment ran down his cheek in front of his ear, discoloring his skin and his silver beard. This fierce-looking incision was a tangible symbol of the violation of Duane's head, our dreams, and our life together.

By Sunday night, Ann had gone back to Duluth. I went home alone for the first time. The quiet emptiness stung like the freezing rain that had hit my face Thursday evening. It was easy to be positive and strong when I was with other people, and especially with Duane. But now I was alone. Panic engulfed me. What would happen to me without him? I wanted to run, but there was no safe place to hide. Despair began to pull me down to the depths of my fear. My heart pounded in my chest, I couldn't breathe, and I began to shake uncontrollably. Suddenly I felt an invisible cloak of protection and warmth wrap tightly around me, and I was immediately at peace.

Our answering machine was filled with messages from friends and family members saying they had stopped what they were doing many times during the day to pray for us. I could actually feel it. That warm cloak was their love and prayers wrapped around me giving me strength and comfort when I needed it the most. I could feel the arms of angels holding me tight, showing me that Duane and I were not alone. The words "Fear not," pulsed with each heartbeat.

Thoughts of my beautiful young cousin Nina speaking at her husband's funeral the year before inspired me: "We cannot control the wind, but we can adjust the sails."

How does a person get through the worst life can throw at her without love and support from others? In these early days of our journey, we were just beginning to experience a flood of this kind of care through unexpected sources. I had heard the words "communion of saints" since childhood but was only beginning to understand the meaning and power of those words.

Never would I have believed how important the Internet would become in our lives. Just the past year I had enjoyed getting reacquainted with classmates from Two Harbors High class of 1964 via email. Lori, my friend since first grade, had notified them of our situation. Most of them had never met Duane.

———

Friday, March 08, 2002 10:20 PM
Subject: Sad News
Mary's Duane had emergency brain surgery today. Duane is truly the love of Mary's life, and she is really in rough shape right now. Please pray for him to get well and for Mary to have the strength to get through this. Damn! Mary is so happy with him! Can't believe this horrible thing is happening! She really needs the support and prayers, so everyone please say some good ones for them! Thanks and take care all! Love to all, Lori

———

This first night I was home alone, one of these old friends re-sent an e-newsletter from career coach Cheryl Leitschuh that I had forwarded to my classmates on Valentine's Day, just a month before:

23

Mary, My hugs, heart and prayers go from me to you. I thought you might want to re-read this now. Love, Kathy A.

YOUR DAILY MOTIVATION

Thursday, February 14, 2002

LIFE IN ABUNDANCE COMES ONLY THROUGH GREAT LOVE

There is no force more potent than love.
Take away love and your world is a tomb.

Your life echoes emptiness without love
With it, your life will vibrate with warmth and meaning.
Even during hardship, love will shine through.

As you look back upon the events in your life
you will find that the moments that stand out, the
moments when you have really lived, are the moments
when you have done things in a spirit of love.

If you have it, you don't need anything else, and if you
don't have it, it doesn't matter what else you have.

Therefore, search for love.
Once you have learned to love, you will have
learned to live.

Happy Valentine's Day
Cheryl Leitschuch and Associates, 2002

I didn't know what the days ahead would bring. All I knew was that Duane and I had a deep love for each other, that we had loving friends and family, and that God had us in his hands. Whatever was to be, we would get through it together. I knew that somehow we would do this, and do it

24

well. Duane called to say good night and to tell me he loved me, and I was at peace. I went to bed and was able to get a much needed night's sleep.

Monday morning an elegant, yet casually dressed, man strolled into Duane's room. He was wearing a black cashmere turtleneck sweater and soft-looking tan slacks with a well-defined crease down the front of each leg. He bore an aura of arrogance that made me apprehensive at the first sight of him; the hair bristled on the back of my neck. He placed his foot on the foot of Duane's hospital bed and leaned forward, casually resting his crossed arms on his raised knee. His pale blue eyes held no warmth as he introduced himself, "I'm an oncologist."

Oncologist. The word reverberated in the deafening silence. Oh God. He was a cancer doctor. With his introduction, our path was set. Duane's tumor was malignant; we didn't need to wait until Wednesday for the results of the pathology report. My stomach felt like it held a million trapped angry bumblebees. He said someone from his office would be coming to see us to discuss treatment in a day or so. This doctor's words were a blur. I don't even remember his name. All I remember is his comfortable-looking shoe placed casually on the foot of Duane's hospital bed — a soft, tasseled shoe of woven leather, the color of caramels—as he delivered such devastating news.

Duane, David, and I sat in stunned silence when he left. Duane spoke first, "Well, now we know. Let's see what we can do about this." He was ready to fight—strong and encouraging with his "we can do this" attitude. It was he who set the tone by being positive, giving comfort and speaking of hope.

The arrogant doctor had told us we would not be seeing Dr. Fischer any more, that neurosurgeons were "hired like plumbers, to do a job and then they leave." David and I were upset at this prospect because she was the one doctor we trusted. She was forthright and honest, and treated us with compassion and respect. When she came by for rounds Monday afternoon, she was outraged. "Of course" she'd be here. Hadn't someone from her office seen Duane all weekend when she was off? The answer was yes. She made us feel much safer, and we were relieved that she would continue to care for us all. I was also relieved that a different oncologist was coming the next day because I surely didn't like this one. When thrust into a situation as serious as this, we had to feel comfortable with the doctors entrusted with Duane's life.

In spite of this terrifying diagnosis, the festive atmosphere in Duane's room continued. Beautiful flower arrangements filled his window ledge, bringing the promise of coming spring and softening the harshness of the sterile room and the reality of the tumor. An enormous basket arrangement of green plants, complete with a small plastic fish and creel, arrived from the Fishing Club, specially ordered to have lots of "guy stuff" in it. A vase of red and white carnations from the little Nystrom girls was another favorite. Duane was overwhelmed by all the support he received not only from friends but also from others he had never met, like my high school classmates. The thoughtful senders of these arrangements had no way of knowing the impact their gifts would have later that day.

"Hi, Babe. The doctor just left." Duane's voice on the phone was quiet and flat, missing its usual amazing spark. After nine o'clock that night when Duane was alone, Dr. Fowler made his rounds. With only the most negative spin, the neurologist emphasized to Duane how gravely ill he was and the hopelessness of his situation, then left him alone and afraid. "For the first time in my life," Duane told me, "I understand how a person can be so low that they can contemplate suicide. Then I looked around my room at all the flowers, especially the ones from Dave's little girls, and started counting my many blessings." Duane had just learned that day that he had cancer — a very aggressive terminal cancer — and he went to sleep counting his blessings. The damage caused by Dr. Fowler's hopeless scenario had already been undone. I never loved Duane more.

Tuesday morning another oncologist strode into the room, his long white lab coat swaying in rhythm with his quick steps. He was not as aloof as the oncologist the day before had been, and we felt somewhat more comfortable as he explained again the diagnosis in detail but gave us options for treatment. We were facing an insidious monster with an unfamiliar name difficult to pronounce. Gliobastoma multiforme — GBM — is a grade IV tumor, the most aggressive kind. As we were told after surgery, only part of it could be removed and feelers were spread throughout the brain; the rapidly growing tumor could reappear at any time. GBM is a primary tumor, meaning there wasn't cancer elsewhere in Duane's body, only in his brain. That was enough.

The first course of treatment would be six weeks of radiation followed by chemotherapy. We learned about the blood-brain barrier that protects the brain from infection and diseases from other parts of the body, a barrier that also keeps traditional chemotherapy from effectively treating brain tumors. The oncologist wasn't overly optimistic about treating Duane's tumor with more traditional forms of chemo and suggested we register for a clinical trial at the Mayo Clinic for a new drug called Iressa ZD1839. The first step would be to place Duane on a waiting list to see if he would even qualify. We had a little time because the staples in Duane's incision needed to be removed before radiation could begin. We were told to "think about it."

"Think about it." Duane's life was at stake; we were dealing with a deadly, aggressive tumor that we knew nothing about until a few days before; and we were relying on unknown doctors we didn't select. How were we to know what was best? Now seemed like a good time to "know someone"; thankfully, David and Meg did. They had both worked with a prominent woman at the Fairview Foundation who had raised millions of dollars for brain tumor research at the University of Minnesota. Her own husband had succumbed to the disease. Meg said she would contact her for a recommendation. In the meantime, we decided we would also apply for the clinical trial at Mayo.

A steady stream of visitors filled Duane's hospital days, a welcome change from the countless doctors, nurses, and therapists. Many were apprehensive when entering the room; they were immediately reassured by the power of his upbeat personality. Negative Dr. Fowler was "very concerned" by reports of the joyous laughter coming from Duane's room saying we weren't being "realistic" or taking the diagnosis "seriously enough." Did he expect Duane to give up in despair? If so, he had the wrong patient.

Barb brought our mother to see Duane. Mom was terribly fond of Duane, referring to him as her "boyfriend." One of my fondest memories of that time is that of my mother, beautifully dressed and sitting in a wheelchair by Duane's bed, and Duane, dressed in his hospital gown and his Will hat, tenderly holding hands.

Visits from Duane's co-workers Willy and Larry were

especially important; these two were living testimonials of hope. Looking strong and healthy, they were both still working and living normal lives after having been treated for brain tumors a few years before. Now they stood at Duane's bedside offering encouragement and sharing a laugh as they caught him up on the events at work. They had not given up, and neither would Duane.

No visitor was more welcome than was David Vikmark, Meg's sister's husband from Rapid City, South Dakota. David had been diagnosed with cancer the past summer. It began in his spine, now was also in his lungs, his brain, virtually everywhere. As ill as he was, he got on a plane to come and offer support and encouragement to Duane. Walking into Duane's room David looked thin and frail but still handsome in his jeans and black leather jacket. Like Duane he had silver hair and a beard. His blue eyes sparkled with warmth as he shook hands with Duane, eager to offer moral support and practical advice.

David had been through it all and had many positive suggestions for Duane about taking supplements and dealing with nausea from the chemo. He cautioned against eating in the same room where the food is prepared. Aromas once considered inviting could now turn his stomach, much like a pregnant woman reacts to the smell of bacon frying. He even warned Duane about depression. The best advice he gave was, "Follow directions." He promised to get Duane in touch with his own doctor at Mayo. The camaraderie that developed between Duane and David was as important to each of them as any treatment could have been.

Dr. Fischer checked Duane daily and encouraged us to plan our trip to Alaska. She emphasized to me, "I bought him some time, but not for him to spend in a hospital bed." By now I had the courage to ask, "How much time?" She replied, "A year, maybe two," indicating by her inflection she was stretching it. At least now I knew, and I vowed I would love him through whatever time we had left. I would gladly sign my name to each day, having given my best.

Thanks to another ice storm, I spent Thursday night in Duane's room rather than driving home. Since Dr. Fowler always came late after family had left, this was the first time I had seen him since Duane's diagnosis. Speaking to him privately, I understood the despair Duane must have felt after his visits.

"This is as good as he will ever be. He will never get any better, only worse. Have you looked for a nursing home? You won't be able to take care of him. This was what I meant when I told you it was time to make serious decisions." Nursing home? I was stunned. The other doctors were encouraging us to go to Alaska as planned. "You absolutely should not go to Alaska. He will suffer from seizures, you won't be able to handle him, and you will be thousands of miles from home." He was also "very concerned" about Duane's positive attitude. As far he was concerned, this was all but over.

Devastated, I called Duane's son in tears. "That man will never see my father again," he fumed. David and I had agreed that we would make all decisions together. The first of many was that as soon as Duane was out of that hospital, we were getting another neurologist. "If Dad is going to die, I want him to die on his boat or in Alaska." We were going to see that he lived a quality life as long as he could and would not subject Duane to any physician who took away his hope.

Dr. Fowler may have known all the medical facts about this tumor, but he knew nothing about the spirit nor the power of

30

faith. He did not know Duane — and he did not know me. Duane was ready to fight for his life, eager to actively attack the beast within his brain. I was ready to devote my life to join him in his fight.

Dr. Raymond Perez, the radiologist, provided options, a plan, and hope. He was a tall thin man with a large hooked nose, intense eyes, and high forehead, reminding me of my mind's-eye version of Ichabod Crane. Soft-spoken and compassionate, he put us at ease as he explained the next six to seven weeks of our lives. After the staples were removed on Monday, Duane would have thirty to thirty-five treatments of full-head radiation. Lying on a slab, his head would be covered with a custom-made mesh mask that would be bolted down to the slab. Red beams of light would then be aimed at specific spots marked on the mask with adhesive tape. Against the wall were little cubicles labeled with a patient's names, just like the ones at my grandchildren's nursery schools where they put their lunchboxes, back packs, mittens, and boots. Each of these cubicles contained specially fitted blocks of lead to protect unaffected areas from the radiation.

This was like living Star Wars. I would have found it fascinating except for one thing — it would be Duane on that table with his head bolted down. Those red beams would be live beams of radiation directed at his brain. His name was already on one of those little cubicles. Was he as afraid as I was? If so he didn't show it. Neither did I. My conversation with Dr. Fowler the night before didn't help alleviate my fear, but it did strengthen my resolve. This was far from over — we were just starting to fight this thing. At least now we felt we were actively doing something about it.

It was another Friday. Could it have been just two weeks since our intimate date night at Toby's? It seemed like a lifetime ago. Just one week ago was surgery. This was our new life, forever to be defined by the previously unheard of "gliobastoma multiforme."

It was also my son's birthday. As hard as it was to accept, I did have a life outside the hospital. Joining Eric and his girlfriend for dinner, I was going through the motions like watching someone else's life in a movie, with the colors and the noises blurring together. As usual, the restaurant was packed with people enjoying dinner out on Friday night, having a few drinks and carefree conversations. Two weeks ago, Duane and I had been doing the same thing. Now I was an observer, trying to be a mom celebrating with my son on his thirty-fourth birthday. I was not only a devoted spouse, I was still a mom. As hard as I tried, I felt incomplete, like a robot going through the motions but void of feeling.

Monday, March 18, was homecoming. On Sunday, Louise, Barb, and my mother had helped me give my neglected house a thorough cleaning, making it perfect for Duane and the anticipated guests coming to visit him. They also brought Duane's favorite foods, homemade and prepared with love. Many things were out of our control, but preparing for Duane's homecoming was something we could actually do something about.

Prior to discharge, Duane had a very busy day ahead of him. His nurse removed the staples from his head with a tiny pliers, leaving his "poorly made baseball" scar looking better than it had when we had first seen it a week before. Then the various therapists came in to go over discharge instructions and to sign off. With his sense of humor still intact, Duane asked about having a drink once in a while, (occasionally— but that didn't mean three fingers of Jack Daniels). Then giving me a wink, he asked "Most important, can I have sex?"

The nurse replied, "Oh you guys! Sure. Go for it." The post-surgery phase was ending, and aggressive treatment was about to begin.

Hospital patients can't just walk into radiation therapy on their own; they must wait for hospital transport to take them, along with their charts, by wheelchair through a series of hallways, elevators, and overpasses to the secured building. Duane was scheduled to begin radiation at 12:30, right after lunch. Lunch was late, and so was the transport. The always-punctual Duane grew impatient. When a hospital worker came with the food cart, Duane asked her if she knew where radiation was. "Sure," she replied in broken English, "I take you." Suddenly Duane was chasing the food cart down the hall, hospital gown flowing in the breeze. What a sight! Fortunately, transport arrived with the wheelchair before Duane and the food cart got to the elevator, and we were taken, along with his chart, to radiation therapy.

The attack on the remaining tumor began. Duane was taken to the treatment room and bolted down to the slab. The doors closed and he was left alone. This was no longer a dress rehearsal — it was the real deal. I was taken to a small room where I could watch the process on TV monitors. I held my breath as live beams of radiation were aimed at the marks on his mask. We were given a code for the secured parking lot we would use the next day, when he would return as an outpatient; then we were on our way back to Duane's room and home.

Duane's eyes misted over as he looked around in awe and relief at seeing the familiar surroundings of his home as if for the first time. I'm sure there were times he didn't think he would ever be home again. I had those thoughts myself. But now he was home. He easily climbed the ten stairs up to the living room and settled into his favorite chair, a blue oversized Lazy Boy recliner. Before long he had a remote in each hand, checking out his favorite programs on TV. He couldn't have been happier on a cruise ship in Alaska.

The importance of my role as his caregiver was becoming increasingly clear as Christi and I poured over the pill bottles and discharge instructions together, making sure we had it right. We set out a day's worth of medication and wrote out what to take when. She took the list home and printed a month's worth of daily schedules from her computer. What a godsend. Keeping Duane's medications and dosage schedules straight was going to be an awesome responsibility. Only a few weeks ago, all he took regularly was a daily vitamin.

Later that evening David, Christi, Will, and Meg celebrated with us for a family dinner, homemade and at our own table. Our home was filled with the plants and floral arrangements of well wishers, and our refrigerator was filled with homemade meals and Duane's favorite mincemeat pie brought by our friend Dariel Allen. Our hearts were filled with love and gratitude as Duane and I went to sleep together in our own bed for the first time in what seemed like an eternity. It had been eleven days.

The New Normal

Waking up with Duane beside me — a few short weeks ago I had taken this for granted. Get up, shower, have coffee, "I love you, have a good day, see you later," then off to work in the rhythm of normal life. Normal for Duane had been working as a service driver at a local car dealership from November through April, a job he took in his "off season" to supplement his summer fishing tournament schedule. I had been an operations assistant reviewing closed mortgage loan files for a large residential funding company. Our working life now seemed like an eternity ago. Tuesday, March 18, I thanked God for another chance as we embarked on our "new normal."

At home we were no longer dependent on nurses, aides, and transports; we welcomed having some control over our lives again. The schedule of medications with unfamiliar names was taped to the bathroom mirror — Decadron to control swelling, Dilantin to prevent seizures, Aciphex to protect his stomach, calcium carbonate to protect his bones, Tylenol #3 for pain, and Ativan for sleep and anxiety. Carefully I counted out his morning pills as Duane devoured his breakfast of homemade pancakes, bacon, and eggs, along with his favorite blend of freshly ground hazelnut coffee.

At 9:15 that first morning after being home, Duane began treatment as an outpatient in radiation therapy. While sitting in the waiting room I began reading a book written by the wife of another GBM patient. Her account gave me a clear picture of what lay ahead but offered no hope. In spite of the certain outcome of the diagnosis, surely there had to be hope. We may not be able to beat it, but if anyone could play this hand well, Duane and I would.

"I can do this," I told myself. Right after surgery, God had told me I could. "Ok, but you've got to help me," I had bargained. Now I was determined to care for Duane, nourish him, keep him from losing weight, keep his medications and appointments scheduled, and encourage him. Since I was now staying home instead of going to work, I also planned to develop Live-It!, my personal coaching business and continue writing my weight loss program, projects begun earlier that year. I was on a mission, full of faith and hope. I would stay positive — I would do it all.

Caring for Duane was now my main, full-time job. There were countless appointments to schedule — follow-up exams, physical therapy, CT scans, the dentist, the eye doctor, and a new neurologist. Weekly I spoke to the health care coordinator from Duane's insurance company; everything was running smoothly. I also became his advocate, a skill perfected while Duane was in the hospital. Now when a doctor's office did not return my phone calls after several attempts, I marched into the office telling the receptionist, "No, I do not care to have a seat. I'll just stand here in everyone's way until someone finds time to schedule Duane's appointment." Never would I have been this assertive for myself, but for Duane it was easy. He proudly referred to me as "Olga the Hun."

The American Cancer Society provided us with all the equipment we would need to make our home safe for Duane — a booster seat with handrails for the toilet, a chair for the shower, and a commode. We had my aunt's walker there, and the beautiful handcrafted walnut cane I had bought my dad for his birthday a few years before. We were prepared. Would my strong, independent Duane actually need these things? It was hard for us to imagine.

Wednesday, the 20th, I went back to my office to meet with my supervisor and a representative from human resources to discuss my leave of absence. Sitting in my cubicle was like stepping back into someone else's life, a life that recently had been mine. Less than two weeks before, I sat at that desk reviewing mortgage files. Everything was as I left it — photos of my four grandchildren pinned to the walls of my cubicle; photos of Duane and me showing off the lake trout we caught at Rossport, Ontario; Eric's and Ann's graduations portraits smiling from a frame on my desk; my calendar with the weeks till Alaska clearly marked off; my lighthouse and loons on top of my file cabinet. Teary-eyed coworkers told me they were praying for us and encouraged me not to make any hasty decisions about leaving permanently. I had no idea when, or if, I would be back.

Thursday, the 21st, Duane and I saw our travel agent to pay the balance due on our Alaskan tour. Only two months earlier we had walked into that same office filled with excitement as we planned our trip, picked out our stateroom with a veranda on the cruise ship, and remitted our down payment, anticipating the adventure that lay ahead. Now Duane walked into the building wearing his "Will hat" and steadying himself with my father's cane. Our agent explained that we were too close to our departure date to qualify for a pre-existing condition; should we have to cancel, we would not be eligible for a full refund. The closer we would be to departure date, the less the refund. Every one of his doctors had encouraged us to take our trip as planned, with the exception of Dr. Fowler, so with a leap of faith we paid the balance and vowed to send him a postcard from every port of call.

37

The last day of March was Easter Sunday. In church I thanked God for the gift of time we had been given and filled out the first of many green prayer request cards on Duane's behalf. When I came home, Duane asked me if everyone stood up when I walked in to the sanctuary. "No. Why?" "Because you look so beautiful." The way he looked at me always made me feel like the most beautiful woman in the room, even now when the stress of the past weeks was etched on my face and the dark circles of interrupted sleep shadowed under my eyes. "Love is blind," I teased him. But I thanked God that Duane still thought I was beautiful. He made my heart skip a beat or two when he would look into my eyes.

As March began, we had celebrated Will's arrival at a baby shower. This last day of March, both of our families joined us in our home to celebrate Easter dinner with all the trimmings. Grandpa Duane held Will in his arms planning for the future, "Ah, Sunshine. I'll pick you up after school and we'll go catch us some crappies. Then we'll go to the Dairy Queen. They're really going to know us at the Dairy Queen." David and I locked eyes communicating our mutual fear that Will would never go fishing with his grandpa. But if anyone could make it happen, Duane could.

Never had Easter Sunday been as meaningful as this one. We celebrated the promise of the resurrection, the hope we had for Duane's life from the brink of death, and the promise of the coming spring.

Recruiting Our Team

He is a wise man who does not grieve for the things which
he has not, but rejoices for those which he has.
– Epictetus

Duane was a man who had controlled his life, living it exactly as he wanted. He had control until he was thrust into the care of unknown doctors while he began to fight a previously unheard of fatal disease. Being able to make decisions regarding his own care was vital to his state of mind and his progress. The first important decisions he needed to make were selecting a new neurologist and getting a second opinion from another oncologist. Where does one start? We had scheduled an appointment at Mayo, but David's and Meg's contact highly recommended Dr. John Trusheim at Fairview, the only neuro-oncologist in this area of the country. His specialty is treating brain tumors.

Duane, David, and I met Dr. Trusheim on Monday, April 1. Dressed in a tweed sports coat, Dr. Trusheim was an easygoing man with sandy blond hair and a full moustache. His compassionate blue eyes smiled at us behind small rimless glasses as he personally led us into his office. Reviewing Duane's case, he didn't sugarcoat the situation but offered more options and hope than we had previously been given. He, too, explained the blood-brain barrier, but thought Duane would be a good candidate for some of the new therapies that were successful in dealing with brain tumors, even GBM. He said that if we needed to go a different route after trying these traditional methods, he would make it possible for Duane to participate in a clinical trial, go to Duke, or to Houston — whatever it took. That made sense to us.

Dr. Trusheim told us he worked as a team member with a neurosurgeon and a radiologist, discussing together the best course of treatment for each patient. What a novel idea — not this "we hire them like plumbers" arrogance we had previously experienced. We were introduced to Kathy Gilliland, his highly skilled nurse, who would be available to us for any questions or unexpected problems. Could this mean I would no longer need to be a nuisance in order to be acknowledged by a receptionist to make an appointment? Duane was impressed, and we were in complete agreement that Dr. Trusheim was our guy.

We asked what we could expect given Duane's condition. "What about Alaska?" Dr. Trusheim agreed that we should be able to take our trip, provided his condition remained stable. "Should Duane drive?" The answer to this was no; Duane was at too high a risk for seizures. This also meant that Duane would not be able to return to his job at the car dealership — he was a service driver. Even though Duane did not feel able to drive at this time, the prospects for the future must have been unnerving. I was the one who asked the next all-important question, "What about driving a boat?" The answer was, "Absolutely not."

It was April Fool's Day. Once again we were driving in a storm as ice and snow fell all around us on our quiet ride home. Late afternoon rush hour traffic had already begun, and we crawled home with our thoughts, letting Dr. Trusheim's words sink in. "Driving a boat?" "Absolutely not." Duane stared straight ahead watching the wipers rhythmically clear the sleet from the windshield. Without turning to look at me he finally spoke, slowly and deliberately, "I guess this

40

means no more fishing." I took a deep breath and replied, "No, I guess not. At least not for a while." He answered quietly, "Well, at least I've had ten good years to fish." Courage, strength, class — he was incredible.

"No more fishing." One can only imagine the impact this statement must have had. Duane not only loved to fish, it had been his salvation. When he was downsized out of his position as an advertising executive, he chose not to go back to the high-pressure corporate world. The men in his family had a tendency to die in their early sixties; if he only had ten or so years to live, he was going to fish. He turned pro and fished walleye tournaments from Lake Erie to Big Stone. He guided trips on the St Croix River. He rarely missed a Fishing Club outing and filled his office wall with plaques commemorating his many club championships. He fished for pure enjoyment whatever the weather, whatever the season, including on the Mississippi River in January. Summer mornings he would leave the house hours before sunrise and drive two hours in order to be on Lake Mille Lacs at dawn. Late September through the end of October would find him alone on his annual six-week pilgrimage to Lake Winnipeg in Manitoba in search of his trophy walleye. He loved life in his fully equipped Warrior 177 Eagle, alone or with anyone who enjoyed fishing. He had lived the past ten years exactly as he wanted with no regrets. When told those days were over, he didn't complain or become angry, bitter or depressed. He didn't mope, feel sorry for himself, or take it out on me, David, or anyone else. He accepted his fate with grace and dignity.

Dr. Trusheim had presented us with the facts, realistic expectations, and options. He had also given us hope. Along with the hope given that first day of April, the side effects of the radiation suddenly emerged. The healthy appetite he had enjoyed on Easter Sunday suddenly vanished as Duane began his third week of radiation. His sense of taste and smell were drastically altered; his food, even his coffee, smelled rancid to him and tasted like metal.

Finding foods Duane would eat became my greatest challenge as he steadily lost weight and strength. He refused to drink the Boost supplements supplied by Dr. Perez. His best meal continued to be breakfast, so I became creative, packing in as much nutritional value into his meals as I could. I made cottage cheese pancakes, sneaked Instant Breakfast into as much as I could get away with, and went to the Ensure website in search of recipes. The morning I tried pancakes made with Ensure, Duane threw them on the floor as I sat and cried.

Meg's sister, Beth, gave me the book *Beating Cancer with Nutrition* by Patrick Quilan, which provided a wealth of valuable information, including what supplements to take. One hundred dollars later, I left the health food store armed with cod liver oil and garlic capsules, minerals, and vitamins. The more I tried, the more Duane resisted. "I take enough pills," he would argue.

He became more obstinate about eating and his weight plunged. His strength waned. My frustration mounted until one night, when he again refused his dinner or a supplement, I finally scolded him, " I've had it. If you don't want to eat or take your vitamins, fine. Don't. It is your life, not mine. But if you ever want to take Will fishing and to the Dairy Queen, you better figure out some way to keep up your strength 'cause I'm fresh out of ideas. You have to do something to help yourself. I can't do it for you."

I went for a walk to calm down and have a good cry. When I returned, he had eaten all of his dinner and drunk two cans of Ensure. "I did it for my babies," he said apologetically, "one for Mary and one for Will."

His hair began to hurt, and then clumps of it remained on his pillowcase. The loss of his hair was a painful, external manifestation of the havoc within. How I loved Duane's silver hair. When I close my eyes, I can still picture him looking handsome and sexy at the Fishing Club Fish Fry the previous October after returning from Canada. He was tan, smiling, laughing, and full of life. His silver hair, unattended by a barber in two months, curled over his black Levis shirt collar. Now as he fought for his life, his skin tone was ashen, and he was losing his hair in the areas affected by the radiation. With or without hair, to me he would always be handsome and sexy.

Let me not pray to be sheltered from dangers, but to be fearless in facing them.
Let me not beg for the stilling of my pain, but for the heart to conquer it. – Rabindranath Tagor

We had faith in the doctors and hoped for the best, but we knew we needed to improve the odds for this difficult journey with dire consequences. The interdenominational Order of St. Luke, a healing prayer ministry, provided the means.

In these early days of treatment, Duane, his good friend Loren Burkel, and I attended a healing service the O.S.L. held at my church. The leader was elegant, tall, and blonde, with the aura of an angel surrounding her. After the service she met with us in a quiet corner of the chapel. She looked at Duane with compassion as she asked him to tell her his story. Choking back his tears, he told her of his tumor, the journey ahead, and his fear. Kneeling in front of him, holding his hands, and looking deep into his eyes, she asked softly, "Duane, what would you ask Jesus if he were here with you right now?"

"Just get me through it," he whispered as tears streamed down his cheeks (as well as Loren's and mine).

Tenderly she asked Duane for permission to lay her hands on his incision, then gently touched him as the rest of us held hands in prayer. As she prayed for healing, for minimal side effects from the treatment, and for strength for us both, Duane felt heat and energy coming from her hands onto his head. I could feel that same heat and energy flowing from Duane through me to Loren as we held hands.

Following the prayers, she suggested that we contact our families and friends and ask them to participate in forty days of fasting and praying on Duane's behalf. "Just send off a couple emails," she suggested. Duane was receptive to this idea, saying it was worth a try. I sent emails to our families, to friends near and far away, to the Fishing Club, to my old classmates, to the Loose Ladies, to my co-workers, and to my coaching friends. I gave them all an update on Duane's progress and asked for their help for the forty days from the end of radiation through the first part of chemotherapy.

———•———

Friday, April 12, 2002
Hi guys,
I want to thank all of you for your prayers, thoughts, and kind messages in the past weeks. We both appreciate the support out there in the real world. Believe me, it helps. Duane has an upbeat, positive attitude (which is why I fell in love with him in the first place). Radiation has been dreadful. Just two weeks left, then he starts chemo.

44

We have a new doctor, a neuro-oncologist regarded as the best in the Cities—in fact, in this whole neck of the woods. (We fired Dr. Negative.) We all trust him and are hopeful. Chemo doesn't have a very good track record with brain cancer. However, it is a place to start, and the new drugs are promising. If they aren't effective, we have clinical trials to try, but it is a crapshoot. We have faith in the doctors, and faith in God. And I'm asking for your help.

As part of Duane's treatment we are participating in a healing ministry through the Order of St. Luke. One suggestion was to have a network of people who would commit to joining us in a 40-day period of fasting and praying for Duane. First, let me explain "fasting"; it is not going without food for 40 days. It would be just giving something up—i.e. morning coffee, breakfast, eating after dinner, or smoking for a day. Or you could do something special—taking a walk, reading something spiritual or positive, anything. Just do it in Duane's name and pray for him. This would be done one specific day a week, or even just do one day during the 40 days from April 22 through May 30 (the end of radiation time and the start of chemo).

My goal is to have at least two people each day for these 40 days who would commit to pray for Duane's healing, for the chemo to work, for us to make the right decisions and to have the strength to get through this. (Throughout scripture 40 days is a significant time period—including the flood and Jesus' temptation in the wilderness. Also, Jesus sent out his disciples two by two.) If this is something you could do, or know of someone else who could help us in this way, let me know what day, or days, so I can be sure each day is covered. If you can't, please just remember us in your prayers. If you have any questions, let me know. Thank you for your help.

Love, Mary

45

We never know how supportive people can be until we ask for their help. How many times do we hear "I wish there were something I could do" and then leave it at that? We were overwhelmed by the eagerness of people from all over the country offering to participate and asking others to help. Friends I hadn't seen or talked to in years, acquaintances, even strangers were joining our cause. People offered to give up coffee, wine, and meals, to take prayer walks and read inspirational books for Duane. Their powerful messages inspired us, giving us renewed hope and strength.

Dennis and I would be honored to join your circle and would like to take Saturdays. This represents the one day we spend totally in each other's company. As we go about our day you will be in our thoughts and prayers. Thank you for inviting us to be part of your healing process. – Robby

I don't know Duane — but I do know you—even if it was years ago. My heart goes out to you both. (I'm all teary-eyed as I write this.) Praying every day on those dates would be little enough to do and I will certainly do it. God can do anything if you have faith. – Elaine

Expect a miracle. Jesus was a miracle maker. What happened 2000 years ago continues to happen today.
– Cousin Kathy

You are doing everything right. Now stay focused and open to all our energy. You will be led through this. – Jan B.

I'm honored you are asking me to help support Duane's healing. I would be more than happy to participate. I will give up eating after supper for 40 days! It will help me, but it feels good to be doing it for someone else too.

You and Duane sound strong. I absolutely know how hard this is on you. I am so proud of you for taking the time to be with Duane, love him and support him. What a gift to both of you! Duane sounds like a trooper and probably adds a lot of inspiration to everyone around him. What a gift!

– Love, Cari

The following letter was sent by a classmate I hadn't seen for thirty-five years. We had known each other since kindergarten but were never close friends. We never hung out together in high school or chatted on the phone. Yet she, like so many others, became a valued supporter and confidant.

Dear Mary,

I went to the beach this morning before work to watch the sunrise. I had time for meditation, no place better than watching the waves and the sunrise from the horizon. The waves remind me of life, the valleys and crests of the waves representing our ups and downs. The turmoil of the current and then how gently the wave comes to the shore. The water gently washes away all the signs of stress and gives way to the glory of God's power.

I walked up the shoreline looking for a shell that might represent a special meaning that I could have to put on my chain as a constant reminder to pray for Duane. As I was in that thought a wave washed up past where they normally were going and in it's retreat it left a small shell. I put it around my neck and this will be with me till he is done

47

with all of his treatments and all is well, then I will send it to him to have as a token of each time I have said a prayer and thought of him.

Prayers are the bestest!

Love, Suzanne

We could feel the positive energy flowing long before the start of the fast. Encouraging words buoyed Duane's spirits as the radiation weakened his body. He believed he would get better. The Brain Tumor Support Group at the hospital reinforced that hope.

Sitting around a large table, we introduced ourselves, told our story, then listened to the others—survivors for three years, five years, seven years, and twelve years out. As people of all ages and all walks of life told their remarkable, inspirational stories, Duane shook his head whispering, "Wow, oh wow," believing he too could once again have a normal life. Granted, none of these people had GBM, but they told us about an eight-year survivor who did. Recently we had heard the usual prognosis for GBM was about six months, so hearing that someone was thriving after eight years sounded to us like a miracle. We left with his address — a post office box in Wisconsin. As soon as we got home, I wrote him a letter telling him our story.

Hope and strength—we would need all we could get the last days of radiation. It had been brutal. It got even worse.

Sunday, April 21, 2002
Update from Mary

Hello, everyone!
Let me start with a heartfelt thank you to each of you for your prayers and for joining us in our forty-day

journey of prayer and fasting for Duane's health. Judging from this past week and weekend, it comes none too soon. Whatever commitment you are able to give during this time is greatly appreciated by both of us. God bless you for your support.

Friday, April 26, will be the last day of radiation. It can't come fast enough. Last Wednesday they redirected the radiation pinpointing a specific area. We thought since his whole brain was no longer affected, he would feel a little better. Wrong. It is worse, much worse; the fatigue, the inability to eat, and the weakness are all worse. The pounds are falling off him. Now he has an infection where he had the root canal late in February and needs a tooth pulled on Monday.

If that isn't enough, he also has an ear infection — all on the right side, the same side as the tumor. This was discovered last night when his son and I had him in the ER till 3 o'clock in the morning. He had a severe headache, and was so weak he couldn't lift his leg to get into bed, the same symptoms he presented the night of his initial diagnosis. A CT scan just showed inflammation from the redirected radiation. Can chemo be worse than this? I'm afraid to find out.

Thank you, too, for all of your messages. We really love hearing from you guys. It gives us strength to know you are all thinking of us and praying for us. It means more to us than I can say. Duane and I are both so thankful to have you as part of "our team."

Hopefully I'll have better news next time.

Love, Mary

This was the first of my "Updates" sent to our network of supporters on our prayer team. The prayers, love, and support in these messages gave us encouragement, strength, and peace. As the months passed, these messages took on a life of their own.

Hi Mary,

It sounds like Duane has a great sense of strength and hope — I'm so happy for both of you! I will begin my "fast " for Duane today. I am a believer in the positive effects of prayer. I will say lots of them for Duane and also for you.

Thanks for the update. I will be thinking of both of you and sending good, positive thoughts your way!

Love, Cari

Mom,

I can't tell you how bad I feel for what you and Duane are currently going through, but I do know that if love truly does conquer all then you two will surely beat this.

Love to you both, Eric

By Tuesday morning Duane was a six-foot, one-inch 185-pound rag doll. Without David's and Christi's help, I would never have gotten him dressed, down the stairs, and into my Jeep. At radiation I had to put him in a wheelchair to get him inside since he was unable to walk, or even stand. As we waited to be called, he sat in the wheelchair with his head tilted back, his mouth ajar, a trickle of drool running down his chin; his blank eyes were rolled slightly back under partially closed lids. I hadn't been this frightened since that first night in the ICU. Dr. Fowler's prophetic words, "This is as good as he'll ever be," echoed in my head as Duane reminded me of a sick old man in a nursing home. Were we headed there already? Were the good days over? Would I ever be able to care for him at home again? As he was wheeled away for his treatment, I was comforted by a lovely woman, her bald head wrapped in a silk scarf of swirling happy colors, waiting for treatment on her cancerous lung.

Nurse Kathy returned my desperate call immediately. She and Dr. Trusheim met us at Fairview Southdale Hospital and admitted Duane to the oncology unit. Oncology. Just the word frightened me, as did the patients with sunken eyes. Clad in hospital gowns and robes, gray slipper socks on their feet, they shuffled along the corridor by the nurses' station pushing their IV poles. Scarves wrapped their bald heads. Would Duane ever be able to even shuffle again?

Just over a month since his discharge, Duane was again hospitalized with IVs pumping steroids directly into his veins. Terrified by what was happening to him, he was relieved to be under Dr. Trushiem's watchful eye. He was safe. He was also in trouble. In spite of the radiation, a new MRI showed that the tumor continued to grow. Duane would need more surgery.

During the lonely drive home, I remembered the forty-day fast and knew somewhere there were at least two people praying for us. Walking into our house that night I felt much like I had a month ago, frightened, alone, and now discouraged after everything had started out so well. Once again God showed me I was not alone. This time my answering machine wasn't full — it only had one message on it. The message was from the eight-year survivor from Wisconsin. "Duane, this is John Schuler, a fellow cancer patient. I was prayed for and now I'm okay. Don't give up, Duane, don't give up!"

I immediately returned his call and was inspired by his story. He too needed a second surgery shortly after the first. His prognosis was six weeks. With nothing to lose, he opted for massive doses of stereotactic radiation. He had chemo.

He developed a thrush infection, and all he would eat was chocolate ice cream. Consuming massive doses of shark cartilage, he used guided imagery, seeing all these little sharks eating away the tumor. "It works if you believe." Most of the credit, however, he gave to the thousands of people praying for him. He focused on those prayers going right to the tumor to kill it. "I was pretty much of a s.o.b. prior to my illness, but now my life has completely changed. God spared me to encourage others and give them hope. That is now my life's purpose."

As we ended our conversation an hour later, I once again had hope. There was no doubt we were in trouble. John Schuler had also been in trouble. He had the same tumor, located in the same area of his brain. He had needed a second surgery shortly after the first, which was also done on a March 8 at the same hospital where Duane had been—eight years before. Now he was telling us both, "Don't give up!"

He had been prayed for, and now so were we. Our family and friends, here and across the country, were participating in the fast. My sister had planted a special, white-bearded begonia on Monday as she and my mother read devotions in Duane's name. David and Christi had given up caffeine. Eric was doing push-ups. Ann had recruited her church choir in Duluth. Duane's brother-in-law, Bernie, had sent a prayer request to the sisters at the College of St. Scholastica, also in Duluth. Duane's name was listed with other prayer concerns in my church newsletter and weekly bulletin. Every Sunday I filled out a green request card for the prayer team at Prince of Peace. Even the young woman who fitted my new glasses asked her church and her mother's church to pray for Duane. John said he had thousands of people praying for him, and now so did Duane.

Within another "bad hand," everything was right. Dr. Michael Rodman, the neurosurgeon in Dr. Trushiem's group, would remove as much of the tumor and scar tissue as he could to ensure leaving Duane with as good a quality of life as possible. The surgery also gave us another blessing; time-released chemotherapy in the form of gliadel wafers would be placed directly into Duane's brain. This treatment, which would last six weeks, was fifty to seventy-five percent more effective in treating brain tumors than traditional chemo and had fewer side effects. It could only be done if surgery was necessary anyway.

"Honey, if I don't make it, you go! You go to Alaska without me. Duane was emphatic. I told him that we were going together or not at all. Now I feared our "dream vacation" would be a nightmare, and was relieved when Dr. Trusheim advised us to call it off. I canceled our trip and was able to get almost a full refund. When Duane was feeling better, we could use the money to take a shorter, less taxing trip or two somewhere closer to home.

On the surface I was holding up quite well — optimistic, strong, encouraging, doing what needed to be done. Underneath, at home alone I was just plain scared. I wrote in my journal at half past eleven at night on Friday, April 26, *Why do I do this, show the world I am so strong, show others that "I'm fine?" All I want is to be held and to cry, to scream and feel the pain. Who will hold me?*

My answer came the next day. Saturday afternoon I met my son at Southdale, a huge shopping mall near the hospital, to shop for presents for my grandson Payton's fifth birthday. When Eric hugged me, I started sobbing, releasing two month's worth of pain, fear, and frustration, oblivious to the hundreds of shoppers passing by in the middle of the busy mall. For the first time in a long while, I felt protected and comforted. Finally there was someone holding me — Eric, my son.

Back at home that night, I once again I reached out to my email support system with another update, recapping the events of the past weeks, the setbacks, the impending surgery, and the hope offered by John Schuler.

So my friends, thank you for concern, for your visits, emails, and phone calls. We especially thank you for your prayers. Just because we are facing another surgery, don't think our prayers aren't being heard and that they aren't working. They are. We are now at a new hospital with doctors of our choosing. We have been given the opportunity for this new treatment. We have been contacted by an eight-year survivor. We are both getting the strength to somehow get through this. So please keep those prayers coming. We feel your support.

Love, Mary

Dear Mary,

Wow, what an awesome miracle of your new friend. God is always so amazing in how He works. The pages of your journey are flipping by, and it is so wonderful to see how God is working and with us second by second.

When our road is smooth it is so easy to thank God for our daily blessings. When He is carrying us, as stated in the poem "Footprints," we tend to think He has forgotten us or given us way too much of a load to carry, we forget He is carrying us.

My seashell is a constant reminder around my neck to pray for Duane. Many ask about it, and it is an opportunity to have even more pray. It is not a perfect shell, so this attracts attention as to why I have it as a necklace, but it represents to me our imperfections and the complete circle it makes reminds me of the circle of life. My prayers continue along with many others being added to the list. I have read that the squeaky wheel gets the oil, and God can't help but hear the requests for this circuit that is filling with prayers from Duane and you. The angels are at the switchboard.

Love and PRAYERS, Suzanne

Oh Mary,
Ron and I both have you and Duane in our prayers. We know firsthand the power they have. I have just heard about two others besides Ron who are doing well. So this cancer thing doesn't have to be all bad. But it sure does take its toll on strength, etc. It is wonderful to hear about the man from Wisconsin. That helps a lot. Keep us posted. We think about you all the time.   *– Linda E.*

My classmate Linda and her husband offered more than hope; they were an inspiration. They had walked in our shoes two years earlier when Ron was diagnosed with a deadly cancer. Like John Schuler, his odds weren't good — but Ron too had beaten the odds. Linda had asked for our prayers, and sent updates on Ron's progress. Now they shared reports of "no new cancer" after every checkup, testimonials that miracles do happen. Perhaps Duane and I would have one, too.

Duane was discharged on Sunday, April 28, six days after being admitted to the hospital. Once again the swelling had responded well to the steroids, and he was strong and steady. Radiation resumed on Monday, with just three more treatments to go. As we were waiting for Duane to be called, a mother came into the waiting room carrying a child, maybe five or six years old, with a horseshoe-shaped scar like Duane's on her bald head. I could tell she was a little girl only by the pink flowers embroidered on her denim jacket. Duane looked at me with tears in his eyes, shook his head, and simply said, "Oh, wow." It was painful to imagine a little child going through this ordeal. Somehow our situation didn't seem quite so bad. Helen, the lung cancer patient who had comforted me on our last visit, was relieved that we had canceled our trip. She had been concerned for me, told me that I would not have been able to handle it. I knew that she was right.

The Hope of Spring

Don't give up, Duane, Don't give up!
– John Schuler

Had it only been six and a half weeks since Duane was scurrying after the food cart in his hospital gown that first day of radiation? It seemed like it had been an eternity, but radiation therapy was finally over. The staff ceremoniously handed him a diploma reading, *"The Lionheart Award, presented to Duane Leach who has shown special courage during medical treatment at Radiation Oncology, May 1, 2002."*

Enduring treatment did require special courage, courage to be bolted down to that slab unable to move as beams of live radiation attacked his brain and ravaged his body Duane started treatment weighing 225; he ended it weighing 179. What hair was left from his right temple to the center of the back of his head was thin and wispy. Two weeks earlier, Duane had been in a wheelchair unable to walk or even stand on his own. He had endured a terrifying setback as the tumor continued to grow, but his spirit and resolve were stronger than ever.

This day he once again walked strong and erect, aided by his cane. Dr. Perez, who had been so kind to us both during these past weeks, instructed Duane to schedule a follow-up appointment for August, then signed the discharge. As we walked out of the secured building for the last time, Duane commented with a touch of optimism, "At least he thinks that I'll still be around in August."

Apprehensive as he faced the second surgery, Duane called John Schuler. Hearing the strong, healthy voice of a true miracle gave Duane a much-needed dose of inspiration. John had just seen his doctor and didn't have to return for a year. Duane kept saying, "Wow. A year! Can you imagine not going back for a year?" We were relieved that Duane didn't have to see a doctor or have some sort of treatment or therapy for five more days.

Pastor Paul Gauche and Spiritual Director Marlene Walston met with us in the chapel at Prince of Peace just days before the scheduled surgery. Preparing spiritually was as important to us as preparing physically, mentally, and emotionally. We discussed Duane's tumor and our hopes and fears regarding the upcoming surgery. We asked for their support. Pastor Paul anointed Duane with oil; he and Marlene placed their hands on the right side of Duane's head and prayed for healing, for God to be in the operating room on Thursday guiding the hands of the surgeon and his team, and for God to be with those of us who waited.

On the way home, Duane said he felt good about the meeting, but there was something else he had wanted; he had wanted Pastor Paul to bless our relationship. He hadn't asked, and didn't want me to ask either. "That's okay," he said, then added, " God had already blessed us."

Not all people who we consider to be our spiritual leaders agree on the right way to live our lives. We had one such an experience with someone I had seen as a spiritual leader at Prince of Peace. Duane and I had been living together for four years. We were married in spirit; our commitment was a strong as any legal marriage we knew. In March of 2001, he had been in church with me when one of our pastors (who is no longer with our congregation) had blasted cohabitation as evil and "wrong, wrong, wrong," saying it was succumbing to our "petty passions." Duane almost walked out of church, vowing never to return to Prince of Peace and fuming, "And furthermore, there is nothing petty about our passion!"

I then met with this pastor, telling him about our life together and our valid reasons for not legally marrying (mostly financial). I told him that, as far as we were concerned, we were married in the sight of God. We had a totally committed, supportive, monogamous loving relationship, something I had not had in two legal marriages performed in church. If what Duane and I had wasn't a marriage, I asked him to please tell me what was. "Whenever two or more of you are gathered in his name," I reminded him, seeking his understanding. I pointed out that we were no longer young; we weren't having babies. Knowing it was highly unlikely, even in a progressive church like Prince of Peace, I added, "If we could come to church with our families and be blessed as a couple without involving the state, we would gladly do it." This pastor said, "Of course that could not be done." By the end of our conversation I felt I had earned his respect and his understanding. He extended an invitation to Duane to come see him as well. In closing, the pastor prayed with me and asked God to bless our union. Duane declined the pastor's invitation; we had not discussed having a blessing since, not until that day driving home from the chapel.

Thursday, May 9, 2002
Dear Friends and Family,

What a day. David and I brought Duane to the hospital shortly after 5:00 this morning for surgery. At 3:30 a smiling surgeon met with us to tell us the surgery had gone "exceedingly well." This was an euphoric statement coming from this conservative doctor. Duane was in much better shape than he had anticipated by looking at the scans. He was able to remove more tumor and necrosis from the radiation than he expected, then placed the chemotherapy wafers in Duane's brain. (They will dissolve over the next six weeks.) His last words to us were, "If anyone has a chance, this guy has a chance."

Praise God! We can't ask for more than a chance. Our new friend in Wisconsin who didn't have a chance eight years ago is now telling us, "Don't give up." His next doctor's appointment isn't for another year. We left Duane tonight in ICU, looking better than he did post surgery two months ago. He will most likely be in the hospital for another ten days.

This is an incredible journey! We heard in a support group recently that healing occurs in many ways. My own life is being healed by this experience. One of the best things to come out of all of this is reconnecting with all of you, and am so grateful to have you on our team. I thank each and every one of you for your support and especially for your prayers. If anyone ever doubted the power of our prayers, look no further. This is working! Please keep them coming. Our lives, and yours, are better for them. We appreciate your support more than words can say.

Love, Mary

⸻

That's great news! Don't give all the credit to us and our prayers. You and Duane have the positive attitude it takes to recover from this. God is powerful, but a lot lies in the person doing the fighting too! I continue to do my spiritual reading on Duane's behalf. I will also enlist my mom. She prays for a long time every night and the results are good. Tell Duane we are still pulling for him and for you to keep the strength. You two are amazing.

Love, Lori and Steve

HI Mary,

Thanks for the update. All of this is in God's hands, as you know, and it looks like a good result as of this afternoon. Congratulations.

I was at my Thurs. a.m. men's Bible study this morning, and I said a prayer for Duane with the group and asked the guys there to remember Duane today. Sure is nice to hear the good news, and we will keep praying.

Thanks, Mary. Our love to you and Duane.

Jack and Katie

Good morning, Guys!

A heartfelt thank you for your prayers, calls, cards, emails, and visits. We are overwhelmed and uplifted by your support; it is working. Duane was released from the hospital on Tuesday, after five days—not the anticipated ten-day stay. Not only was the surgery a huge success, he is not sick from the chemo. He is tired, and still doesn't have an appetite, but he isn't sick. Tuesday he said he felt better than he has in months. All those prayers are being heard. A few weeks ago he was in a wheelchair, now just uses a cane, or occasionally a walker. The goal is to get rid of both.

Last Thursday he was undergoing his second brain surgery; yesterday we drove to Red Wing to enjoy the river and went out to lunch. Unbelievable. We decided that while he is feeling good we would take a well-deserved getaway to Door County in a week or so. It *isn't Alaska, but right now it sounds perfect. We know how quickly things can change.*

The next appointment with the oncologist is June 12. Then we'll see how this treatment is working, and find out what the doctors will do next. In addition to the chemo we are still watching diet and vitamins, using guided imagery, and I am learning about Qigong, an ancient Chinese therapy. Whatever works. We have just begun to fight.

Thank you again for all your support. Please keep it up. Pray that the chemo gets rid of that thing. We welcome hearing from you. Your messages and visits really keep us going.

Love, Mary

———◆———

The last weeks of May we embraced life once again, enjoying a trip to Duluth for my granddaughter Nadia's third birthday party and a trip to the zoo with Annie, Nadia, and her big sister, Elina. Old friends from my former neighborhood in Duluth, Don and Judy Goodermote and Ron and Ruth Tryon, joined us for dinner in Two Harbors. I had met them when I was pregnant with Ann more than thirty years before; they had met Duane shortly after we began dating. From then on, he was an integral part of their lives.

We dined at the Vanilla Bean, owned by my childhood friend Jan Bergman and her husband, Paul, friends who were vital links to our prayer chain and who met Duane for the first time that evening.

Duane thrived on this time away from home enjoying a "normal life" again. He was feeling good and we were now ready to take on Door County.

Door County

*If you pile up enough tomorrows you'll find you've
collected a lot of empty yesterdays. I don't know about
you, but I want to make today worth remembering.
– Harold Hill in* **The Music Man**

———◆———

Duane had been the one to plan our vacations, making
all the arrangements and scheduling our itineraries down to
the minute. Loving to surprise me, he would keep our
destinations a secret. One time I asked, "Can you at least tell
me are we going north, south, east, or west so I know what to
pack?" Giving me his most disarming smile he simply
responded, "Yes." He took me on the Circle Tour of Lake
Superior, going in all directions.

This time it was up to me to make the arrangements. We
agreed Door County, Wisconsin, was the perfect choice. Door
County is the "thumb" of Wisconsin, a peninsula situated
between Lake Michigan to the east and Green Bay to the
west. It offered all we enjoyed on vacation — lakes,
lighthouses, and beautiful scenery. The landscape is dotted
with apple and cherry orchards. In addition, Door County is
an artists' haven, blending a unique mix of painters, potters,
performers, weavers, artisans, and galleries. It is also a
shopper's paradise. Its charming small towns are filled with
quaint shops and delightful restaurants.

I selected the Egg Harbor Lodge for our stay; it was
centrally located, "adults only," and handicapped accessible.
It had a pool, a patio, a Jacuzzi in our room, and private
balconies overlooking the lake. It boasted having "the best
water view in Door County." If I wanted to go exploring (or

shopping) and Duane was tired, he would have a comfortable place to rest with plenty of amenities. This trip we had no schedule and no itinerary. We were just going to "play it by ear," something we had never done on vacation before.

In the past, we traveled in Duane's truck, a red Ford F150 4X4. He did all the driving, including the entire Circle Tour of Lake Superior when he drove a stick shift while having a broken wrist. A big man, he was more comfortable in a large vehicle; he also liked to be in charge. As I loaded my Jeep for our Door County trip, I was thankful I had traded in my little Nissan for my Grand Cherokee. Not only was it more comfortable for him, it had ample room to haul all the necessary equipment that might be needed to keep him comfortable and safe—room for the wheelchair, the walker, and the raised toilet seat. He graciously accepted his changing role from captain to co-pilot and navigator, and enjoyed telling me where to go.

Our days in Door County were enchanting and busy. Duane felt he had rested plenty over the past months and was not about to sit around any more. Together we traveled the back roads and on a ferry in search of lighthouses. A special triumph was seeing majestic Cana Island Light north of Bailey's Harbor. The small island a few blocks off the mainland was accessible by a rocky path with the water low. A blanket of fog hid the island from view, so we couldn't see how far the walk was, but Duane was determined to try it. Using his cane he set out on the rocky trail with me to see the lighthouse — not an easy task for him. We took our time and were soon thrilled to see the lighthouse, rising tall and gleaming white in the fog. Reaching the island was a personal triumph, well worth the walk.

After he devoured every bit of information available in the

museum, he rested a while, then walked back to sit in the car while I took a few more photos and did a little shopping. I bought him a blue denim shirt with the lighthouse logo on it at the gift shop to celebrate his success. He proudly wore it every day for the remainder of our trip.

Each evening we made a point to end the day relaxing on our balcony and enjoying the spectacular sunsets over the lake. The trip to Door County was amazing. Duane was amazing. One month earlier he couldn't climb the stairs to his own living room and bedroom. Three weeks earlier he was in the hospital undergoing brain surgery for the second time in less than two months. Now he was enjoying Door County with me, going everywhere with only his cane for support.

We had been on some beautiful vacations together in the past, many similar to this one. We had seen numerous lighthouses all around Lake Superior and had marveled at the beauty of the Great Lakes and the golden sunsets reflected on the water. Now he had a look of awe in his eyes; I looked at everything differently too, seeing it anew through Duane's eyes. We were blessed to even be here together, and we knew it. The forty-day fasting period ended on May 30, the day we were at the Cana Island Lighthouse, but we knew that the prayers of so many would not end.

One evening after sunset we were watching *The Music Man*, one of our favorite musicals, on TV. At one point in the story, Harold Hill tells Marion, the librarian, that if "you pile up enough tomorrows, you'll find you've collected a lot of empty yesterdays. I don't know about you, but I want to make today worth remembering."

Our days together would be well worth remembering. No matter what lay ahead, we were not going to have any empty yesterdays.

The Death of a Dream

We weren't supposed to be here. It was Wednesday, June 12, and Duane and I were supposed to be in Fairbanks panning for gold on our first day in Alaska, not discussing chemotherapy options in Dr. Trusheim's office. Was this a bad dream from which I would soon awaken? No. This was real. Our Alaska dream had died.

The doctor was cautious. Although he was impressed with how well Duane looked, the way he walked, his balance, and his reflexes and cognition, he was concerned about the aggressive nature of the tumor. The fact that Duane already needed a second surgery was not a good sign. The gliadel wafers placed in his brain during surgery appeared to be controlling the tumor at this time, but they would be completely dissolved and out of his system by the end of June. Regular chemo needed to start early in July. Now we listened intently as Dr. Trusheim outlined our two options.

"Plan A"— oral chemo — would cause fewer side effects, and require no hospitalization. Duane would simply take a pill for five days each month. This method, however, also provided a lower success rate than "Plan B."

At this time Dr. Truesheim leaned towards Plan B — inter-arterial chemo — while Duane was strong enough to handle the side effects. He would be hospitalized a minimum of three days each month while the chemo was administered through a catheter in his groin. Then he would receive daily injections at home. This method provided a ten-percent higher success rate than the oral chemo, but also produced more severe side effects. In addition to nausea, fatigue, and hair loss, his white blood count would be at risk and would have to be monitored constantly. Travel of any kind was discouraged, in case Duane would need immediate hospitalization.

"Would travel to Two Harbors or Duluth be okay?" Dr. Trusheim said that would be fine because he could always send a helicopter to airlift Duane back to the hospital if necessary. He wouldn't recommend going any farther than that. Airlifting? Duane was terrified of height and refused to even discuss a helicopter tour over the Badlands of South Dakota a few years before. The look he gave me told me that we would stick close to home once he started chemo. We left with literature on each type so we could review and discuss them in order to make an informed decision.

I don't know what I was expecting at this appointment, but this wasn't it. Maybe I was expecting a miracle. We knew this was coming but wanted more time — time that Dr. Fischer bought him "not to spend in a hospital bed," more time like the last few "normal" weeks when he was enjoying life again. For the first time in months he felt good, and was strong and steady. I didn't want him to be sick again already. But that wasn't an option; he would be sick again no matter what. The tumor would see to that, and we had to fight the tumor as aggressively as Duane wanted — and as aggressively as it was attacking Duane's body.

We had two weeks before giving the doctor Duane's decision — two weeks not to be wasted sitting at home. Squeezing in one last mini-vacation, we headed for the south shore of Lake Superior. We had begun our Circle Tour of the lake in the summer of 1999 and had been everywhere we wanted except Bayfield, Wisconsin, and on the cruise around the Apostle Islands. Now was the perfect time to complete our tour.

We rented a cozy cabin, complete with a fireplace and hot tub for two, just outside Bayfield. It was the ideal place to relax after poking around this charming town with its marina filled with row after row of sailboats, quaint shops, and trendy restaurants.

The words "Island Princess" were painted on the side of the little cruise ship we boarded for our tour of the islands. Fortunately I needed to wear my oversized "Jackie O" sunglasses this bright, sunny day, so no one could see the tears welling up in my eyes, especially not Duane. This very morning we were to be boarding another princess, a cruise ship of the Princess Line in the Inside Passage in Alaska. My heart ached in silence as I mourned the death of our dream. I never mentioned to Duane how I felt, nor what we would have been doing that day. Did he remember? He had known our cruise dates as well as I did, so he must have thought about it. But he had dealt with the death of many dreams lately; this was just one more. Today he was apparently content to be on the Island Princess hearing the stories being told by the captain as we passed each island and lighthouse. Once more he was at home on the water, feeling the sun on his skin and the lake air blowing his hair — enjoying an idyllic day on Lake Superior.

Like the days of our lives, idyllic days on Lake Superior are not to be taken for granted. The weather changes quickly and often. Our calm sunny day in Bayfield was sandwiched in between days of cold rain and fog. When we left Bayfield the next morning, we encountered the first rain of our vacation days that spring.

Our Circle Tour had now been completed. As we drove along the south shore towards Duluth, memories of those trips replayed in my mind — the panoramic vistas of the North

Shore, the inspiring Terry Fox Memorial in Thunder Bay, the Rendezvous at Old Fort William, charter fishing in Rossport, Ontario, the variety of beaches, the waterfalls, the stirring Shipwreck Museum at Whitefish Bay, the lighthouses, collecting rocks along the way, and sitting on the shore together mesmerized by the lake. Would we travel together again when this year of chemo was over? Or had this been our last vacation? Only time would tell.

The chemo decision was foremost in our thoughts during those two weeks. Knowing we would need all the help we could get, I sent an update to our network asking for their participation in another forty-day fast. I asked for their prayers that we make the right decision and for the success of the chemo. Once again our growing network of supporters rallied to our cause.

My dearest Mary,

What ever you and Duane decide to do, I'm sure will be the right decision for the two of you and I support you. Mary, I know how much you love this Duane of yours and if only for that reason, I pray that whatever Duane has to endure to get rid of this terrible disease, he comes through successful, happy, and confident that God was indeed on his side. Tell him how much he is loved by a lot of people and to fight with all his might. Tell him that the devil has not seen anyone fight until he sees Duane fight and the army of friends surrounding him so watch out!

Love you both!

Your friend Gerry

As we prepared to assault the tumor, once again our prayers were answered.

Good morning!

This may be a little long, so please bear with me.

A while back I asked some of you to join us in a forty-day fast and prayer for Duane. (The response was overwhelming — again thank you.) That first Monday my sister and my mom planted a white-bearded begonia for Duane. Barb is a master gardener. She cared for this plant, prayed for it, and was horrified when it failed to grow while the other begonias planted with it flourished. She was afraid to tell me that Duane's plant wouldn't grow.

Yesterday Duane, David and I met with Duane's oncologist to discuss the results of Monday's MRI and the next course of treatment. Dr. Trusheim was upbeat and smiling, amazed that the MRI looked better than he anticipated. David and I, remembering all too well the huge mass we had seen in March, were ecstatic. Now there was only an outline of existing tumor left where it had once been. Dr. Rodman had actually removed most of that hideous thing. Once again Duane is doing better than expected. Now Dr. Trusheim is more optimistic about the effects of oral chemo. Two weeks ago he leaned towards inter-arterial. Now a good case could be made either way—a ten-percent margin of effectiveness vs. quality.

Did Duane want to risk side effects or go fishing? I asked, "Doc, if this were your tumor, what would you do?" "Given Duane's age, if this were my father I'd recommend the oral." If we need to be more aggressive later, nothing will be lost. At least now we feel we have more choices and more control. When we left the office I broke into tears. Duane said to me with tears in his own eyes, "No wonder the news was so good. I have all these people praying for me!"

71

So to all of you, thank you, thank you, thank you for your prayers. Thank you for asking others to pray for us. It works. We just need to decide the next course of treatment and how aggressive we should be with the chemo. We haven't forgotten how aggressive this tumor is. We need your prayers now more than ever. Please pray for us to make the best decision.

Yesterday some court said "under God" in the Pledge of Allegiance was "unconstitutional." Heaven help us. What is next? "In God we trust?" As for me, who else can I trust? Please continue your prayers and all your support on our behalf. If you can participate in any way in the next forty days starting July 1, or if you have any questions about it, please let me know. Your help is so greatly appreciated.

Oh, as for the begonia, my sister and I had decided—independently of each other—it represented the tumor that refused to grow—not Duane's health. The events in our lives are not "good" or "bad" themselves. They just are. It is how we perceive them and what we do about it that matters. Duane and I have just begun to fight this thing.

We cherish and make the best of every day. We enjoy our time together. We just came back from another mini-vacation to Bayfield and Duluth where we looked for lighthouses and enjoyed the lake once more. Duane goes fishing with the guys every chance he gets. And oh how he loves that new grandson.

Thank you all so very much for your support in our journey. Please forward this message to anyone who would be interested, email, call, come to see us, etc. It means more than you could know.

Love, Mary

Dear Mary and Duane,

Reading your first part of the letter on Duane's update nearly made me start to cry, I was thinking that you were going to give me bad news. How right that the begonia refused to grow as the growth is also refusing to take hold.

I have a bit to add about the shell I have been wearing around my neck to remind me to pray for Duane. I was at a dock party last Tuesday night and while fingering the shell it broke in half. I was in the midst of 4 other people and to their shock I started crying at my broken shell. My thoughts were that it was bad news, and after relaying the story of the shell and Duane, their immediate response was that the broken shell represented a good omen . . . . Duane didn't need those prayers any more. How right they are. That doesn't mean I will stop praying, I will just find a different reminder seeing that he has moved on to a different path.

Now we have 4 new lines going to heaven for Duane because of the broken shell and I had acquired many before because of questions on the shell. God will give me a new approach I am sure.

Keep up the great recovery, Duane,

Love and prayers, Suzanne

Hi Mary,

Just a note to check in with you and Duane and see how he is doing. I was thinking about him (and you) this morning as I couldn't sleep. As I watched the sun come up over White Bear Lake I said another prayer. Hi to Duane, and tell him his old 'rassling buddy was thinking of him.

Mike Pappas

"I have all these people praying for me . . . ." As the prayers of friends and strangers impacted Duane's life, his faith grew. Whenever possible he attended the outdoor church services at Prince of Peace with me, where he was able to remain in the car and still participate in the service. He realized the importance of prayer and kept his own prayer list on hand in a small green notebook. In it were the names of others that he prayed for on a daily basis — John Schuler, my cousin Nina fighting breast cancer for the second time, a friend undergoing treatment for prostate cancer, my co-worker's six-year-old nephew with a brain tumor, and many more. He kept this list with him at all times, adding to it as warranted, having the names written down so he would not forget anyone. Others prayed for him, and he in turn prayed for friends and strangers in need.

We were also given the opportunity to help others sharing our journey. While leaving Dr. Rodman's office, we noticed a younger couple seated at the appointment desk. The man also sported a horseshoe-shaped scar on his shaved head. We introduced ourselves to them in the hallway; then we all had a cup of coffee and a chat. Lisa and Richard Anderson lived in Iowa. Richard had also been diagnosed with GBM in March, had a first surgery in Des Moines, and was now a patient of Dr. Trusheim. They had just scheduled his second surgery complete with gliadel wafers, this time with Dr. Rodman.

Duane was now able to reassure this couple how successful his own surgery had been and how confident he was under the care of these doctors. We had been helped and encouraged by many others — Willy, Larry Pedersen, David Vikmark, and John Schuler; it was an honor to be able to help and encourage someone else. We exchanged many stories, ideas, and practical information. Richard had recently applied for Social Security Disability, and gave Duane all the necessary information. Exchanging phone numbers and email addresses, all four of us felt a little less alone in our battles, as we had discovered new allies who were in the midst of this nightmare right along with us. Duane added two new names to his growing prayer list in his little green notebook.

Turning Sixty

She had been right. The compassionate woman at the support group had taken me aside after the June meeting saying, "I can tell you two really like each other." Having lived with her husband's tumor for seventeen months, her experiences were beyond anything I could have foreseen. While her husband visited with Duane, she had advised me to be patient and forgiving with myself as I cared for the man I deeply loved. Still in my "I-can- do-it-all" state of denial, I listened to her words but couldn't comprehend how they would pertain to me.

She cautioned me that caring for Duane would stretch me more than I could possibly imagine, that I would discover the best and worst in myself, handling the situation like a saint one day and a bitch the next. "We caregivers discover that we are stronger, more patient and loving than we ever thought possible," she said. "We also discover the limits of that patience, and at times resent our loved ones, even though we never thought we would."

I remembered being impatient with Duane once or twice in the last months, but I thought surely I could never resent him. Not me. "I can do this; I can do it all," I naïvely said to myself. However, my patience and strength were put to the test as my responsibilities and frustrations became greater and greater. The calm we had enjoyed since the second surgery vanished as Duane's problems with balance and equilibrium suddenly returned.

It began without warning on July 2. Early that morning, Duane and Dave Nystom were heading to Lake Mille Lacs for a day of serious fishing. These guys had fished Mille Lacs, the premier walleye lake in Minnesota, numerous times over the years, including competing in the prestigious invitational Wave Wackers Tournaments. Duane would pre-fish early in the week staying at a combination restaurant, motel, and bait shop. When Dave would arrive for the two-day tournament, Duane would know where and how to catch fish. Going back to Mille Lacs with Dave, Duane was eager to visit his former life. In his haste he barely said good-bye to me as he headed for Dave's truck. Like a mom running after a school bus with a forgotten lunch, I chased them to give Duane his cane, "just in case." He hadn't been using it lately, but it was always good to have nearby if needed. Was I being overprotective?

Later that afternoon, Duane called me to pick him up at Dave's. "Honey, could you bring me my walker?" His walker? Did I hear that right? Earlier that morning I had felt overprotective bringing him his cane, and now he was asking for his walker, which he hadn't used since April. His equilibrium problems had reappeared without warning as Duane and Dave were heading for the boat after eating breakfast. Dave had to hold him as he walked. By the time they returned home Duane was steady again, but the indication was clear that those good days would not last indefinitely. Fortunately, chemo was due to begin on Monday.

It is hard to imagine what must go through a person's mind when facing the onset of chemo. As the day neared, Duane was very quiet and pensive. His sister, Everell, was frequently on his mind and he spoke of her often. In the years we had been together, he seldom mentioned her; she was sixteen years older and had died of breast cancer in her mid-thirties, leaving behind her husband, Bernie, and their three young sons. Now when I'd find him in tears, he'd say, "Oh, I was just thinking about my sister. She never complained, not once." A private person, Duane kept many things to himself, but I know that his big sister was his inspiration, his strength, and his angel as he faced the challenging and terrifying days that lay ahead.

Another person ever present in his thoughts as he contemplated chemo was his co-worker Willy. He spoke of him often, telling me how Willy had changed while on chemo for his brain tumor, exhibiting a violent temper and becoming angry and mean, "and you know what a nice guy Willy is." This was Duane's greatest fear — not the pain, not being sick, but changes in his personality. I met Willy for the first time when he and Larry came to visit Duane at the hospital following the first surgery. I sensed an aura of kindness and compassion surrounding him. Now he was a frequent visitor at our home, and was as concerned for me as he was for Duane. He gave me his cell phone number with strict instructions to call anytime I needed him, day or night. Willy angry . . . violent . . . mean? Could this possibly happen to my Duane? Thinking of Willy, Duane choked back tears as he apologized to the entire family in advance should he share a similar fate. "If I get real nasty on this stuff, I'm sorry! It isn't me. You know I don't mean it! Please forgive me."

Duane had decided on the oral chemo to enjoy more quality time. When I called Nurse Kathy to notify her of his decision, I asked, "What would you recommend if this were your husband?" "That's a tough question," she said. Yes it was, but we were in a tough situation and we needed to be sure, at least as sure as possible. She agreed that Duane had made a good choice, and that the new treatments were very encouraging in treating GBM. Okay. We would start after the upcoming July 4 weekend.

I too was afraid of the chemo. I was also frustrated with Duane's new passive attitude; the stress was building. I didn't want to upset Duane, but needed to vent, so I once again turned to my computer, this time writing a letter to "Sunny," my "future self" and alter ego discovered a year ago in a coaches' training exercise. At least by writing it, I could get it out and deal with it.

Recently I read somewhere to find out what I'm thinking to just write and write and write every day for a month and then read it — not before. Maybe that is a good idea. I need to put my fears into words 'cause I basically keep them to myself. So, my dear Sunny, I'll confide in you. I know you are the strong one, at peace — you've already lived through this mess.

I try to remain positive, and think I would be doing ok—if this were my tumor. But it is not; it is Duane's. I want him to fight. Why does he seem so passive? Is he relying on me to make this better? I want him to take some initiative here. Maybe I'm just getting tired. I need to do everything, even unplug his toilet.

I want him to take his vitamins — try; I want him to eat more, at least try. I want him to try! I tell him he is the one who has to do it. John Schuler is an eight-year survivor because he didn't have a Mary to do everything for him. He made the decision to take massive doses of shark cartilage; he didn't complain about how many pills he had to take.

So what do I do with this? I am also scared of the Thalidomide. If we ever have sex again he'll have to wear a condom. Sex — that wonderful night after our date at Toby's — was it good-bye? It was so tender, so intimate. Now I see myself putting up this wall around me again. I put off going to bed trying to protect myself from the hurt that is coming. I am afraid. I am grieving the loss of my strong yet tender Duane even though he is still here. I miss intimacy; I miss his laugh, his arms around me, his protection, and time to myself. I miss us.

80

Sunday July 14, 2002
Duane Update

Hello Friends,

Guess I better get busy and write this. Yesterday an old friend called, concerned because I hadn't sent an update in a while. What can I say? This week has been frustrating. When I get down, it's hard to write. Aren't you guys getting tired of hearing about this this? I guess not. Well, we can't be cheerful all the time, and that's okay. Some days are better than others. This is a new day, and a new week, so here goes.

Duane started oral chemo on Tues. As I counted out his pills, I was well aware that I held life and death in my hands—a fearsome responsibility. For five days he took Temodar, which kills cells. He doesn't take any more for twenty-three days. Along with this he takes a daily, increasing dosage of Thalidomide which keeps the cells from dividing (yes the stuff responsible for all those horrible birth defects decades ago). Just getting this stuff is quite an ordeal. Duane had to fill out a three-page questionnaire regarding his sexual practice among other things, returned it to his doctor who had to sign it before the drug could be ordered. Each month Duane has to complete a phone survey before it will be refilled, even if we are old farts not producing babies. Scary stuff. Condoms are mandatory. There are photographs of deformed babies and warning labels not to allow pregnancy all over the packaging and on each and every capsule. These two drugs used together have proven to be very effective in treating GBM. Except for the chronic fatigue, Duane feels fine thanks to the new anti-nausea drugs. If this stuff does what it is supposed to do, this is the way to go. The doctor will monitor him constantly, keeping an eye on any changes in the tumor.

81

The problem Duane is having is with balance and walking — mostly caused by swelling in his brain again. Dr. Trusheim has doubled his anti-swelling medication, but this time it isn't helping. There are times it gets worse, much worse. Ever since the second surgery Duane has walked quite well unaided. Then he started using a cane again, and now needs the walker and even the wheelchair occasionally. It isn't weakness, it's more of an equilibrium problem. Duane is actually eating much better and has gained five pounds. (Unfortunately, so have I — at least.) Another MRI may be needed this week. Dr. Trusheim's nurse assures me this isn't a setback, just something that "happens." Whatever it is, it sure is frightening, and frustrating when he is otherwise feeling so good.

Sadly, this past week Duane lost a member of his support team—his brother-in-law and fellow cancer patient David Vikmark in Rapid City. (David was the husband of Duane's ex-wife's sister — such a beautiful couple with two young children together.) His cancer had spread everywhere, including to his brain. In spite of his own declining health, David flew to see Duane after the first surgery. He called Duane weekly offering suggestions and moral support. We saw him just before the end of May in Rochester when he was at Mayo for treatment. How he will be missed! As much as Duane wanted to go to Rapid City for the funeral, he was too unstable to make the trip.

So, for all of you who think I'm always strong and in good spirits, I'm not. I don't dwell on the disappointments, but this whole thing just stinks. This is tough. So many uncertainties, so many ups and downs. Someone sent an email stating, "God doesn't give us more than we can handle. I just wish He didn't trust me so much!" Amen to that. We both remain optimistic and are very hopeful, concentrating on the many good things happening each day. Per Rabbi Kushner, this isn't "good" or "bad," it just is. It is how we deal with it that matters. Your prayers and support give both of us strength. I need them every bit as much as Duane does. Your messages, calls, and visits really help. Once again, our heartfelt thank you.

Love, Mary

Dearest Mary,

I hope you are writing a book. If not for publication, at least for you and Duane to read one day and see from the "other side" of this horrible disease how brave and steady and faithful you both are. And I believe with all my heart that with your spirit and faith and love for each other this will all be over soon and the two of you are going to live a long and happy life together.

So, when you're having one of those down days, let the rest of us out here do the praying for Duane, and for you. Just lean back and rest for a moment knowing that others are lifting you up in their thoughts.

God bless you both in these weeks to come.

Jan B.

We had received many such letters of encouragement. One scolded me:

Oh Mar, when I read your email I wanted to scream and cry and yell and anything else to get your attention. I'm sorry but that had to be a Catholic that said that to you about God not giving us more than we can handle. God doesn't give us this stuff—what he does is give us all the strength through him that we need to handle whatever life gives us! I'm so sorry that you are having a difficult time emotionally.

Mar, pardon me if I seem not to understand but gosh I think it's great that he has medication that helps with any

side effects and has his appetite back to a certain extent. If
balance is all he has to put up with right now, hey, hang on
to that wheelchair and make the most of it. It's not every day
that you get to ride around and have someone push you.
hahahaha

    Love ya

    Just me, your friend who loves wheelchairs

I was dumbfounded. I realized that the balance problem
wasn't just a nuisance, it was life threatening. If I was going to
get the support from my friends that I so desperately needed,
they had to understand my situation and my fears. Seeking
compassion and understanding, I responded to my friend.

Ouch. I can't win! I've also been scolded for not
acknowledging when I feel frustrated and scared. I've
been told its normal and to be expected. I sure don't
dwell on it, but it happens. I'm more concerned than
anything — why is his brain swelling? When this
happened before it was because the tumor was growing.
We can never forget that this tumor will never, never go
away, it will come back, and it is totally unpredictable.
It is my responsibility to be completely aware of any
changes, every nuance, and consider them serious until
proven otherwise. Neither Duane nor I has a problem
with the wheelchair; that is not the issue. The issue is
that suddenly, without warning, he could not walk,
could barely stand and had no control over his legs in
the middle of our driveway — and I had to keep him
from falling, get him to a safe location, and then get him
safely back home. He cannot fall. If he breaks a bone

he won't heal. We are both concerned as to why this is happening.

Re the "God doesn't give us . . ." quote: that was an attempt at humor. A good Methodist friend of Duane's thought we'd get a kick out of it. We did. I know where my strength comes from and that God has Duane and me in his hands. He will not let us down, no matter the outcome.

Sometimes we just need to get things off our chests and be understood.

<hr />

What was the most productive way I could deal with the frustration and apprehension of our current situation? Celebrate the positive — celebrate Duane. Tuesday, July 16, was his sixtieth birthday. I would make it the most memorable birthday he would ever have. "Plan A" was a surprise trip to a B&B on the river that featured a candlelight breakfast. His best meal continued to be breakfast, so this would be a perfect beginning to his day. The week before his birthday it became obvious that he was too unstable to go. Maybe another time when he was stronger . . . . So, on with "Plan B"; I was now an expert at "Plan B."

When he came into the living room his birthday morning, he was greeted by a dozen red roses in my best crystal vase on the coffee table and a huge "Happy Birthday" balloon tied to his favorite chair. The living and dining rooms were aglow with candlelight, and soft music played on the stereo. The dining room table was set with my best china, silver, and linens, with more candles. I played "Happy Birthday" to him on the bowed psaltery he had made me for my birthday a few years before. He savored all of his favorite foods for breakfast, including heart-shaped pancakes. We couldn't get to the B&B for a candlelight breakfast, so we had one at home. Surely the B&B couldn't have done better at providing a memorable and romantic breakfast.

Saturday, July 20
Duane's Update

Hello friends!
This has been a roller coaster week. We have been very concerned about Duane's fatigue, constant wooziness, and difficulty walking. Dr. Trusheim thinks he is having seizures, due to either too high or too low levels of Dilantin in his brain. We now go for a weekly blood test, every Monday at 6:40 pm, to check these levels, along with blood counts, etc. Everything was fine. So Keppra, another anti-seizure medication, was added to his arsenal of pills. Doc also scheduled another MRI saying, this isn't "unusual—not to panic." Easy for him to say! After nervously awaiting the results, the news came back—"No change!" Whatever is causing this, thank God it is not the tumor growing again. Duane said, "I didn't think it was the tumor. It couldn't be, not with all those people praying for me." So, thank you again for your prayers. Don't ever doubt they are working, they are. So, the anti-seizures meds have been increased again, and they are scheduling an EEG and hopefully this will get figured out. Other than this, he feels good. Now if he could just stay awake!
Funny story: When Duane first was released from the hospital in March, his insurance coordinator told me about another Duane about our age who has GBM, lives with his girlfriend, has the same doctor, etc. I called Harriet (the girlfriend) one day and we had a nice chat. In spite of the many things we had in common there was

one huge difference — her Duane was considering going back to his ex-wife to "please his (adult) children" and create peace. Since then Harriet and I have played phone tag a couple times, but haven't connected. Last Monday Duane and I went to the clinic for his first weekly blood draw. The man just ahead of us was about our age, also has a brain tumor, has the same doctor, and his name is Duane. So I, of course, asked the lady with him, "Oh, are you Harriet?" "No," she replied icily, "I'm Joan." Oooppppsssss! My Duane has been laughing about this ever since! (And so has Meg, his ex-wife!)

Duane turned sixty on Tues. He mentioned once he thought it would be nice to have some fish to look at, so, ignoring good advice to the contrary, I bought him an aquarium. He wasn't strong enough to go to a B&B so I created one for him at home. Later that evening our families joined us for dinner out at the Red Lobster. It was a memorable day, hopefully the start of a memorable year. No matter what lies is store for us in his next year, we will make the best of each day.

Have a good week, everyone! And keep those prayers and positive thoughts coming our way.

Love, Mary

"Absolutely not! No party!" Those had been Duane's strongly stated words to me regarding his sixtieth birthday. He had never had a party in his honor, and he was positive he did not want one now. Reluctantly, I promised to abide by his wishes. However I didn't promise not to help David plan one. Now more than ever we needed to celebrate Duane.

Saturday, July 27, Duane stood in awe at our association clubhouse surrounded by 100 of his closest friends, enjoying every minute of being the center of attention. "How did you pull this off? Everyone I know is here." And they were—all of our family members (his, mine, and Meg's), the guys from the fishing club, co-workers, and friends from all over Minnesota and even from Illinois. Most of those in attendance hadn't seen Duane for at least a few months and were shocked to see how thin and frail he was now. Yet Duane walked around unaided, talking to everyone — no wheelchair, walker or cane, running on pure adrenaline. A few hours earlier he was in bed unable to stand. Now here he was the star of the show, and of course showing off his little grandson.

Duane's sixty years of life flashed before us as David displayed photos on the clubhouse wall — pictures of Duane as a child, a high school student, an athlete, an FFA officer, and a young dad with David, and on fishing trips with friends from the Boundary Waters to Florida. Then there were our photos, the wedding where we met, David's and Christi's wedding, events with my family, playing with my grandchildren, holidays, the two of us on vacations — all from another life, seemingly long ago. Duane had been big and strong, full of life with his vibrant smile and dancing eyes.

In my mind I replay many memories of that day — the fellowship, the food, the pinata for the children, the festive fish decor gracing the walls and hanging from the ceiling, the fresh flowers on each table. The picture that remains is Duane posing with his co-workers and fellow brain tumor patients Willy and Larry — smiling, supportive of one another, and happy to still "be looking at the grass from the top down."

Duane's condition deteriorated rapidly in the days after the party. Tuesday he had a previously scheduled EEG to see if his problems were being caused by seizures.

Hi Kathy,

Thanks for the invitation, but I can't get away for lunch anytime soon.

Today was a day from hell — "opportunity for growth" doesn't come close. Duane slipped off his shower bench this afternoon and for the first time I was totally useless, unable to help him. No way could I get a 6'1", 190# wet man, with no strength, up from the bathtub floor. I made a few calls, then called 911. Since Duane wasn't injured, they didn't consider it an emergency. Before the police could get here, two of his co-workers, (including Willy, great guy undergoing treatment for reoccurring cancer himself) came to our aid. (Followed closely by my nephew Jason who works in Bloomington). They had to take the shower doors off to lift Duane, covered only by a towel, out of the bathtub to the safety of our bed. I called Doc's office and learned the EEG he had yesterday was fine — no indication of seizures. So, the MRI is great, the blood tests are great, and the EEG is great — and Duane is anything but. What the hell is this and what can we do about it? Do I sound just a little frustrated?

Sorry, it is all those fucking meds! (Obviously, these are not things I would say in an "update" or maybe I should. I did get a reprimand once for not being "positive" enough about having to use a wheelchair. So tomorrow the doctor, his nurse, and I will chat about what to do next. I have requested help at home. Don't worry about my not asking for help; I'm not. I am screaming for it. Thank God Duane's son and daughter-in-law live just two miles from us. They are in this with me — just not 24/7.

Love, Mary

July started with Duane heading to his beloved Lake Mille Lacs with his fishing partner on a beautiful summer morning, forgetting to bring his cane. The last night of July he lay exhausted in our bed after having been rescued from his own bathtub. How did he handle it? Was he scared? He was terrified and discouraged; we both were. He was embarrassed. He had been helpless and knew I was unable to help him. Yet he handled it with his usual grace and dignity, grateful to his friends and my nephew for coming to his aid, and to me for trying my best to help him.

Moguls

Not to know is bad . . . but not to wish to know is worse.
– West African saying

⸻

Discouraged and apprehensive, Duane was readmitted to the eighth floor at Fairview Southdale Hospital the following day, August 1. Now not only was he unable to stand, he was also having trouble swallowing. What was going on? The possibilities were frightening — no matter what they might be, we had to know. All I could see in my mind's eye was Duane helpless in the bathtub the day before.

Reading Psycho as a teenager, I had feared turning to the last page to discover the source of the terror hidden in the depths of the Bates Motel. Now I felt a similar dread, but it was even more terrifying—this was not a fictional story but a catastrophic reality. Maybe now with Duane hospitalized, the source of the terror hidden within his tormented body would finally be revealed. The answer was near as the next page.

When this journey began, I boldly told myself, "I can do this. I can do it all," and believed it. For years I had been telling Duane and my kids that I wanted "Lord knows I tried" engraved on my tombstone or I'd come back to haunt them. Now all I could think was, "Lord knows I'm trying." I couldn't do any more. I could not fix this.

In March I had bargained with God, "Okay, but you've got to help me." God did, every day, every time. There was no way either Duane or I could have gotten this far on our own. Now I was too exhausted and afraid to even pray.

When you're having one of those down days, let the rest of us out here do the praying for Duane and for you. Just lean back and rest for a moment knowing that others are lifting you up in their thoughts. Jan B.

My childhood friend Jan had recently sent this reply to an Update. Now I leaned back and rested for a moment, knowing that others were lifting us up in their thoughts and prayers.

Hi Mary, I just marvel at his and your stamina and courage. What fighters. Lesser people would have thrown in the towel. Randy

---

Stamina and courage? Is that how others saw us? Duane, yes—he was still the strongest, most courageous man I knew. Me, I was tired and scared. If I had it, I sure didn't see it in myself. Somehow Randy, a Fishing Club friend, did. We had never met before Duane became ill, but now his email message lifted me up and gave me strength.

God sends "angels" to remind us that we are not alone. Sometimes they appear to us in dreams; sometimes they speak to us in soft whispers during quiet moments if we are open to receive them. More often, he sends angels in the form of fellow travelers on our journey. We had angels surrounding us, sustaining us in unexpected ways.

Dr. Trusheim called me at home after examining Duane early the next morning. His words "I wish Duane was doing a little better," hung over my head like a rain cloud as I entered the hospital elevator heading for the eighth floor. An excited young couple got on the elevator with me — he was holding an overnight bag, and she gazed lovingly into his eyes. The elevator door opened on the maternity floor and they left to deliver their first child.

Choking back tears, I said to a woman remaining on the elevator with me, "At least someone is going to a happy floor." This woman, wearing a hospital ID, passed by her own floor and sat with me on the eighth floor landing, holding me in her arms as I told her about Duane. I was no longer attempting to suppress my tears. Taking my hands firmly in hers, she prayed for Duane and me and assured me she would continue to do so. God had sent another gentle reminder that we were not alone. This angel, a stranger on the elevator, lifted me up and gave me the strength I needed to walk down the corridor to Duane's room.

Mary, my heart goes out to the two of you in this time of desperation. "Why?" is the most asked question when things just aren't coming together in the desired manner. Duane's body will work this out. More than likely by now the two of you have test results explaining the "WHY?" and I pray it is the correct answer. Every update leaves me in awe of your strength and courage.

There is nothing more foreboding than knowing one of us has to continue without the other. But that is life and you have given it thought. But in your case Duane is going to be the victor. Mary, he is so lucky to have you. So on with the prayers and loving thoughts which pass through my mind at no specific time every day.   — *Robby*

Friday, August 02, 2002 10:53 PM
Updated Duane's Update

The results of the MRI are in; the problem is caused by the brain swelling again. Thought so. He is presenting like he did when this happened in April. Dr. Trusheim says the swelling is caused by either the tumor dying and creating more scar tissue, or the tumor is still growing. There is no way to tell without further surgery, which isn't an option right now. He has increased the steroids to decrease the swelling and put next week's chemo on hold to see how Duane reacts in the next few days. Duane is sicker now than he has been in months. To think, a week ago I was worrying because I didn't know how to get him to his surprise party. We won't know where he will go when released from the hospital until Monday either. So many unknowns. Please continue to pray for us.

Love, Mary

Go with the first version of why he is dizzy. Makes sense. Like your sister's flower that died. Think about it. – Robby

Barb's white bearded begonia — I had forgotten! That must be it. The tumor was dying, not growing. It had to be scar tissue causing the swelling and creating all this turmoil. Once again I was optimistic.

94

Tuesday, August 06, 2002
Duane update

Hi guys!
When I worked at the Weight Loss Clinic, I had clients visualize their goals as skiing down a hill and keeping their eyes on the bottom (a trick my friend Don taught me when I was trying to cross-country ski. I never could make it all the way down the hill without falling 'cause I just looked at the tips of my skis. It was only by keeping my eyes on where I was going, not where I was, that I made it to the bottom of the hill on my feet.)

This week I heard that dealing with brain cancer is like skiing moguls; just take one hill at a time before taking on the next one — and the one after that — and the one after that. We have just handled an unexpected mogul on our feet. It is going to be a long, bumpy ride all the way to an unseen bottom of this mountain.

Thanks to massive doses of Decadron, Duane is rallying once again after a terrifying relapse. This morning he said he felt "real good." I don't remember the last time he said that. His doctor and all the therapists are amazed at his resiliency. Today his therapist was teasing him about not being able to keep up with him as he raced down the halls. We both know his progress is thanks to all your prayers and support, and we are overcome with gratitude.

Dr. Trusheim is also encouraged. Duane will start his second round of oral chemo tomorrow, complete with Thalidomide. (Seems it wasn't the cause of Duane's problems.) The cause of the swelling, (whether it is scar tissue or tumor growth) is still not known. If it is indeed tumor growth, it is only about five percent so that is good. Doc feels the course of treatment we are on is containing the tumor, so we will continue with it for now.

His most welcomed news is that, as of today, he can have thin liquids again. When he was admitted, he needed all of his liquids, including coffee, "thickened" because his swallowing reflex was so slow. Liquid was getting into his windpipe, putting him at risk for choking and pneumonia. There are few things in this life Duane enjoys more than a strong, flavorful cup of coffee. This morning even hospital coffee tasted good to him. "Thickened" coffee that he had to eat with a spoon just didn't cut it.

He is still at Southdale, but will be moved to Methodist Hospital tomorrow for acute rehab (three hours daily) for maybe a week or so. He will be working on strength, balance, and endurance — walking, stairs, dressing, getting in and out of the shower/bathtub, swallowing, working on cognitive skills, numbers (the phone, his checkbook, etc), everything. By the time he gets home, he should be much stronger and hopefully safer. All of this was getting pretty hard for him, and I don't want a repeat of the bathtub incident anytime soon.

What a ride. I'm exhausted and my emotions are shot. I had to come home from the hospital this afternoon 'cause I have a slight tickle in my throat. I can't get sick, and neither can Duane. So, I'm hanging out with Buddy, my "foster dog" (a golden retriever I acquired in my son's divorce), and getting a little R&R while I can. So, to all of you who have been harping on me to take care of myself, I'm trying. I'm letting the well-trained hospital staff take care of Duane all by themselves while I get some rest.

Thank you once again for all your encouragement. It really helps getting messages from you on those tough days. God bless you all.

Until later,

Love, Mary

God bless you and Duane,
 Just read your update; it really is a tough battle. I am praying every day with you. I also have asked God to take you both gently off the mogul hill and move you to the
 Bunny Hill. It is smoother and when you fall it doesn't hurt so much.
 You are in our prayers everyday.
 Love, Jack and Katie

If one is going to ski moguls, or even the bunny hill, he has to train and get in shape. Duane was determined to get home as soon as possible, pushing himself and making steady physical progress as he struggled with rehab. His cognitive skills were another matter as he continued to have difficulty with a checkbook and simple math. In the past Duane could do complicated math in his head faster than I could turn on a calculator. Another problem for always-punctual Duane was having to wait for the transport that never picked him up at the scheduled time.

To Dave Nystom, Dan McCanney, Jack Naylor:
 Good morning guys. Thought you'd get a kick out of this. Yesterday Duane was just a bit "impatient" (Duane?) waiting to go down for physical therapy. "If I'm just going to be just sitting here I might as well be bass fishing!"
 He's doing better — already planning on going to Lake Vermillion with you guys for next month's fishing trip and to Canada in Oct. 2003. He's coming home Wed. Come see us anytime.

Thanks, Mary, I just got a chuckle on what you just said.
Yep, nothing wrong with his attitude, but did he really want
*to go **bass** fishing? I'll call soon. – Jack*

Duane's hospitalization at Methodist allowed me to have some much-needed time at home alone to reconnect with friends. I needed Dee. Dee and I had met two years before when I took her life-coaching class. We bonded immediately, discovering we were so much alike we must have been sisters in a past life. Often when meeting for lunch we would be dressed the same; sitting across the table from one another, our body posture would mirror the other.

One of the many things we had in common was Duane, whom she had dated more than twenty years before. We agreed that their prior relationship was a "non-factor" as she became my mentor and trusted friend. As Duane's illness progressed, her wisdom, compassion, and understanding provided incomparable support. Once when she discussed our situation with her husband, he made a request. He said that if he became ill, "Don't bury me before I'm dead." These were words I would keep in mind in the months ahead.

Dee encouraged me to take control of my life in the few areas where I could. Now with Duane in the hospital I actually did have some control in my own home. "It is the only place you have control right now. You can eat — or not. You can listen to music or watch TV — or not. Go to bed — or not. Every other area of your life is being controlled by outside events. Control what you can." It was important for me to realize that in some things, no matter how seemingly insignificant, I could have some control over my own life.

When you're going through hell, just keep going.
                                    – *Winston Churchill*

Duane was discharged after one week of therapy, weaker and more tired than I expected. He mentioned spitting up a little blood into a tissue that morning. Had he told anyone? No, he dismissed it, saying it must be happening because the room was too dry. I didn't make an issue of it, but kept an eye on the situation.

Friday, August 16, 2002 2:50 AM
Duane's Update

Hi guys,
I started to write this earlier. I guess by now that would be yesterday morning (Thursday)—an entirely different letter than the one I am writing now. In my last update I wrote about this cancer journey being like skiing moguls. Truer words were never spoken. Skiing moguls isn't easy. You never know when one will knock you right on your ass. One just did.
Duane came home Wednesday from his two-week stint in two different hospitals. It was a long haul, and he welcomed being home, looking around with tear-filled eyes when he settled into the sanctuary of his recliner. He enjoyed a favorite dinner, a visit with David, Christi, and Will, and phone calls from good friends. We stayed up late (10:00) and talked about how lucky we are. It had been a beautiful day.
Thursday morning he woke gasping in pain on his left side, like he had a broken rib. Dr. Trusheim's nurse asked if the pain was worse when he took a deep breath. He said no. She told me what to do — pain medication, alternate cold and hot packs — and if he didn't feel

99

better to go to ER for a chest x-ray. He got worse, so David and I brought him to Fairview Ridges Hospital (three miles from our house) to get checked out. I thought it might be muscle spasms from the weakness on his left side. (He is now too weak to support himself in that treasured big recliner of his and needs to be propped up with pillows). I also feared a possible touch of pneumonia, thanks to the swallowing problem.

This was unbearable. Having a lung scan, this strong man was screaming out in pain. After two brain surgeries, this was the worst thing he'd endured. For the first time I couldn't stand to watch and had to leave the room. My hands feel like lead as I type this. He has blood clots in both lungs. (I understand thickening blood is a possible side effect from the large doses of steroids he takes — necessary to reduce the swelling in his brain! Catch-22). Having blood clots is bad enough in itself. It is worse if one has a brain tumor. The drugs that thin the blood to dissolve the clots can also cause the brain to bleed; I was too afraid to ask what will happen then, but I can about imagine. If he doesn't take the drugs, the blood clots will kill him. You know you're in trouble when the ER doctors look scared.

There are no words to tell you how I feel tonight. I left the hospital at 1:30a.m. after he was safely tucked away in intensive care — only one day after he was released from another hospital. David, Duane, and I discussed our options and decided to go with a less aggressive form of treatment, one that will thin the blood with less chance of serious problems in Duane's already traumatized brain. We were all in a state of shock. The only difference between now and March 7 is that in March Duane didn't realize how much trouble he was in; tonight he does. We promised each other we would not give up.

I don't remember when I've felt as alone as I did just walking out of that hospital. David had left a little earlier to go home to his family. I don't remember seeing other vehicles on the road driving home — of course at that hour most people were sleeping. But being able to sit down at my computer in the middle of the night is a comfort. I don't feel quite so alone. I also have my beloved foster dog, Buddy, here at my side.

To ask you once again for your prayers goes without saying. Even tonight Duane said to a nurse, "Someone must be praying for me right now. I have people all over the country praying for me." And I need your strength, support, and prayers now more than ever. As many of you know, I was never athletic and have never been a particularly good skier. But with your help I will make it through these moguls. Right now, I've never been more scared. I never anticipated this. It is now the 16th. One month ago was his 60th birthday. And, oh, how I love this wonderful man. Please pray for us.

Thank you!

Love, Mary

Caregiving is watching what your loved one has to suffer; it may involve such shock and horror and helplessness that the sobs and unshed tears build up and suffocate you without your realizing it, wracking your mind and body only later when it is all over. – Jessica Schaver

(wife of a seventeen month GBM survivor)

A few hours later I sent a "Revised Update" to a select number of our team — to my closest friends:

Hi again.

It is now 4:30 in the morning. I took a shower, reread what I just sent you and I want to throw up. My earlier state of shock has worn off. To a select few of you on this list, I want to add a P.S.:

P.S. I want to scream and throw things. Dammit! I have done such a good job at playing this game, and now not only have the rules changed, they changed the whole damn game! I was never good at sports as it was. Brain cancer — fine — we can deal with that. OK. But now it's life-threatening blood clots in his lungs! I know "Life isn't fair," and "The fair comes in August." But Dammit! It is August! And this isn't fair!

Tonight having that lung scan was sheer torture. David held his father's hands and comforted him while Duane lay flat on his back, arms over his head being told to "take a deep breath, hold it and don't move." I have never known anyone as strong as Duane, and tonight he was screaming in pain. Afterwards he told us that what got him through was thinking, "This is for Will because I don't want that little boy to grow up without his grandpa." Later, when we all knew what we were dealing with, David said, "Dad, why don't you try to get some rest." Duane replied, holding my hand, "I just want to look at the two of you." Once again my shattered heart was overflowing with love for my man.

I don't know what strength is anymore. I don't walk on water, never have. My cousin Louise asked me just to have a good cry. I don't have tears left. My hair is falling out; I just polished off a jar of peanut butter, and have gained 10 pounds. Not only that, I am enjoying a glass of Christian Brothers brandy on the rocks at 5:00 a.m. Does that qualify as a "nightcap"?

As Paul Harvey says, "And now you know the rest of the story!" Thanks for listening. I feel better.

Time to get ready to greet the day.

Love, Mary

My bed remained untouched as I left for the hospital just five minutes away. By now Duane was resting comfortably in ICU with IVs and monitors recording his vitals. "Duane, is this your wife?" asked his nurse as I tiptoed into his room. He reached for my hand and looked at me with adoring eyes, "No. She's my angel."

Friday evening I had planned to get together with the Loose Ladies at Kathy's. As another challenging day unfolded after a sleepless night, I decided not to go. How could I leave Duane? Kathy suggested that the Ladies met at my house instead; everyone would come equipped with cleaning supplies to "help me." I appreciated her offer, but declined. I didn't have the energy to figure out what they could do to help, even though by this time I needed help with everything.

"You go! You need to be with your friends." Duane insisted that I take a night off. I wouldn't listen to anyone else, but I did listen to Duane. I also listened to my friend Terry. She knew I'd had a sleepless night and insisted on driving me across town to Kathy's. We would leave whenever I'd had enough. Reluctantly, I agreed.

The last time I had seen any of my girlfriends was at the hospital in March. Now they welcomed me, telling me how "good" I looked. Surely they were lying; I had been crying half the night and hadn't slept. My futile attempts at applying makeup did little to camouflage the dark circles beneath my swollen eyes. My attempts at casual conversation were equally as futile, only reminding me how far away my former life was to me now. Our get-togethers had always been times to laugh off the stresses of work and our lives. Now I felt like a warped piece of a jigsaw puzzle; exhausted from a sleepless night and consumed with worry, I no longer fit in my usual space. I excused myself early, thinking at least I had tried. My concerned friends did their best to support me, but home was the only place I wanted to be. I had control at home. It was my haven. Here I could cry — or not; scream and throw things — or not; go to bed—or not. At home I could just "be."

Once again in the sanctuary of my home, email provided the inspiration I needed as I read the responses to the last update. Messages of love and support from friends and family filled my computer screen and comforted my soul.

———

Mary, saying I'm sorry is of no use to you, but it is the best I can give at this time. Do not beat yourself up. Duane will endure as much as God wants him to and so will you. Not to sound stupid, but I'm crying. Drink your brandy and the hell with the world! And then have another one for Duane.

We all handle issues differently and you have been and remain a wonderful testimony to love and strong belief in God. But now let it all go before you are in serious health trouble. Advice is cheap, but you need to now take care of you. And keep "venting" like you just did. It is good for you and there are no friends in this world that don't understand and are more willing to listen than the ones on this list. You are loved and thought of daily. – Robby

———

Over the years Duane has been a distant cousin. Nevertheless, he has always been present at key events in the Deegan family. We are so grateful that Duane has someone like you in these impossible times. He deserves a loving, caring companion — and he found the best. Our tears well up with every email — and we never forget Duane and you at Sunday Mass — your strength is amazing and God will reward you both. – Gene and Nancy

Dear Mary,

I think of you several times a day and I tell myself to write. But the words are never there. There is no way I can possibly understand what you and Duane are going through. To say that my thoughts and prayers are with you seems shallow, but know that it is true.

Stay as strong as you can, Mary, and please take care of yourself. Our thoughts are with you.   – Dick Wright

A devoted friend of Duane's for over thirty-five years, Dick had been forwarding my messages to their mutual friends. Messages from former colleagues touched Duane deeply, bringing not only a tear to his eyes, but also a smile to his face.

Having skied downhill (but never with enough courage to try moguls) I understand your description of Duane's journey We are all praying that he gets one of those exhilarating top-of-the mountain views soon.

I appreciate the updates on Duane's condition that are forwarded to me by Dick Wright. I, in turn, forward them to Al Heitala and others who know or have known Duane over the years. Tell Duane that he is being prayed for in many quarters.   – Ron Sorenson, Publisher

Please tell Duane to hang in there! Having worked with him over a decade day in and day out, I know he is not the kind of guy to give up and he will ultimately prevail. Remind him of the time he went on a salad-only diet for months and months and months, and lost a lot of weight. That's the kind of will power he has. Tell him I'm looking forward to seeing him at our annual Good Friday get together at the Officers Club. My prayers and thoughts are with him. – Al Heitala

A letter from a stranger was the most touching of all.

Mary and Duane,

E-mail, how it has changed the world and how it brings us all together to support and take care of each other. My friend Dick is in pain right now because he fears for his friend Duane. I will be there for him, and you can count on that!

Your message touched my soul with the reality that life is not all roses. It passes out the moguls you describe so vividly. My prayer gift to you is to know that there are many out there that wish there was a miracle to throw your way, to boost your strength, to help you sleep when it simply won't come, and to tell you that you are not alone. We are simply people trying to reach out and change the world for you. If we can make a difference, we are here!

Loneliness is feeling you are forsaken, and you are not — neither of you. A perfect stranger wakes in the night and sends as much strength to you as she can possible muster up. If I can light a candle, I will do it! – Judi H., Ely, Nevada

Dear Judi,

One of the books I've read recently talked about angels on earth — how God uses mere people to show that he is here with us in our trials and pain. Thank you for being one of his messengers. Your beautiful note brought tears to my eyes, and to Duane's. Last night, when he was telling me how this clot situation has him terrified, I reminded him of your letter. Thank you for sharing your comfort and strength with us. It makes a difference. I hope we won't always be strangers. Any friend of Dick's is a friend of Duane's, and of mine.

Love, Mary

One of the most profound statements of all came in a phone conversation with my daughter:

Duane has given David this incredible foundation — he has shown him what it is like to be a man. — Ann Walchuk

That he did. He showed us all, crisis after crisis; he faced fear, pain, setbacks, disappointment, and disability with strength, courage, faith, and gratitude. He fought each challenge with resolve and confidence, never giving up or giving in.

August 24, 2002
Duane's update
Hi guys,

Guess I'm a little late on this update. I'm getting some "what's going on?" calls, so I guess I better get busy. After yet another full week in the hospital, Duane came home on Wednesday. Last Friday morning he had more tests done to determine the extent of the clots. Even while performing the procedure, the tech was able to see a large clot in his pulmonary artery. In addition to the clots in his lungs, he had several clots in his legs. So on Friday afternoon he had a surgical procedure to insert a filter up through his groin, placing it just below his heart to block any clots from his lower body from getting into his heart and/or lungs. (A "Greenfield" for any of you medical types out there.) Amazing. I would have found this fascinating if it didn't involve Duane. (Speaking of medical types, a RN asked me if I were a nurse or a doctor. Guess I've learned a thing or two in the last few months.)

He was in ICU until Sunday, and on bed rest, oxygen, and heavy-duty blood thinners till Wednesday. It seems

*it takes "a while" for the clots to dissolve. Too bad —
they are very painful. Two brain surgeries and this is the
worst thing he has had to endure. The good news is he
was able to be discharged without oxygen, and he has
cut back on pain meds since he has been home.*

*Until Duane is strong enough to go out for therapy,
we will have it at home. He has had a home health
nurse visiting the last two days to check him and draw
blood to measure his Coumadin levels, plus various
blood tests needed to measure the effects of the chemo
and the thalidomide. He will also be getting PT and OT
at home for now. Today we had a Lifeline installed on
our phone so if he has a problem on the rare occasions
when he is at home alone, he can get help right away.
Managing all this, setting up all these appointments,
keeping all these meds straight, following up on
everything, I feel like the CEO of a large company. How
do sick people do this without someone like me around?*

*After all this, Duane is better physically. Emotionally
he is devastated. He has a long way to go to be where
he was even a month ago. This is the first time he
hasn't wanted visitors. Sure hope that changes in the
next few days. Phone calls and visits are vital to him.*

*Big week coming up — MRI on Monday and the next
visit with Dr. Trusheim on Thursday to check on the
tumor and decide what to do next. I sure hope
everything is ok. We could use a break. This past
episode really took the wind out of our sails. Yes, I
remember, "We cannot control the wind, but we can
adjust the sails." They just feel a bit tattered these days.*

*We have received many messages from "new" people,
so thank you for forwarding my little messages to
others. Thank you for your concern, phone calls, cards,
messages and your prayers. They are what make
this "do-able."*

Love, Mary

Dear Mary,

I like your comparison to sailboats. I just finished watching the Wednesday night races in Annapolis. We are right at the finish line and the wind is blowing good tonight. Each sail was filled with wind, some tattered, and they all looked like they were on a collision course, but not one upset!!! You are right; you will come out of this together with the gentle winds at your back and the whispers of the lapping water on the sides that this storm shall pass for much calmer waters.   – Suzanne

Mary

Your courage is an inspiration to all those that you have touched. Hang in there — I know that you are sustained by a higher power and all who know you are thinking of you and Duane constantly.   – Bob

Thursday, August 29, 2002
Duane's Update

Good news! We went to see Dr. Trusheim today with Monday's MRI in hand. Whatever was left of the tumor/scar tissue is smaller. It looks much better that when he left the hospital (Southdale) three weeks ago. Per Doc, "The pictures look good, very good." There is still swelling, but that is being controlled by the Decadron; (Duane's dosage of that is gradually being reduced so I no longer need to set the alarm for the middle of night to give him his meds! Yippeeee!) Next week we will start round three of the oral chemo — one pill per day for five days, plus the Thalidomide. If all goes well, we don't need to see the doctor again for a month or two.

109

So the only concern is the clots. Doc says they often happen with brain tumors. "Lucky" Duane, his case was worse than most. We'll just keep a close eye on that situation as well. He has a nurse come here for a blood draw (INR) a couple times a week to monitor Coumadin levels. But tonight we are very relieved, and once again hopeful. It's time for him to get a break. Thanks again for all of your support.

Love, Mary

Stretched to the Edge

"And it came to pass . . ."

———

Scripture repeatedly affirms "and it came to pass." Nothing comes to stay, it comes to pass — even the moguls of August. Shaky and scared, somehow we had endured by clinging to one another and relying on the prayers of others. Could we possibly spend some time on the Bunny Hill for a while?

Before the tumor, Duane read two or three books at one time. If he had five minutes to spare, he was reading. He no longer read; it was too much of a challenge. I devoured the many inspirational books that had been sent or recommended to us, then bought them on audiotape for Duane. Powerful books — *Love, Medicine and Miracles* by Dr. Bernie Siegel, *When Bad Things Happen to Good People* by Rabbi Harold Kushner, *It Isn't About the Bike* by Lance Armstrong, and *Nothing Is Impossible* by Christopher Reeve — motivated and encouraged us both. Duane would listen intently at home, in the car, wherever he could, just as he had once read.

One book in particular captivated him. He listened to *The Isaiah Effect* by Gregg Braden over and over again. The premise of the book emphasizes the power of living in a constant state of prayer — a constant state of gratitude. It points out that our thoughts change our energy, therefore effect our health, our lives, and our world.

Gratitude. How can one be grateful having experienced

the moguls of August? In spite of the painful ordeal Duane had endured, he continued counting his blessings. Not trusting his memory, each day he consulted his little green notebook that listed the names of those on his prayer list. He was faithful about praying for others and didn't want to forget anyone on his list. Duane's state of gratitude was a blessing to us and to all with whom he was in contact.

Frightened? Of course he was. Discouraged? Without a doubt. Yet, with gratitude Duane welcomed the RN and physical therapist from home health care into our home when he was not able to get out for required blood draws and therapy. Leaving home for necessary doctor's appointments was as challenging as running a marathon.

September 10, 2002
Duane Update

Hi guys!
It is my pleasure to report an uneventful week. I'm almost afraid to say it. We saw Dr. Loken, Duane's primary physician, yesterday for a follow-up of his hospitalization for the clots. She was very pleased with his progress, and explained that any type of cancer, no matter where, causes changes in the liver that affect the blood clotting tendency. She is not overly concerned about Duane's clots because he is on Coumadin, which is monitored regularly, and the Greenfield filter keeps any more clots from getting into his lungs. The existing clots appear to be dissolving, as he rarely has lung pain anymore, doesn't experience shortness of breath, and isn't spitting up much blood. So dare I say it looks good for now.
His body is slowly recovering from the weeks in the

112

hospital. Physically he is spent; his weak legs can barely support him. Although his appetite is improving he has no energy, and he experiences waves of exhaustion and fatigue. At-home health care is a godsend.

This last episode set us both back emotionally. While in the hospital, he admitted he was "scared shitless" and is now more concerned about the blood clots than the tumor. He hasn't wanted visitors lately, but when he has had a little company it has done him a world of good. So please come see him, or call, write, email — lets keep his spirits up! It will be a while until he can get out again.

This weekend I'm taking a little break — my first since Duane was diagnosed in March. I'm going to Two Harbors for the weekend. My best friend from high school, currently a resident of Sacramento, is participating in an inline skate marathon from Two Harbors to Duluth. (Hard to believe someone my age doing this, but then, she was a cute little cheerleader in high school — I wasn't. I didn't become a "cheerleader" until years later!) Anyway, she has dedicated all of her training and her race to Duane and his recovery. Pretty neat — they have never met. It will be great to hang out with her for a while, and to get some cool Lake Superior air to restore my soul.

Duane's son will stay with him this weekend so I can get away. It will be good for them, too, and of course Duane will enjoy spending time with grandson Will, now seven months old.

I need the break. Next week my sister leaves for a two-and-a-half-week trip to the British Isles, so I'll also have our mom — age ninety-two — to care for while she's gone. Yikes! Lord, give me strength and patience. Please keep those prayers coming.

Tomorrow is September 11. In the grand scheme of things, our problems seem minimal compared to what others have endured. Their pain and their courage are inspirational. So many lives changed that day — all our lives changed. A few hours after the attacks, my office building was evacuated due to bomb threats. Duane came to get me and I felt safe. He has been my rock and my strength through national crisis and family crisis. Just as our country came together and our resolve became stronger during this tragedy, Duane and I will get though our current crisis as well.

I recently finished reading Lance Armstrong's inspirational book. Fabulous! If Lance can come back from the depths to not only survive cancer but also win the Tour de France — 4 times — and become a father, we can get through this. It isn't easy, but we are getting through it. Once again, your thoughts, prayers, and all your support make this journey of our doable. We couldn't do it without you.

Love, Mary

Lake Superior was calling me home. I missed the peaceful September days when sunlight dances on the water under sapphire skies. I needed to be invigorated by deeply breathing crisp lake air while sitting on the rocky shore near my house in Two Harbors. If only I could fill tanks of Lake Superior air to inhale as needed, like others receive necessary doses of oxygen.

He leads me beside the still waters. He restores my soul.
– Psalm 23:2-3

Having endured the stress and anxiety of the past months, and facing the uncertain months that lay ahead, I was desperately in need of restoring. Devoting all of my energy to Duane's care was hurting me.

Not wanting to be a burden, Duane strongly encouraged me to go to Two Harbors. My time away was equally as important for him as it was for me. Before we met he had lived alone for most of the past twenty years. Sharing his home I respected his sanctuary in the garage and in his den, and of course his needed time alone on fishing trips. For the past six months he seldom had had time alone — even in the bathroom. This was as much of a loss to him as his health. This loss, too, he accepted gracefully. Now, psychologically, he needed to know I could leave him for a couple days. He also needed time to hang out with David and Will.

Like a mom leaving an infant with a teenaged babysitter for the first time, I left pages and pages of detailed instructions and doctors' phone numbers for David. Pills were counted out and placed alongside the medication schedule. At-home exercises with instructions for Duane's legs were highlighted; they needed to be wrapped to the knees with ace bandages and elevated a couple of times a day. Heat needed to be applied. He needed to have his legs measured at the thickest part of the calf daily to make sure he wasn't swelling, indicating blood clots. I also left homemade pancake batter in the refrigerator, along with an abundance of his favorite foods. Meg had brought over hot, home-made cinnamon rolls. Leaving him that Friday, I knew Duane and David would be fine. Still, I knew no one could take care of him like I could.

I also needed to be cared for; I needed my old friend. Mary Del and I had gone our separate ways after high school graduation. No matter how many years passed between visits, we would continue where we left off as if we had spoken yesterday. During Duane's illness, she was an insightful and invaluable source of support, having walked a similar path herself years earlier when her four-year-old daughter had lost an eye to a rare cancer. A few years ago she had shared the journey with her sister and brother-in-law as he fought — and lost — his battle with cancer.

Now with a leg injured in a fall, she was skating a marathon along the shore of Lake Superior for Duane. When she doubted she could go on, thoughts of him kept her going. She told herself, "You can do this. Don't quit. Don't give up! Keep going. Just a little more. One more mile for Duane, one more hill, just a little more for Duane."

Louise and I were waiting for her as she triumphantly crossed the finish line, proudly proclaiming to be "the most obnoxious woman in my age group!" Together we called Duane on my cell phone, "Honey, you're going to be fine! She finished for you!" The excitement and tears were evident in his voice as he cheered and thanked a woman he had never met.

Later as a group of us toasted her success with champagne, she presented me with her finisher's jersey for Duane; there was not a dry eye among us. This particular event is one of the largest in-line skate marathons in the world — over 4000 entrants. Thousands of finishers celebrated their success that Saturday at Duluth's Canal Park, but none more enthusiastically than those of us cheering for Mary Del and Duane.

Angels had been surrounding us for months, reminding us we were not alone. They gave us strength, peace, and hope. They did not appear in the form of winged beings with glowing halos, but spoke to us through ordinary people in our daily lives. This day they spoke through my old friend, a fifty-six-year-old woman with an injured leg who completed the twenty-six mile race in two hours and fifty-six minutes, telling

116

us, "You can do this. Don't quit. Don't give up!"

This angel also gave me much needed encouragement as we leisurely strolled along the lakeshore the next morning. She reminded me that the first thing we are told on airplanes is that, if there is a problem, we must put our own oxygen masks on first before attempting to help anyone else. I had been trying to do everything without putting on my own mask. Returning from our walk, I felt relaxed and invigorated, and I had a better perspective. I felt better able to handle the weeks ahead.

Being back in Two Harbors with my best friend was the best therapy and inspiration I could have had. How could I be discouraged now? Duane and I would finish our marathon with equal class and style. As for now, it was time for me to go home and begin my own marathon, two and a half weeks caring for both Duane and my mother.

I thought I was prepared. I thought my respite trip to Lake Superior had fortified and invigorated me, giving me the strength to take on the challenge of proficiently and patiently caring for two. I thought I could do it all. I was wrong. I discovered that as patient and loving as I tried to be, it was not enough.

What were those painful red blotches on my eyelid and forehead? Five days after my mother arrived, the entire left side of my face was throbbing. Was I experiencing acne from a change in my hormone replacement therapy? Oh no. It was shingles — undoubtedly caused by stress — diagnosed on my birthday. My left eye, hidden behind my over-sized "Jackie O" sunglasses, looked like that of the beast in Beauty and the Beast. Fortunately only the eyelid was affected, not the eye itself. In spite of the pain, in spite of how grotesque I looked, it could have been much worse.

Obviously I wasn't taking as good care of myself as I thought. The responsibility of caring for one more person was both overwhelming and exhausting. Dee had organized my friends to help with meals, but the day in, day out responsibility was all mine.

Like little children having to vie for my attention, both Duane and my mother demanded more and more of me, taking less and less responsibility for their own well-being. I was sleeping on the couch to be able to hear Duane in the bedroom and Mom in the guestroom downstairs. Mom fell the first night in my care and had badly bruised herself. I couldn't let her fall again. The sleeping pills given me by my dermatologist remained unopened on the bathroom counter. In spite of my doctors' urgings to get some rest, I was on call 24/7 and could not sleep.

As cooperative as Duane usually was, now even he was exasperating. One night he fell trying to use the urinal, spilling its contents and the contents of his bedside water glass all over the floor. I was thankful he wasn't hurt and that I was able to get him back into bed without injuring myself. After sopping up the carpet, I needed to go to the bathroom myself. While sitting on the toilet, I heard Duane yelling for me, "Mary! Water! I need water! I need water now!"

"My God, Duane! Can't you wait one minute?" I scolded. "Can't I even take time to pee?" No wonder I had shingles.

He gave me the silent treatment for a day; then the next night as I was getting him ready for bed and giving him his nightly meds, he sheepishly explained, "Last night when I was calling for you, I thought I was going to die. I thought I was choking and couldn't breathe. I thought I wouldn't be able to breathe again. I needed water. I was scared and I needed you."

"Why didn't you tell me this last night?"

"You yelled at me and didn't give me a chance."

Frustrated and angry, I had yelled at him, something I had never done. I had known he was upset about the fall and the mess, and thought he was just being demanding. I didn't know how frightened he had been. Now terribly ashamed, I cried until I threw up. I wrote in my journal, *What more can I do? I don't dare go to sleep! I am not Superwoman; I'm sick myself and overwhelmed. A nursing home couldn't give him better care than I do. I can't do any more but it's not enough.*

Concerned friends responded to my next update with a wealth of suggestions, some easier said than done: herbal remedies, avoid caffeine and red meat, deep breathing, walking, glasses of wine, meditation, yoga, and setting aside a two-hour block of time daily for myself.

Okay, now here is a little of your advice to me back. I quote "You are no good to anyone if you don't take care of yourself first." Duane has other family too. Let them step in and carry more of this. Put yourself first now. When we martyr ourselves we usually don't ask if our loved ones expect us to do so. Sure they enjoy having a slave on hand but they didn't ask us to do it. So quit it.

Love, Lillian

Dear, dear Mary,

I can't imagine how it might feel to be in your shoes these days. Well, maybe I can guess a little — exhausted, discouraged, hopeful, angry, frustrated, lost, disoriented, determined, responsible, loving, purposeful, and scared. Did I hit any of your emotions? As you know, it IS important that you put on your own oxygen mask first.

Sending prayers and love to you both, Dee

She hit them all, everything I had been feeling and things I hadn't thought of. There was one more — guilty. Somehow seeing the words, acknowledging the words and their associated feelings took away their power.

Ahem. Something was caught in my throat, something I couldn't dislodge. My wise friend Dee noticed that I kept clearing my throat when we spoke. What was stuck? What wasn't I saying? Robby had encouraged me a few weeks before to keep on venting. Dee pointed out there was much I had not expressed in the last six months. I had not verbalized or named my fears. She was right. In my efforts to hang on to the positive, I had not truly expressed my fear. Oh I knew it was there. Maybe if I didn't acknowledge it, it would go away. It didn't. It erupted in shingles on my face; it caught in my throat.

Okay, I was afraid. Of what? Name it. Say it. Write it down. Face it.

I was afraid Duane would die. What would happen to me without him? I was afraid of how much he would deteriorate and suffer — and for how long. I was afraid of how much he might change. I was afraid of not being able to take care of him. I was afraid of how long I could go without a job.

What else? Besides the fear, I was already experiencing grief and loss. Late at night I began to write in my journal, the words coming slowly at first, like the first fingers of water breaking through a dam holding back a pent-up river. Then more came, faster, until the dam exploded and the river ran free:

Shingles. Nerves. What am I not saying? There must be a lot, as I am heartbroken and afraid as I try to remain positive grasping onto hope wherever I can find it. Duane, I love you with all of my being. There is so much I miss. I miss who you/I were. I need to accept/love who you/I are now. I guess this is what I cannot say — I can't say goodbye to who we were.

I miss leaning on you.
I miss needing you.
I miss being your lover.
I miss feeling like a woman.
I miss falling asleep in your arms.

I miss your laugh.
I miss your recording your TV programs
even La Femme Nikita.
I miss your going fishing.
even when you got up at 4:00 a.m.
I miss your silver hair on your black shirt collar.

I miss riding in your truck and
having you open the door for me.
I miss your laughing at me as you pull out the step stool
making it easier for me to climb up into the cab.

I miss going out for dinner.
I miss our dreams.
I miss pillow talk.
I miss having "life" to talk about.
I miss our having a life

I miss my kids and grandchildren.
I miss my friends.
I even miss going to work.
I miss feeling secure.

I miss time alone, time to relax
even when you go to sleep.
Then I want to slap myself for being such a brat!
You are still here! You didn't die!
Then I would have plenty of time to be alone.

I miss being able to plan
    — like meeting you in Winnipeg.
I miss our wonderful life.
I miss you/us the way we were.

Having purged my thoughts and feelings with pen and paper, I felt cleansed, freeing what had been buried. The catch in my throat soon disappeared.

What did Duane miss? He never talked about it; he only dealt with life as it was each day. It was late September; he should have been in Canada in search of his trophy walleye. How he loved this time away — how he must have missed his independence. I don't know how Duane felt, I could only imagine. Knowing Duane, he was counting his blessings.

Days of Red and Gold

Every day we need to adjust to the "new normal."
Duane, I miss who you / I were. I need to accept / love you
for who you / I are now. I guess that is what I can't
say - I can't say goodbye to that part of us.
– Journal entry September 27, 2002

———

"Normal" — what was that? For Duane in October it had been freezing his buttocks sitting in his boat somewhere in Manitoba. Now he was sitting in his favorite chair propped up with pillows supporting his weakened left side. Was he back in Canada now as he sat with his eyes closed deep in thought on these crisp autumn days? Was he remembering our rendezvous the previous October?

Halfway through his six-week fishing trip, I had flown to Winnipeg to meet him for a long weekend. At that time I thought my life was in shambles. Our country had been attacked on September 11. There had been three bomb threats and evacuations at my place of employment. My son had separated from his wife. Nothing in my life felt secure — not in my country, in my workplace, nor in my family — not until I arrived at the Winnipeg airport and Duane was holding me tight. I was safe in his strong arms; nothing could hurt me here.

For five idyllic days we enjoyed museums and art galleries, quaint shops and restaurants, the sculpture garden, and the zoo. We drove in a snowstorm to Selkirk, where I witnessed firsthand the boat landing overflowing with trucks and boat trailers, proof that others actually did enjoy fishing in the cold October snow. When he kissed me good-bye at the airport, my independent Duane whispered in my ear, "I think we should make this an annual event." I readily agreed.

Now I looked back on that last October, missing who we were and trying to find peace with who we had become.

Friday, October 11, 2002
Duane Update

Oh what a gorgeous fall day — the kind that makes us grateful to be living in Minnesota. A day like this is always sandwiched in between those that aren't so gorgeous (for example, we had a little snow on Monday and are expecting even colder temps — in the twenties — this weekend.) But today is warm with red and golden leaves shimmering in the sunlight against a clear blue sky; all we need to do is be thankful and enjoy it while we can.

This is how our journey is right now — we are enjoying good days and sunny skies. After a month of home health care, Duane is now back at Ridges Hospital for physical and speech therapy three days a week. Being able to "get out" even for therapy has been a major psychological boost for him as he sees progress and knows he is able to do something about getting better. He is stronger and steadier every day, his appetite has improved, and his positive attitude has returned.

I have recovered almost completely from my shingles—no more pain, a few minor scars on my forehead, and no damage to my eye. Was I lucky! Thanks to all of you who offered suggestions on how to better care for myself. Funny, I thought I was doing a pretty good job. My mistake was not being perfect and feeling guilty about it.

Sunday afternoon Duane and I had a "date," our first outing other than to a hospital in months. Duane had given me tickets to **South Pacific** *for my birthday. How handsome he looked dressed in his gray-striped Ralph Lauren sweater and charcoal dress pants, a refreshing change from his usual comfortable loungewear. He squeezed my hand as Robert Goullet's rich baritone filled the theater with "Some Enchanted Evening." Like the enchanted evening when we had met as strangers at Rich and Kay's wedding, we knew we were part of something special. Holding hands in the darkened theater that rainy afternoon, we felt truly blessed.*

Duane's two co-workers who also had brain tumors have both had relapses recently. Our new friend from Iowa with GBM is angry and hostile towards his wife. I am thankful for crisp, clear sunny days in October. I am thankful that Duane is still Duane, still loving and appreciative. He is working hard to regain his strength and get better. Every day he tells me he loves me and that we are going to get through this. I can't ask for more than that. All any of us has is today to do our best — to give thanks when we do, and forgive ourselves when we fall short.

Once again thank you for your support. It is our comfort, our strength, and our hope.

Love, Mary and Duane

The Bunny Hill

The Bunny Hill . . . is smoother and when
you fall it doesn't hurt so much
– Jack Naylor

———•———

Could we possibly enjoy some time on the Bunny Hill? For six months Duane and I had lived among the moguls, each new hill more challenging than the last. Returning to the levels Duane had experienced during the spring and summer months would require hard work, months of therapy, and maybe just a little luck.

During the early days of outpatient therapy his progress was inconsistent. Days of steady progress would be followed by bouts of weakness, and then slow and steady progress once again. We also made some startling discoveries.

Watching Duane attempting to complete a simple math worksheet, Pamela, the speech therapist, realized he was suffering from "left neglect," and was unable to see the left side of a page. Duane started his assignment by working on the problems in the middle of the page. Disregarding the varied signs to the left of each problem, he added them all. Writing the days of the week on a calendar, he only saw Wednesday through Saturday. No wonder he had difficulty reading!

Sadly, his amazing math skills had vanished. Dr. Trusheim suggested this condition was most likely permanent. Pamela gave us home exercises and computer games to retrain him to look to the left and aid in concentration, and suggested that I highlight the left margin of the newspaper and magazine articles to make reading easier. Frustrated and discouraged, Duane exercised his strong will by refusing to play computer games or let me highlight the newspaper. As hard as he worked to strengthen himself physically, he would not frustrate himself to strengthen his cognitive skills.

"Going through what we are right now, I realize what is truly important in life is our family, our friends, and our memories, " Duane reflected after attending a ninetieth birthday party for a family friend in Winnebago one Sunday afternoon. Duane didn't have many close family members left. Most of his remaining relatives were scattered across the country and only seen at funerals. That changed in late October as relatives and old friends filled the church basement and fussed over Duane, welcoming him as if he were the guest of honor. His hearty laughter filled the room while he reminisced with his cousins and shared stories while showing off pictures of David, Christi, and Will. Cousins that I had only corresponded with via email warmly welcomed me to their family. The love and support he experienced that afternoon buoyed his spirits and mine. I was grateful to have met these warm, caring people at a happy occasion, and not at his funeral.

10/30/02
Happy Halloween everyone!

Oh how I used to enjoy this "holiday!" In my old neighborhood in Duluth, my friends and I used to dress up and "trick or treat" for drinks — had a blast! (We were much younger then.) I had a "killer" witch outfit that I enhanced every year — the slinky black dress with cape, the hat, the wig, the prosthetic nose with warts, and the green face paint, and the perfect accessories.

The first Halloween I knew Duane, I came to his house fully attired in my perfected ensemble, rang his doorbell and thought he was duly impressed. He got out his camera and took my picture, but when he had them developed he ripped them up. I then found out he hates costumes. He couldn't even look at me with my green face, hook nose, warts, long black wig, etc.

This year my costume is packed away — but with the brace I wore on my neck after my surgery, the brace I wore on my leg when I broke my knee, the long white socks left over from his surgeries, his "Will hat,"ace bandages, and the mesh mask from his radiation, we could come up with quite a frightening costume.

To think he couldn't even look at me wearing a witch costume. See—real life is much scarier than our fabrications could ever be.

The last couple of weeks have been very busy — physical and speech therapy sessions three days a week in addition to weekly blood draws and more doctors' appointments. Pretty much the story of our lives these days. We did discover a few new things. First of all, Monday's afternoon appointment with Dr. Trusheim to see the results of the last MRI showed no new growth. Thank God, once again the tumor is contained! The oral chemo treatments are still working, and Doc is very pleased with the results. So tonight we began our fifth month of oral chemo. For now it is doing the job. More aggressive treatments would be much, much harder on him. Please pray for the continued success of this treatment.

Last Friday night he participated in a sleep study. The diagnosis was severe sleep apnea. He was actually going two minutes without breathing and was "waking up" at least fifty times an hour. No wonder he was always so tired! (This condition is quite common and causes serious heart and lung problems. Any of you who has—or has a spouse who has — a problem with snoring might want to check on this.) Monday he got a new machine (a CPAP) with a mask to wear at night forcing air at a prescribed pressure into his lungs so he gets a better night's sleep. (Me too!)

Monday night he slept so soundly (and quietly) I kept checking him to make sure he was still breathing. He immediately had more energy and was more alert; he also looks and feels much better. Today he accomplished more in PT than he has been able to do in weeks. Sure, he isn't crazy about this thing, and complained quite a bit at first (this is still Duane you know) but too bad. Whatever it takes. A small sacrifice like this is well worth the increase in energy.

Our goal here is quality of life. Thanks to this device, and a couple adjustments in the meds, we look forward to his perking up, getting out more, and being able to enjoy life a little more than he has lately.Guys, I can't tell you enough how important your messages, calls, and visits are to him. He loves them. He needs them. Please keep them coming. Our door is always open. Duane has always cherished his friends and loves to visit. Now that he is feeling a little better, he needs you more than ever.

The same goes for me. I cherish you guys. You keep me going when the days, and the nights, get long. Since my bout with shingles, I am really trying to get out a little more and take better care of myself. If there were just more than 24 hours in a day — and I had a lot more energy. But I am listening to my body more, and learning to say "no" once in a while. I can't do everything and that is ok. If I screw up, that is ok too. (Big change for me.) Today I had to drive out to the sleep institute because I couldn't figure out how to put the filter on Duane's mask back on; seems I had it backwards and it goes together "just so." ("Respiratory Specialist" — yet another line I can add to my new resume.) Anyway, finally got it right and Duane is sleeping like a baby.

Sooooooo, that's it for now. In many ways life has been uneventful (and that is good) with baby steps forward. Let's just hope it continues.

Boooooo!!!!!!!!! Happy Halloween!

Love, Mary

The effect of the CPAP machine was truly miraculous, putting us securely on the Bunny Hill. Duane enjoyed the best months he'd had in a long, long time. He had gained weight and was more alert. His strength, energy, and endurance skyrocketed. Julie, his physical therapist, was amazed how rapidly he progressed as he completed his tasks, navigating in and out of a line of tall yellow cones placed on the floor. He was able to weave around them, making tight corners without knocking them down, then bend over to pick them up one at a time. Before long, he was able to easily climb flights of stairs.

When I sat down at the computer to send our Thanksgiving message, I had never been more thankful.

Tuesday, November 26, 2002
Duane Update/Happy Thanksgiving

Hello Everyone,
Duane and I send our best wishes for a Happy Thanksgiving to the best support team ever. May you be surrounded by family, good friends, marvelous food, and God's Blessings! To say that we are "thankful" this holiday is the understatement of the year. We are

consumed with gratitude from the depths of our souls. We are both overwhelmed.

For the past weeks life has been great. Monday morning at PT, I watched with tears in my eyes as Duane and his therapist walked down the long hospital corridor together. To my right was the hall leading to ICU where he lay with blood clots in his lungs three months ago. Now he was walking tall, steady, and sure of himself unaided by even his cane. He hasn't used his walker in over a week. His progress in this past month alone is unbelievable. Of the many things for which I am thankful, his CPAP machine for sleep apnea is at the top of the list. It is amazing what getting rest and a good night's sleep will do.

Last March the neurosurgeon who did his first surgery told me, "I bought him some time, but not for him to spend in a hospital bed." Now, after that awful setback in August, we are finally enjoying a more "normal" life. Duane actually acknowledges he is getting better. (For the longest time when I would encourage him, pointing out his improvements, no matter how small, he would just shake his head and say, "But I don't feel any better!" Now he does. Admitting it a huge step forward.)

Recently he went to the U of M wrestling match with his buddies Jon and Mike. These three have had season tickets together for many years. These great guys gave Duane his season tickets for his birthday and assured him they would get him to the home matches. They helped him navigate the hundreds of steps in the Excel Energy Center; powered by pure adrenalin, Duane did well. (Was it only a few weeks ago he couldn't climb the ten steps in our townhouse?) Anyway, this was his first night out to do "guy stuff" since last January.

He didn't get home until after midnight, (a far cry

from his usual 7:30 bed time) happy and fulfilled, not even upset that the Gophers had been badly beaten by rival Iowa. This outing did more for his morale than any therapy or meds could possibly have done.

We also enjoyed dinner at the home of my old school chum Lori and her husband, Steve. How blessed we are to be enjoying normal life again. Oh, and have I mentioned he has gained twenty pounds this month? His appetite is back! And so is most of his hair — and it's dark. He says he can't remember when his hair was this color.

You guys are at the top of our Thanksgiving list. I can't tell you enough how your thoughts and prayers, your messages of support have helped us through this ordeal. You have made all the difference for us. When I talk to my young friend from Iowa (whose husband has the same tumor as Duane) and she is in such despair, I am grateful to all of you. You have picked me up, encouraged and comforted me when I've been down, celebrated with us when things have gone well, and permitted me to share my pain, fears, hopes and joys with you. Thank you!

We know we still have a long road ahead, and things can change at any time. I will be holding my breath for the MRI and doctor's appointment in December. He will be halfway through his year of chemo. But today we are enjoying today — Thanksgiving — and are anticipating a memorable Christmas season together.

Happy Thanksgiving everyone!

Love, Mary and Duane

I have no doubt that this message brought a collective shout of "Praise! And Thanksgiving!" from all who received it. Mary, this is all such incredible news! You know that book you're writing? The one with all these emails as chapters? It is going to be a best seller — and it's going to have a happy ending. With you two as the main characters there can be no other outcome.

Thanks for keeping us all updated. I'll look forward to seeing you both back here on the North Shore when all of this is behind you.

Love, Jan B.

Thank you so much for this wonderful update and making this Thanksgiving Day truly what it stands for. I was in tears reading this. I am so glad Duane is going to really be able to enjoy this day! You'll have to let me know if his hair comes in curly as well!

Love you & Happy Thanksgiving!!!!!! Sherry

Mary and Duane,
Such wonderful news! You are testimony to the notion that miracles do happen. Continue to take care of yourselves and have a wonderful holiday season. – Robby

---

Mary and Duane,
Praise God from whom all blessings flow! I am still out here praying. – Elizabeth

---

Just thrilled to hear everything is going so well. It looked pretty dark there several times. It is amazing what prayer and faith can do!!!!! Wishing you both a very pleasant holiday season. – Elaine

―――

Thank you for your news! I always find your letters so encouraging, filled with hope and love. I will continue to pray. Hope you have a wonderful holiday.   – Mary S.

―――

What a wonderful report! You made my day! I'm grateful for all the answered prayers you two have received and for the reprieve. Enjoy each day! Blessings to you both!
Dark hair? Oh my!
Love, Dee

―――

Duane and Mary
What a wonderful Thanksgiving message—you two have been an inspiration for so many people and we're SO happy that things are going well. Mary, remember the exercise at CTI when we were learning to live in the moment? Sounds like you and Duane have had a major experience to reinforce that learning — and we all need to learn more how to cherish each moment. Thank you for the messages.
Happy Thanksgiving! Bob

―――

The following came from Mary Del, my old friend who had had her own cancer journey with her little daughter several years before. Once again, God used her words to tell me what I needed at the right time.

What wonderful uplifting news. It sure made my day to hear how all is well with you all. You mentioned "holding your breath" for an appointment in December and then followed it by living for today. You know, you really can't do both. You have to live for today and enjoy today's good health and fortune and not even think about the next appointment. Holding your breath for it means it is taking up too much of your thinking.

I don't say this as a lecture thing. I lived it with Kristen for a long time until I learned how to think differently. Every three months she would go through a battery of tests and I would just hold my breath waiting for the results. When the results came in and they were positive, I would let the tension go for too short a time before I began worrying about the next battery of tests.

I was driving myself crazy until I faced my fear. The results could come back negative and Kristen might die. And then what???? I figured out that how I reacted wouldn't make a bit of difference.

My job was to enjoy her and the moment, and the hell with the next test. It's a small thing but it made a huge difference in my being able to handle all the rest of the crap you have to go through.

"I don't know what tomorrow will bring, or next week, but today is mine." That's what I chose to celebrate. And, can you believe that some people thought I was not being realistic???

I have a wonderful family, friends, a loving boyfriend, and a nice place to live. I don't have a job, but I'm thankful for and will celebrate the rest. Feel pretty darn lucky.

A most joyous Thanksgiving to you!

Love, Mary Del

————

Thank you for a profound message, as usual. You are absolutely right, and you have been there. I really don't dwell on the next MRI, I just know it is coming, and how quickly things can change. I too have been accused of being unrealistic. I don't go to support groups, or listen to horror stories about GBM, and I don't spend all my spare time on the internet looking into the "what ifs."

Bottom line, Duane is going to die, but then, so am I
someday. All we have is today. Thanks for the reminder.
I love you, girlfriend. Happy Thanksgiving.
Love, Mary

Our Thanksgiving was a joyous celebration. David, Christi, and Will came for breakfast, the highlight of Duane's day. Later we went to Barb's and had dinner with my family. "My cup runneth over" with joy and thanksgiving. No matter what might lay ahead we celebrated the day, it was ours.

Christmas - 2002

Life was good on the Bunny Hill. With the advent of Christmas, we anticipated more of the same. If anything was "for sure" on this journey, it was that nothing was for sure. Like everything else, our Christmas would be defined by Duane's tumor. No matter what, we were going to celebrate and make it memorable.

Duane loved the Christmas season. His extensive collection of Christmas tapes accompanied him on long road trips in his truck no matter what the season of the year. The day after Thanksgiving would find him shopping for the most beautiful poinsettias he could find, then personally delivering them to his friends.

Yet he spent many lonely Christmases before we found each other, dining on Popsicles while watching TV in his treeless home.

When we got together, he bought a twelve-foot tree that graced our vaulted living room. It would take us weeks to assemble it, string it with hundreds of lights, and decorate it with perfectly placed ornaments. We reminisced as we tenderly unwrapped each ornament, retelling its story. Some of the ornaments were made by our children — David's red cardinal, Eric's bell made from a plastic cup, Annie's red wooden rabbit. And there were others that Duane and I had brought with us from our previous homes. There were also the special ornaments we had given to each other or purchased together to remember our trips. The results were enchanting. No one enjoyed that tree more than Duane, who each year would sit mesmerized, lost in its magic. He delighted in seeing my grandchildren's eyes fill with awe when they looked up at our magnificent tree, its star reaching to the vaulted ceiling.

This year he navigated the store aisles in a wheelchair as we selected a smaller, seven-foot tree, one that I could put up alone. Adorned with our special ornaments, it was still beautiful, and Duane enjoyed looking at the tree more than ever. But I knew that he would never have the chance in years to come to delight in seeing his own grandson look up in awe at our magnificent twelve-foot tree.

Something in his system was changing. The strength of November rapidly abated. Duane was not only too weak to attend the next wrestling match and planned holiday events, he missed three weeks of PT as well. Blood draws previously done once a month were now scheduled for three times a week.

Mary Del's advice from her last email permeated my thoughts as we awaited Duane's next appointment with Dr. Trusheim, scheduled for December 20. "You have to live for today, and not even think about the next appointment. Holding your breath for it means it is taking up too much of your thinking." This was easier said than done. For all these months I had been keenly aware of every nuance; I had to be. Even the slightest, most subtle change meant something serious was happening. When Duane had problems with balance and equilibrium, his brain was swelling. When he spit blood into his tissue in August, he had blood clots forming in his lungs.

This month the changes had been anything but subtle. We were both anxious to know what was happening in his rapidly weakening body, fearing that either the swelling had returned or the tumor was growing again. I was scared. We both were. Fortunately, his MRI showed no new growth; in fact the tumor was smaller; there was also no increased swelling.

"Why am I so weak?" Duane asked the doctor. Dr. Trusheim explained that while Decadron was controlling the dangerous swelling—its long-term effect was the weakness Duane was experiencing in his legs. He said that in order to control the swelling, this muscle weakening was something we were "just going to have to live with." He lowered the dosage, hoping Duane would be strong enough to go to Duluth with me on Christmas Eve.

"Could I have a glass of wine?" Duane asked. "I'd just like to have one glass of wine with Annie." Duane adored my daughter and was looking forward to going to her home for Christmas Eve. The doctor said yes, one glass would be fine. We left Dr. Trusheim's office that Friday afternoon apprehensive about the effect Decadron would have on our Christmas celebration.

Reducing the dosage only made matters worse. On Saturday, Duane's strength diminished even more. His legs buckled underneath his weight; he said his sense of balance was like "trying to stand on his boat in a hurricane." Duane tried to conserve what little energy he had to celebrate Christmas with Eric and his boys, Chase and Payton, later that day. Early that afternoon our friends Rich and Kay also stopped by. They had planned a short visit, but Rich couldn't leave his old friend. They had spoken on the phone a few times in recent months, but seeing Duane sick and frail shocked and saddened Rich. They laughed, reminisced, and swapped fishing stories for hours. Would they ever visit again?

However, when they left, Eric needed to help me get

Duane into bed; his strength was zapped. He was unable to join us for dinner or presents afterward, so Eric sat at his bedside until he drifted off to sleep. My son was as worried as I was. This was hard on all of us. Seeing Duane weak and feeble also frightened my grandsons. The last time Chase and Payton had seen him, they were proudly showing Duane their room at Eric's new apartment in October. Duane loved those little boys as his own grandchildren and had eagerly anticipated our Christmas party with them. Now all he wanted was to be strong enough to be at Ann's on Christmas Eve. It didn't look good.

How would he ever make the trip to Duluth? "Plan B" had been decided earlier; if he couldn't make it, David and Christi would take Duane to Meg's on Christmas Eve. I needed to be with my own family. Except for Chase and Payton, my whole family would be together. Ann was giving a testimonial at her church, and I couldn't miss that.

Duane was so ill over the weekend that Dr. Trusheim needed to increase his dosage of Decadron again. Christmas Eve morning it was obvious the trip was impossible for Duane. We held each other and cried. Knowing how much I needed to be with my family, he insisted that I go. Leaving Duane Christmas Eve morning was one of the hardest things I ever had to do. Since we met, we had never been apart for Christmas. I sobbed in the car as I left our home, dropped off his "Santa's helper" gifts for the Nystrom girls on their front porch, and then drove to Duluth.

Our "Plan B" Christmas Eve blessed us both. David, Christi, Meg, and her family will long cherish the memory of sharing Will's first Christmas Eve with Duane, while enjoying Meg's traditional fondue dinner. Duane brought home thoughtful gifts—a 2003 calendar Meg had made of Will's photos, another made by David and Christi, jars of Meg's step-mother's delicious peaches, and a mix of "brownies in a jar" from Meg's sister, to name a few.

As much as I missed Duane, without having him to care for, I was able to enjoy rare quality time with my own family. We filled the first two rows at First Lutheran Church for the five o'clock service as we listened to my beautiful daughter share her testimony of faith on Christmas Eve. Barb videotaped the service for Duane so he would not completely miss hearing Annie speak. In spite of Duane's illness, I felt truly blessed sitting in this candlelit church with my family around me. Little Nadia was sitting in my lap; Elina snuggled close; my beautiful, healthy ninety-two-year-old mother was beside me; and my Annie shared her faith that holy night.

It was impossible to be in Ann's and Tom's home Christmas Eve and not share the excitement of my little granddaughters in their new velvet dresses. Amid the turmoil and uncertainty in my life at that time, my family provided love, stability and continuity. The antique red and green candelabra illuminated my daughter's table with seven candles, just as it had done in my grandmother's childhood home in Sweden. Dining on our traditional dinner of Swedish meatballs, I felt joy and peace surround me.

Early Christmas morning I left the sleeping household to join Duane for breakfast at David's. Relaxed and content, I sang along with the entire Messiah on the two-and-a-half-hour drive to Apple Valley. As Duane excitedly shared the events at Meg's the night before, I realized that even though this was not the Christmas Eve we had anticipated, we had been blessed in ways never expected.

We exchanged gifts. The last gift I was given was a small

box from Duane. Inside I found a necklace with a silver heart pendant with my name engraved on one side and "Lord knows she tries" on the other. Duane said, "You're either going to love it, or think it is the stupidist thing I've ever done." David and Christi, who provided the legwork to get this for him, agreed it was the stupidist thing he'd ever done. I thought it was the sweetest, most thoughtful gift I had ever received and vowed never to take it off.

December's Update recapped the events of the past month:

> *The New Year is just around the corner. A friend recently asked me what I was hoping for in the New Year. I said I didn't want to even think about it. Looking too far ahead terrifies me, but as my friend Mary Del told me, think of the worst thing that could happen and say, "Okay, and then what?" We go on. We'll just continue to take each day as it comes, do the best we can. We hope for more good days, more good times together. Each day is a gift. Please continue to keep us in your prayers as we continue our journey together.*
>
> *Again, we hope all of you had a blessed Christmas. Thank you for all your cards, messages, and visits. We wish you a happy, healthy New Year—and Peace!*
>
> *Love, Mary*

Thus we ended 2002, a year begun with so much hope. As I prepared a walleye dinner for Duane and me on New Year's Eve, I thought back to one year earlier. That New Year's Eve we had planned to have our Duluth friends come to our house, but I had cancelled our get-together. Duane had pain from root canal surgery and generally didn't feel up to par. He retired early that New Year's Eve with a splitting headache. Who knew? We looked forward to a happy, eventful 2002 — the birth of his first grandchild, our trip to Alaska, the best days of our life together that lay ahead. We could never have imagined what we would be facing by year's end.

Now, counting down the hours and minutes to 2003, as optimistic as I tried to be, I didn't want to think about what lay ahead in the New Year. I knew that more than likely we would be faced with "and then what?"

New Year ~ 2003

I don't know what tomorrow will bring,
or next week, but today is mine.
— Mary Del Euretig

———•———

Journal entry:
Saturday, January 4, 2003

I helped Duane with a hard day today. His legs were weak; his walk was unsteady. He decided not to go the wrestling match with the guys — we were both relieved. Although he had been looking forward to it all week, he was apprehensive about his ability to get around the huge Target Center, even with his friends Jon and Mike helping him. He said, "If it were just you and me, I think I might make it." In all these years, I have only attended one wrestling match with him, I'm not familiar with the Target Center, and I hate driving downtown Minneapolis! Yet he would have rather gone with me than with Jon and Mike. Taking my hand in his, he tearfully added, "Sometimes I just want to be here with you." He felt safe/secure/loved here with me. We held each other and cried, something we had done only one other time — Christmas Eve morning when he couldn't go to Duluth with me. I'm thankful he can share his pain and vulnerability with me more easily now, but this is heartbreaking. It was a difficult day for both of us, but a day I'd sign my name to.

———•———

I always dreaded the long hours of darkness in January. This year the nights seemed longer, darker, and lonelier than ever before. Duane was terribly discouraged, admitting "I'm just not interested in much these days." Was it from the weakness, was it depression, or was it something else? Remembering David Vikmark's warning about depression, I was concerned. Yet who could blame him for being discouraged? Our only social life was going to the clinic for his numerous blood tests and doctors appointments. At night he went to bed right after supper, no longer interested in watching TV or a movie with me. I grew more and more frustrated — and lonely.

Journal entry:
Sunday, January 5, 2003

I need to write this down or I won't believe what happened tonight. I feel helpless, impatient, angry, lonely, guilty, and scared all at the same time! I don't understand! I think I'm losing my mind!

I was busy today — took care of Duane, walked the dog, did the laundry, and prepared a nice dinner. In the morning I asked Duane to call David to come over and program the new phone Duane bought me for Christmas. I've been concerned because David and Christi haven't been around much lately. They have had colds, but Duane needs to see them — especially that baby — and I need some help and moral support here!

I came upstairs with the fresh linens for our bed at 4:45. Duane was undressed on the bed — for the night. He didn't want dinner (the chicken breasts were just about thawed). At 6:00 he had an Ensure along with his pills. He didn't have the energy to get up so I tried to make up the bed with him on it.

I had him roll on his side while I eased the bottom sheet underneath him. The next thing I knew he was screaming at me, yelling at me how I had hurt him.

I was shocked! I told him he'd better not scream at me again or he'd have to hire someone else — he couldn't afford to lose me. We had a terrible fight. I spilled my guts, said things I probably shouldn't have — that I want and need David to be here more, to help more. I stressed how much I love him and would never, never do anything deliberately to hurt him. All I could do was cry. I'm at a loss and so very frightened!

While I was grabbing a few bites of my over-baked Lean Cuisine, Duane kept looking for his pants — he was getting dressed. Then he wrote me a note telling me he loves me. The next thing I knew I was at the front door trying to keep him from leaving. He was hell bent on going outside — it is dark — and cold — and slippery. I was terrified. He didn't even know where he wanted to go — just "out." Somehow I convinced him to go back upstairs and eventually to bed — he is sleeping now.

God, I feel awful. The last thing I want to do is hurt him in any way. I've devoted my life to caring for him — I love him so much. This is tearing me apart. I am sorry this got so out of hand — and I don' even know what the hell happened. We both apologized. I feel alone, helpless and afraid — and so sorry — but what did I do?!   God please help us!

Sunday I was still so upset I could barely talk.   When David, Christi, and Will came over later in the day, Duane said, "Mary, if you have a problem with David, you'd better tell him now." I did.

"Okay. David, I know this is hard for you, but you have to come over more often. Your dad is depressed and he needs you. He gets little company these days and needs some joy in his life. He needs to see Will. That baby is his "Sunshine," his reason for fighting to live. Not only that, I need some support here. I can't do this all by myself."

David looked down at the floor, hands in his pockets, then said softly, "I'm sorry. I know we need to be here more. We'll come more often from now on." Then he gave me a hug, both seeking and giving comfort. I could feel his pain as he held me tight against his six-foot, four-inch body. David and his family were back on Wednesday for a nice long visit and continued to visit more frequently, making it possible for all of us to get the love and support we desperately needed.

I understood why David stayed away and why, when he did come, often he didn't stay long enough to take off his jacket. Christi had told me, her voice choked with tears, " It tears him apart to see his dad like this — to see him so weak."

I empathized with David. My own father was in his late eighties when illness transformed my handsome strong dad, the man I had turned to and relied on my entire life, into a failing old man. He died the month before his ninety-second birthday. I was in my fifties, and I agonized as I watched my dad decline after a long, healthy life.

Duane was only sixty; David at thirty-one was losing his handsome, strong dad. No one who knew Duane liked seeing this once robust man struggling and declining. Judging by the few visitors that he had these days, I knew some of his friends felt the same way; they couldn't take it. They too saw him as being weak.

That was not how I saw Duane. A weak man would have given up. A weak man would have pitied himself. A weak man wouldn't fight. A weak man would have been angry and taken it out on others. A weak man would have lost his capacity to love, to pray, to be thankful. Duane continued to be the strongest man I had ever known. Living this 24/7, I saw that it was only his body that was weak; every day I witnessed the strength of his spirit. This is how I saw Duane, but he was David's father. David was experiencing this in an entirely different way.

Thursday, January 23, 2003
Duane's Update

Happy New Year!
This has been yet another roller coaster of a month. I should be getting used to them by now. It is one damn thing after another. I haven't looked at my computer in weeks and have had several inquiries as to how things are going. I guess a lot of you guys actually do read this stuff. Thanks! Your concern encourages us both.

Soooooooooo, here goes. Duane has had a tough time again, in spite of the "success" of his treatment. He just hasn't perked up like he did in November. Now he has developed sharp pain in his back and side. After a battery of tests, it was determined he has a broken rib. What next?

To make matters worse, I had to leave him alone for a couple hours the other day (when my sister and I admitted Mom to the hospital for congestive heart failure and severe back pain). It was only a short time before David could get here from work. Duane spilled his pills and tried to pick them up off the floor, then fell and couldn't get up. He explained, "I thought I could do it. I don't have any trouble picking up the cones at PT." He further hurt himself struggling to pull himself into his chair. He has taken more pain pills than at any time in the past year.

The pain left as quickly as it began. For the last two days he has felt better than he has in weeks — just in time. He started round seven of his chemo last night. We see Dr. Trusheim again next month.

Once again God gave me the help and perspective to do what I need to do. Earlier last week, old friends from Duluth lost their son suddenly due to a brain aneurysm. Ron and Ruth would have done anything to care for their son and couldn't. How lucky I am that I can still care for Duane.

Hopefully the day will come again when we can enjoy a little "quality" of life here again — just to get out and visit with friends. Duane is discouraged, and who can blame him. I get a little down myself. Months of doing nothing but doctoring and still not feeling well are taking its toll. It isn't that we aren't so very grateful that he is still around and doing well containing the tumor, etc. Maybe it's just 'cause it's January. But Duane could use a lift. So could I. We both need our friends.

So, that's it for now. Please continue to remember us in your prayers.

Love, Mary

———◆———

My Dear Sunny,

You are always in my thoughts and prayers. I can so hear your struggles of late. I wish I could alleviate some of the pain and burden from your shoulders.

It is a mystery why we are handed these things in life to cope with. I'm sure many times our challenges are placed before us to help us grow and become more aware. Can't we do that in less dramatic ways — I wonder! I wish we could.

Last night a great teacher in my life told me to ask myself the question, "What nourishes me best?" It is such a life-

giving question, isn't it?   The answers come from our body and soul and they are to be honored and not ignored. Can you ask yourself this question and see what comes to light for you?

I had another teacher/friend talk to me about "blessings" yesterday.   We were having fun sharing our blessings with each other.   Perhaps you'll feel compelled to share some of your blessings with me? I hope you do.

Take care my sweet Sunny—I am thinking of you always! Love, Cari

----

"What nourishes me best?"   What an inspiring, thought-provoking question! The answer was being loved.   Being loved by Duane made everything worthwhile.   Our being loved and supported by our friends and family gave us strength and encouragement.   Our being loved by God gave us peace and power. We would be lost without love.

Dear Cari,

Here they are, per your request.   Thank you for a "life-giving" task.

Sunny's Blessings:
1. *Hugs and holding hands*
2. *Duane's loving eyes*
3. *My grandchildren's' laughter*
4. *Nurturing friends*
5. *Good coffee*
6. *Crackling fires*
7. *Sunrises/sunsets on a lakeshore*
8. *The call of loons*

9. *Listening to or singing good music*
10. *Uplifting books*
11. *Fresh snowfalls*
12. *September blue skies*
13. *Teddy bears*
14. *The smell of freshly baked bread*
15. *"Sunshine on My Shoulders"*
16. *The sound of wind in tall white pines*
17. *The unconditional love of my awesome family*

I could go on and on. There are so many blessings, many more than the troubles in our lives. Thanks!

———

On the tough days, Duane and I had to keep in mind the many blessings we still enjoyed. Duane had done that the night he first learned he had an aggressive cancerous brain tumor. He still did. He continued to listen to *The Isaiah Effect* tapes, which stressed the impact that living in a state of gratitude can have on our health, our lives, and our world. Duane lived a life of gratitude.

As the wearisome days of January continued to pass by, it must have been increasingly difficult for him to be grateful. The remaining season tickets to the Gopher wrestling matches went unused. I did attempt to drive him to the one afternoon match scheduled on the University of Minnesota campus. (All others had been in the evening when his energy was spent.) Getting to the arena was a frustrating and frightening experience. Duane, who had driven to this arena countless times over the years, could no longer remember the way as he tried to direct me through the freeways and streets of Minneapolis. "Turn here, no that's not it. I think it's this way; no, not here — maybe it's the next turn. No. There, turn there!" When we finally arrived at the arena, Jon was waiting for us on the street — the afternoon match had been canceled, rescheduled for 7:00 p.m. Duane opted not go. He was exhausted.

This man who once commanded such control of his life no longer had control over most of it. There was one area, however, where he demanded control — the dining room table. When we first met, the dining area in his home was his "office" and the table was always piled with stacks and stacks of papers. This was sacred ground, and I knew better than to touch anything on it. When I moved in with him, he moved his office area to a small bedroom that became his den and his sanctuary; only then could I set the table and place bouquets of flowers or an arrangement of candlesticks on it.

Now that he could no longer maneuver in the den, our table was once again filled with his papers — his "stuff." He was more protective of his turf than ever, and on a few occasions actually yelled at me about touching his stuff on the table, something I only did when I needed to pay bills. He had to take control somewhere, and this was it. The disarray of piles of papers made sense to him; he knew where everything was. I removed anything that was mine from the table and bought TV tables, so that when anyone came for a visit we could eat in the living room. The "stuff" on Duane's table would not be disturbed.

Duane also needed to exert some control over his own well-being. Moving the treadmill into the bedroom provided a way for him to once again do something about improving his own health, not only physically but mentally as well. Both Drs. Trusheim and Loken emphasized the importance of strengthen his leg muscles as much as possible. Should Duane be bedridden for any length of time, he risked never being able to walk again. Determined to build up his strength, no matter how tired or weak he was, he faithfully put in at least a few minutes every day on the treadmill. Five minutes became six, then eight, and before long ten. With every step, Duane's spirits escalated.

January 31, 2003
Duane Update

Wow, you guys! Since my last update just a week or so ago, amazing things have happened. I know that a lot of you must be offering prayers our way—there is no other way to explain this. Duane is so much better! A week ago he struggled with the walker. Today at physical therapy he was walking down that long corridor (past the hall to the ICU where he was in August), walking strong, erect, sure of himself, with just his cane, much like he did before Thanksgiving. He did this after 13 minutes on the treadmill this morning, (something he has barely touched in weeks) and finishing chemo on Sunday. His therapist was amazed. We've been here before, and know how quickly things can go the other way, but for now, today, we've had the best day since November.

When I told him I was going to send another update tonight, he said to say "Thank you" and "Tell them not to give up on those prayers." You guys make all the difference. There is so much power here! So much strength. Such comfort. Thank you. This is incredible. God bless you all.

Love, Mary

Hey Mary! Nice to get a somewhat good update. Sorry to hear of all the past month's ups and downs tho. I think of you a lot and your tests and trials. Life has really thrown you some curve balls but you keep on swinging. I'm in awe of you two. I know things will get better for you soon. In the meantime, keep the faith. Our prayers are always with you and Duane.

Much love, Barb D.

Can anyone still hold doubts that we are all connected by the omnipresent Universal Mind? When we are all affirming and giving thanks for total health and nothing less than complete recovery. Duane's progress can only move in one direction.

Thank you for keeping frequent updates arriving to jog each of us into holding him in thought consciousness. I'm envisioning individuals on this email list opening your message at different times of the day and night, rather like a relay, which assures the affirmations and prayers are constantly being sent into the universe.

After affirming right decisions by doctors and perfect results from medications and therapies, the final vision I hold is Duane striding into the Vanilla Bean one day with you beaming at his side. I know that day will happen very soon.

Much love, Jan B.

"I am still out here praying and am so glad things are going well. There is lots of evidence that prayer heals and that distance is not a factor, nor is the person knowing that he is being prayed for or even believes it. Our souls are reaching out and being with your souls. When we operate in the soul dimension, time and space are not a factor. I am with you now and sending lots of healing light and love.

– Elizabeth

157

Elizabeth,

I know for a fact that what you say is true. In the past few months since Duane was diagnosed, I have read this over and over, from many different sources. The bottom line is always the same — the power of prayer, the connection of souls, the connection we all have to God. We are just beginning to understand the connection here. There is so much I don't understand— quantum physics et all, but I do know that it works. I can feel it; it sustains me and it is positively impacting Duane. My dear old friend, thank you for your prayers and your support in this journey.

Mary

January's last day was the best day we had had since November. Is was almost midnight when I finally read my daily devotional from *Grace for the Moment* by Max Lucado. The entry for January 31 spoke of God's "peace beyond logic." It said that when we are faced with seemingly insurmountable challenges, God's empowering gift of peace enables us to prevail. God knows "we can't, but he can." Mr. Lucado cited several examples of the power of his peace from scripture including, "He gave it to David after he showed him Goliath; he gave it to Jesus after he showed him the cross."

He gave it to me in March after he showed me Duane's tumor.

In a Spirit of Love

The space shuttle Columbia vanished upon re-entry to the atmosphere on Saturday morning, February 1. Instantly seven talented, exuberant people were lost. Watching the newscasts of this tragic event put my own life in perspective once again. I had been blessed.

If things had been different a year before, if Duane hadn't seen the doctor on March 7, he too would have been gone in an instant. Had he stayed in bed with that debilitating headache and not been in the hospital getting steroids to reduce the swelling in his brain, I would have awakened the next morning to find him dead beside me in our bed, presumably from a heart attack. We would never have had the opportunity to fight the tumor, or spend this time together — the good days and the bad. It was now February, and we were coming up on one year. Dr. Fischer had said, "A year, maybe two." Every day I thanked God for another day to be with Duane. In spite of our trials, or maybe because of them, our love and relationship grew stronger and deeper every day.

I didn't need a brain tumor to remind me how lucky I was to be loved by a man like Duane. My ongoing conversations with Lisa, my new friend from Iowa, were a constant reminder that others were not as fortunate. Her relationship with her husband, Richard, had deteriorated as his tumor grew. He was angry, violent, and unpredictable. She lived in a constant state of frustration and fear.

Thank God neither Duane's tumor nor his treatment had robbed us of our love and tenderness. Every woman should have a man like Duane to love her — a man who is strong and independent, yet sweet, thoughtful, true, trusting, trusted, sensitive, appreciative, and a tender giving lover. How blessed we were to have found each other. The loving, supportive relationship that Duane and I had nurtured prior to his diagnosis carried us through the current crisis.

On Valentine's Day in 2003, bittersweet memories of the past mingled with the reality of the present. Memories of our first Valentine's Day together in 1996 had troubled me for months. Duane had been on his way to have dinner with me when he had stopped at Dave Nystrom's house to drop off papers for the upcoming tournament season. Walking back to his truck, he fell on some ice hitting his head on the sidewalk. He was more than an hour late for dinner when he finally called me saying, " I'm somewhere in St. Paul. I don't know where I am or how I got here." Dave found him at a gas station and I took him to the hospital. Duane had no memory from the time he left Dave's house until he arrived at the gas station an hour later. A CT scan showed he had a slight concussion, but everything else was fine. Was it? Could something deep within his brain have been injured that night, eventually causing the tumor? The doctors said "no," but they also have no idea what caused the tumor.

One year later, my mom, sister, and I were with my father in the hospice unit of St. Luke's Hospital in Duluth on Valentine's Day. Duane got up at half past three that morning to go to work at UPS, then drove to Duluth after his shift to hand-deliver flowers not only to me but also to my mother and sister. He only stayed a short while — just long enough to give me a hug, tell me he loved and missed me, and give us all some much needed moral support — then left to drive another three hours home to Apple Valley. After all, he had to be up early again the next day. I always knew what a sweetheart Duane was; now my mom and my sister (not to mention all of the men in our family) knew it too.

On Valentine's Day in 1998, Duane handed me a letter asking me to move in with him. (Whenever Duane was emotional about something he needed to say, he wrote it down.) Reading his message, I readily agreed. He said he hadn't wanted to ask me to share his home and his life until he was absolutely sure he was ready to commit 100 percent to this next step in our relationship. Now he was sure, and so was I.

Duane loved to plan surprises. On Valentine's Day in 2002, my instructions were, "I need you available after five o'clock. This includes dinner." Our date was to see *The Music Man* at Chanhassen Dinner Theater. He looked so handsome sitting across the table from me in his new dress shirt and gray sports coat. We thoroughly enjoyed the evening, but he had another bad headache. He hoped he would feel better after his next root canal surgery scheduled for the following week.

Now on Valentine's Day in 2003, I played Cupid for him all day. From the roses and heart-shaped pancakes for our candlelight breakfast to our candlelight walleye dinner, our day was filled with romantic touches. I gave him DVDs of our favorite musicals, which he watched all afternoon. Within the largest card I had ever received, he gave me a ticket to see an Elton John /Billy Joel concert in April along with Christi and her parents. He had no interest in going himself but knew I would love it.

In 2002 I had sent an email to my friends:

Life in Abundance Comes Only Through Great Love

> *As you look back upon the events in your life*
> *you will find that the moments that stand out,*
> *the moments when you have really lived,*
> *are the moments when you have done things in a*
> *spirit of love.*

Our Valentine's Days were examples of our many days together lived in the spirit of love, days to which we would sign our names.

Wednesday, February 19, 2003
Duane Update

Good news!

Yesterday's appointment with Dr. Trusheim was the best yet. The latest MRI again showed no new growth in the tumor. It wasn't just the words Doc said that encouraged us; it was the way he said them and the satisfied look in his smile and in his eyes. He said it is probably starting to die off now. We were both surprised, wondering if it would do that. Doc said, "Oh, yes! That is the plan!" He is very, very pleased with Duane's progress. He did remind us that we are dealing with a "very aggressive tumor." (Like we needed to be reminded!) I also remember the relatively low success rate of the course of chemo we are on — 30 to 40 percent. But it obviously is successful for Duane. That "very aggressive tumor" is not growing or branching out anywhere else. Thank God!

The eight nightly capsules of Thalidomide cause fatigue. Doc says we may not need them for controlling the tumor anymore. They may have done all they are going to do there, but that if it were his tumor he would continue taking them. We said, "Keep doing what we're doing — it's working."

This past weekend we had our first night away since going to Bayfield, WI, in June. We enjoyed a retreat with my Duluth neighbors at the Radisson in Roseville (a suburb thirty minutes away on the other side of the Cities). Duane wasn't able to go in the sauna or the whirlpool, but he savored a beer sitting poolside with the guys (his first beer in a year). Per his doctor, he can have one "on occasion." Spending quality time with our old friends was an ideal occasion.

One year ago yesterday Duane became a grandfather. When we heard baby Will had arrived, we left for the hospital immediately. Duane made three wrong turns on the five-minute drive. At the time I thought he was just excited about the baby. Now I think it was the onset of confusion caused by the tumor. From that day forward, I can think of other little things that all add up. Just one year ago . . . .

We will soon mark his first anniversary. (March 7 diagnosis, March 8 first surgery.) We heard the prognosis of GBM is six months, or maybe a year. Here we are a year later and the tumor is showing no new growth. Yes, he has had talented surgeons who skillfully removed as much of the tumor as possible, a gifted oncologist who knows the best way to treat what was left, and caring doctors and therapists who have treated all the other problems encountered this past year. We also know that the reason they have been successful is that we have the best support team out there praying for us. Do not under estimate the impact of your prayers, friendship, and support this past year. We couldn't have gotten this far without you. Duane believes it, knows it — and that is why he has been able to survive this. We still have a long way to go, but look at how far we have come. Please continue to pray for us, send messages, call, and drop by. It is all working. We are so grateful to each of you. "Thank you" doesn't seem like enough. God bless you all.

Love, Mary and Duane

News of Duane's good report again brought joyous hurrahs from our "team."

———◆———

Hello my friend!

I'm thrilled to hear the wonderful news! Tell Duane to think of us when he's on the treadmill and maybe name each and every one of us while he walks. Maybe that would help pass the time and help strengthen his steps. I know how hard it is, so I don't minimize the strength it takes to make himself do it. Yes, at the front end a year seems like a long way away and yet, here you are one year later and looking back on what you've been through and where you are right now. You've truly been through the ride of your life and are coming out the other end stronger and with a deeper feeling for each other than you had/were before, huh. If nothing else has been accomplished besides beating this dam tumor thing, it's served to strengthen your relationship. And that's always a good thing. My wish for you is to have a long and happy life together with the knowledge of what you've been through together to seal that relationship. Can you just imagine life as normal people once again! We take so many things for granted, don't we.

Have a wonderful day/week/month/year!!!!!!!!! Bye now!

Love you both,

Gerry

———◆———

Dearest Mary,

I'm rather excited by your last update. No new growth and possibly some shrinkage of the tumor is certainly good news!

I am in awe of you and Duane and your courage. I am also now more convinced than ever that you will overcome this thing. God is most definitely working with you as we are working for you through Him. I certainly believe in the power of prayer! Hang in there, Mary, and God bless.

Love, Barb D.

Duane's old friend Dick Wright from Chicago sent the following message. Whenever he was in the Twin Cities on business, he made a point to visit our home. Duane always enjoyed Dick's long visits, remembering past escapades and laughing at Dick's arsenal of amusing stories. Dick had forwarded my email messages to mutual friends of his and Duane's across the country and also to his son, Rick. I had never met Rick, and Duane had met him only once when he was a child. Now years later he was in college and took the time to write us. Dick proudly passed along his son's message to us.

Hi Mary,

The following letter from my 'lil boy' brought a tear to my eye. I know Duane will love it.   DW

Dear Duane and Mary,

It is fantastic to hear that you are doing so well, Duane! My father has been sending me all of the updates that you send out and I have been reading them with much pleasure! Duane, it warms my heart to know that you are doing so well. Keep on the path to recovery! Mary, you are a fantastic individual to go through all this with Duane and keep a smile on your face!

God and I don't talk too much. I don't ask him for much and he just keeps it chill with me, but you two will be in my prayers.

Godspeed to recovery.

Rick Wright

Hi Dick,

Thank you for forwarding Rick's message. Your "lil boy" brought a tear to our eyes too! You were right— Duane loved it. He was amazed that your son would remember him and deeply touched that he would take the time to write. You made his day. Let that nice son of yours know how much we both appreciated his message. Sounds like a wonderful young man. Hope to see you again before long.

MC

In the midst of going through all of this with "a smile on my face" and receiving comments from others who were in "awe" of my courage, there were times I felt like a big phony. The truth was, sometimes when the news was good, I felt down. My new friend Lisa was the one person I knew would understand what I was experiencing now.

Friday, February 21, 2003
Hi Lisa,

One of the things that is so perplexing and so misunderstood is this business of feeling down when things are good. It has been on my mind for weeks,

166

months. I'm sure that you and I aren't the first caregivers to feel this way, or the first to admit it. Here are my thoughts for now:

First of all, you know how much I love Duane; he is my soulmate, my spouse, and the love of my life. I waited almost fifty years for him and he was worth the wait. Tuesday we saw Dr. Trusheim, and the MRI was awesome. The everlovin' tumor is less and less a problem. The drugs, well that's another story.

Yesterday we discussed the doctor's visit with Duane's physical therapist and he was discharged. After seven months of PT, some in the hospital, a month at home, and as an outpatient since mid-September, it is over. The goals set months ago have now been met. All great news, right? Well, in a way but not really. I haven't exactly been euphoric, to say the least. There is nothing more they can do for him.

One year ago this weekend, we went shopping for baby gifts for little Will. Whenever I think back on it, what I remember most was how fast Duane walked with such purpose, so sure of himself. He was incredibly strong. One year later, he struggles to climb our stairs. On a good day he walks with a cane and can sometimes go unaided a little bit, provided there is a wall or something else close by.

His release from PT simply means this is as good as it will get. We will continue daily exercises at home, but PT has nothing else to offer us. Today he did seven minutes on the treadmill; considering he is just beat from chemo, that's pretty good. He didn't have his head in the toilet all day, he doesn't have to go to the hospital, and doesn't have to give himself shots. And, bottom line, this course of treatment is controlling the tumor.

So, maybe that's it, at least for me. As good as it

gets isn't as good as I want. I want him back the way he was two years ago. The strength, the independence, the romance, the passion. Then I remember the article you sent me a while back about 'Blessed be the Caregiver' and accepting him and loving him for who he is now. The independence is gone, but I have never seen him stronger. As for the romance and passion, sex is long gone but he still makes me weak in the knees just the way he looks at me, or when he struggles to walk across the room to give me a hug. But oh how I miss him, his silver hair curling over his shirt collar, and our dreams, Alaska, and all the other places he wanted to take me. Retirement, growing old together. Enjoying our grandchildren.

It could be so much worse. He could have died many times this last year. A year ago I would have called myself a brat for not being overjoyed with how things are now. Now I am more forgiving of myself, realizing I am doing the best damn job I possibly can and there is nothing I can do to fix this. It is okay to grieve for what I have lost, and still be thankful for what we had and what we still have. I am not a brat, nor a bitch, nor am I a saint. I am just human and don't have to be perfect. I can't be, and neither can anyone else.

If you think this will help, please share this with Richard. I have talked to Duane about this and he understands. He feels much the same way. This is difficult for all of us. But a burden shared is so much easier to carry.

We share your burden, just as you share ours.

Love, Mary

Hi,

I just finished reading the last part of your message, and that is exactly how I feel and exactly what I was trying to put into words a month ago.

It's almost a year ago that we all were all thrown this big ball of Jell-O with a huge lead ball inside. Now we know what's inside this big ball of Jell-O, but the huge lead ball inside keeps shifting its weight so we are continuously darting and diving and juggling trying to adjust everything, every second of every day, just to be able to hold onto our lives. It's the "not knowing" that beats the hell out of me. It feels like "post-traumatic stress" & "traumatic stress" & "pre-traumatic stress" all at the same time!

Love, Lisa

———————

Duane was also having down days. All the emotions I was feeling, he was feeling too. Simple things like getting dressed were increasingly difficult. He would put his underwear on backward and his shoes or slippers on the wrong feet. He would shake his head in amazement that I knew which shoe went on what foot.

David wanted his dad showered and dressed every day; showers, however, once an automatic part of Duane's daily ritual, were less frequent and more challenging. No matter how warm it was in the bathroom, he always got cold. Even with the new clear plastic shower curtain and all the bright lights on, Duane said the shower was too dark; even with the shower bench and handrails, he felt unsteady and afraid. Memories of his being helpless in the bathtub the past July were ever present in both of our minds. I helped Duane with daily sponge baths, but he only got a shower about once a week, at my insistence. When I suggested having David help,

Duane said, "No, we can handle this ourselves."

After I had helped him with his shower one morning, moisturized his torso, arms, legs, and feet, then helped him get dressed, he said, "You have done everything but wipe my butt. You do this every day." How this made him feel, I can only imagine; I tried to always treat him with gentleness, respect, and the utmost compassion and love. Still, how frustrating it must have been for him to not even be able to clean or dress himself without my help — Duane who had always been so fiercely independent.

One evening I walked into our bedroom as he was sitting up in bed with tears in his eyes. I took his hand in mine and sat down beside him, "Hey, Sweetheart, what's goin' on?" "Oh," he said, "I was just thinking of all the things I wanted us to be doing now instead of this — all the places I wanted to take you." He talked about the East Coast, the Carolinas, D.C., places he had lived or visited and wanted to show me. "I wish we had met years earlier and that we'd had a couple little girls."

To ease his growing frustration and rekindle his waning hope, I urged Duane to attend the healing prayer service held at Prince of Peace on Thursday nights. He agreed, and as difficult as it was for him to go out in the evening, he made the effort to go the last Thursday of February.

The altar area was dark, with a single spotlight shining on Pastor Dan Anderson seated at the piano. Pastor Dan softly stroked the keys as he slowly recited the Twenty-third Psalm, verse by verse, with time for reflection in between. "The Lord is my shepherd . . . . I shall not want . . . . He makes me lie down in green pastures . . . . He leads me besides the still waters . . . . He restores my soul . . . ." Reflecting on the words of the familiar psalm spoken slowly, deliberately in the darkened sanctuary was immensely powerful. Duane's grip on my hand tightened as Pastor Dan continued, "Yea, though I walk through the valley of the shadow of death . . . . I will fear no evil . . . . for thou art with me . . ." The psalmist's words seemed to sooth Duane; he appeared to be calmer, less anxious. The words wrapped around both of us like a cloak of peace and protection, assuring us that God was with us now as he had been throughout our entire journey. We knew he would continue to sustain us in the days ahead.

After the service, we were invited to go to stations near the altar to pray with members of the prayer team. As Duane struggled with his walker, two members of the prayer team came to meet us where we were. A woman with short gray hair and loving eyes asked Duane to tell her his story. He began to talk about his tumor, then suddenly she interrupted, "What is your name?"

"I'm Duane."

She turned to me and asked, "Are you Mary?"

"Why yes, I am."

"Duane!" she exclaimed, "I've been praying for you for months!"

Every week that I had attended church services in the past eleven months I had filled out a green prayer request card on Duane's behalf and placed it in the offering basket. Tonight before us was a beautiful, spiritual woman who had been praying for both of us for almost a year because of the green cards I had filled out. Her name was Myrna, and her husband too was now going through treatment for a newly diagnosed cancer. Duane and I left the church that evening, awed by the love that surrounded us.

The Anniversary

When the heart grieves over what it has lost,
the spirit rejoices over what it has left. .
– Sufi saying

"With us it's so special." Duane whispered these words to me the last time we made love in our bed the night of March 1, 2002, after our date at Toby's on the Lake. That night will forever remain as one of my sweetest memories— the calm before the storm that lay ahead. One year later, on March 1, 2003, I wrote in my journal:

Duane and I are so lucky! We were lucky on March 1, 2002, and we are on March 1, 2003. Our relationship has flourished this past year; every trial has only brought us closer together. We no longer get out for date nights — we have them at home. Sex is gone, but he tenderly holds my hand and makes love to me with his eyes, and with us it is still so special.

Dr. Fischer had said, "A year, maybe two." One year had now passed. Memories of the previous March replayed daily in my mind like reruns of *Casablanca*. As the anniversary date neared, I was as thankful for time we had spent together as I was anxious about the time we had left.

Early in March, Lisa had asked me to meet her at the hospital chapel when Richard was in for his monthly treatment. Their relationship had deteriorated to the point that she was now concerned for her safety. Preparing to meet with hospital personnel to discuss her options, she called me for moral support. With Duane's blessing, I left immediately to offer whatever help I could to our troubled friend.

It was almost a year to the day since the night of Duane's original MRI. Walking across the skyway leading from the parking ramp to Southdale Hospital, memories of that night came flooding back — the ice, the fear, the strange look in his eyes, the way he had dragged his foot. Now trembling with grief and pain, my body succumbed to pent-up sobs suppressed deep in my heart. I wanted to bolt and run out of that place and never return.

How I longed for our life before the tumor! How I longed for my healthy, vigorous Duane. Sitting in the lobby trying to regain my composure, I could feel his arm around my shoulders as it had been that night; I heard the sound of his voice saying, "I must have been a saint in a past life to have gotten you." The truth is, I must have been the saint to have gotten him. Putting one foot in front of the other, I somehow made my way to the chapel, thankful that, unlike Lisa, I was going home to my sweet strong man who cherished me.

Saturday, March 8, 2003
Subject: Duane's Anniversary.

I am overwhelmed tonight as I reflect on the past year. If you are reading this, you have played a vital role in this letter even being possible.

People have said, "What an awful year you have had!" Funny, we don't see it that way at all. Challenging, yes — awful, no. Our lives have been blessed in spite of, or because of, the obstacles thrown our way.

One year ago the surgeon told us she had "bought him some time but not for him to spend in a hospital bed." Although he has had several subsequent hospital stays, we have embraced life this year as best we could. Some doors closed, like our planned Alaskan cruise, but new ones opened in their place. Visiting Door County and cruising the Apostle Islands gave us the opportunity to enjoy sunsets on the water, lighthouses, and most importantly, each other. Remembering Harold Hill's line from **The Music Man**, I have to agree that we don't have any "empty yesterdays."

Today our families joined us for a celebration in Duane's honor. By far this was the most relaxed and successful party I've ever given. Once I would have been overly concerned about the appearance of my house and a perfectly set table. My priorities have changed. Today I put food on the counter announcing, "Here's the food, here are the drinks, and there are the plates. Eat when you want and sit wherever you can find a spot." Without being asked, Duane had cleared his papers off the dining room table to make room for everyone. He "hosted" his own party. A good time was had by all, and we agreed to make this an annual event. My son Eric summed it up best saying, "I've never seen anyone so strong."

Last week we saw Dr. Loken for Duane's monthly follow-up exam. Duane said, "You know, Doc, although nobody really said so, last year I had the feeling I had about six months." She replied, "Yeah, that's about right. I really didn't think I'd be seeing you in a year. Gee I love it when I'm wrong!"

One year down and we're going for two. This year has blessed us beyond belief. We have re-established relationships with old friends, former classmates, and far-away relatives. We have grown closer together and closer to God. We have experienced an outpouring of love and support from family, friends, and from total strangers. We have been held up by your prayers when we had no strength. From the first night that I came home alone last March, terrified and heartbroken, your prayers have been a cloak of comfort and strength wrapped around me. From the night Duane learned his prognosis and lay in his hospital bed hopeless and afraid, they brought him comfort and peace. We could feel them then, and we feel them now. Whatever the days ahead hold for us, we know that cloak will be there for us both.

Saying "thank you" for what you have done for us this past year seems inadequate. We honestly could not have survived this alone. Whether the news of the latest MRI was good or Duane was lying in an emergency room screaming in pain, he would say, "I have all these people praying for me."

Thank you, too, for allowing me to share my thoughts/feelings/fears/frustrations/ joys/ and triumphs of this past year with you. Hey, I don't have a job and I can't afford a therapist. God bless you all!

Love, Mary

Going For Two

"And then what?" After our triumphant anniversary celebration, the letdown hit us both hard. "A year, maybe two." Now we were going for two. Something told me Duane would not be another John Schuler.

He was becoming impatient with me. The bathroom was too hot, or cold, or dark; I couldn't get his pillows fluffed just right; he couldn't get comfortable. If he couldn't see me, he couldn't remember where I was. If I said, "Honey, I'm just going downstairs to throw in a load of wash," the next thing I'd hear was "Maryyy! Where are you?" After I'd dash up the stairs reassuring him I was home, he'd say, "Oh, I thought you'd left me alone." He was sad, weak, uncertain, lethargic, and irritable. I was not only scared, I was frustrated! I was devoting my life to him and was being scolded because I couldn't fluff his pillows correctly.

Fortunately, this situation was temporary. About two weeks or so after the party, he felt better, his disposition and memory improved, and he was up to twenty minutes on the treadmill. Midway through his current round of chemo, Duane was upbeat, steady, and strong again. But we were getting on each other's nerves and we needed a break.

Wednesday, March 26, 2003 11:15 pm
Duane Update

Hi Guys,
You have to love March in Minnesota. Sunday was 72 and gorgeous! Today we have winter storm warnings. Just when spring seems within reach, we get another dose of winter.

Everything was going so well. Last Sunday I was able to leave Duane alone while attending a ninetieth birthday party for an old family friend with my mom and sister. He enjoyed an entire afternoon by himself watching the "Sweet Sixteen" of college basketball without a mother hen hovering over him. It was a beautiful spring day — 72 degrees, bright and sunny.

There was, however, a storm warning. Sunday night he asked for a pain pill for the first time since January. The pain in his ribs had returned — but not in the same place. It was up higher this time. He said he almost had asked for one the day before, and he also said that while doing the treadmill his arms were hurting. I gave him his pills and put one of those thermo-wraps around his chest. He felt better.

Tuesday morning I ran to Target for a few groceries. It was warm so I didn't wear my jacket; my cell phone was in its pocket. Oh well, I'd be right back. What could happen in a few minutes?

Returning home a half hour later, I heard his frightened, agitated voice saying, " . . . and I can't reach her on the phone!" I dashed up the stairs to find him prostrate on the floor talking to a 911 operator in a neighboring county. A pair of wall sconces was on the floor beside him; glass splinters of shattered candle cups glistened dangerously in the surrounding carpet. With the slightest movement he screamed in pain. I grabbed the phone, assured this operator he was not alone, and called 911.

This is what I think happened. Whenever I leave the house, I have everything set out for him — the remote, the phone, his prayer notebook, his walker — anything he might need Before I left he asked for his phone directory. Done. For the first time in well over a year he was making plans to surprise me — he was buying us tickets to a matinee performance at Chanhassen Dinner Theater. They must have asked him for his credit card number. Not thinking, he got up to get his wallet from the dining room table without reaching for his nearby walker, then lost his balance when he turned. The man at Chanhassen (in Carver County) had connected the 911 operator.

A police officer who had ticketed me for expired tabs in January was the first to arrive, then the fire department and paramedics. Only after a generous shot of morphine were they able to carry him to the waiting ambulance via stretcher and take him to Ridges. Being back in the ER where he had endured the agonizing lung scan in August, Duane was terrified. He was admitted to the hospital, diagnosed with broken ribs from the fall.

That made no sense to me at all. I am no doctor, nurse, or therapist; I'm just a loving caregiver who has lived this nightmare being aware of every nuance for a year. As in January, the pain came days before a fall. Okay, once was a fluke. Twice is setting a pattern. Duh—does anyone else question what is going on here? I felt like I was talking to doctors from another planet in the ER. Although I thought I was being fairly articulate, they didn't seem to understand that he had been in pain for four days before he fell. The pain was not caused by the fall, whether or not he broke his ribs. It was from something else. Why didn't anyone understand what I was saying?

After he was admitted to the hospital, a new doctor — a hospitalist — ordered a CT scan of his chest. Duane and I feared the cancer might have spread to his bones. Thank God there was no new cancer. According to the radiologist who read the CT scan, there is also no evidence of broken ribs. Okay. So what is this? They

179

are keeping him hospitalized until Friday for observation and some rehab.

Guys, this is a huge mogul that caught us completely off guard. No, it isn't life threatening, but it is spirit threatening. Duane is devastated. He cries a lot, apologizing to David and me telling us how sorry he is, that he didn't mean to fall, that he should have been more careful. He thinks it is his fault.

Everything had been going so well, just like March in Minnesota.

It goes without saying, we count on your prayers now more than ever. Thank you for allowing me to vent. One thing about the snow in late March, it eventually does melt. Spring always comes. Let's hope it comes soon.

Love, Mary

One year ago I asked God to help me. "I am just this weak little nothing!" "Who are you to question God?" "Okay, but you've got to help me." He always did. Every time I needed help there was someone — an angel on earth — to lift me up — always. Now leaving Duane again in the hospital, I felt especially alone and afraid. God sent another gentle reminder that he was still here. We were not alone. This time the angels lived on our block.

When I lived in Duluth, my neighbors had been my best friends. Here on our little street in Apple Valley, I was only acquainted with Wes and Mary, neighbors from two doors down. Our relationship consisted of a wave in the courtyard or a pleasantry exchanged at the mailbox. I didn't even know their last name. Duane, who had lived here over twenty years, knew them much better. Mary, a breast cancer survivor, had recommended *The Isaiah Effect* to Duane a year before when we met at the mailbox. Other than that, we hadn't had any contact with them until now when I checked my email messages:

Hello Mary (and Duane),

Today we heard about the ambulance and a fire truck near your place. Has Duane been taken to the hospital? We don't seem to have your telephone number or would have called you. We are hoping and praying that nothing too serious occurred. Please update us when it's convenient as we offer you any help we can during these tenuous days/nights for you two. Don't hesitate to call us for relief, be it help with the dog or whatever, okay?

Know that we are concerned, a bit worried, and just a phone call away from helping. Okay?

Love & hugs, Wes and Mary

They had our email address. How, I didn't know and didn't care. All I knew was that I wasn't alone anymore. There was someone right here on our block offering help.

One year ago, I would never have asked for their help. One year ago, I felt strong. "Oh I can do this — I can do it all." I slapped on those "Wonderwoman" cuffs on my wrists and put a big "W" on my chest and prepared to take on the world. All I needed was the cape, the tiara, and the boots (and certainly the perfect body). An aggressive brain tumor was no match for me. My love was so strong, there was nothing I wouldn't or couldn't do for him.

That was a year ago. Now I knew better. I could not stop the inevitable, the unpredictable, unrelenting tumor or the havoc that it would raise. I welcomed the God-sent neighbors from the mailbox into my life with open arms.

Duane was scheduled to be discharged on Friday afternoon, and would be provided with at-home health care once again. Early Friday morning the social worker from Ridges called me at home saying the occupational therapist had just seen Duane and was concerned about his coming home. She recommended that he be discharged to a nursing home instead. Dr. Fowler's insensitive words from a year ago resurfaced. I was not ready to give up caring for Duane — not without a fight, not yet.

I was as concerned about Duane's mental state as his physical condition. Now he was crying frequently, more discouraged than he had been in the entire year. I pleaded with the social worker to let me bring him home. We discussed the success he had had with home health care in September. I described our downstairs living quarters — a bedroom, a full bath, and a family room; he had stayed there following his April hospitalization. He would never have to navigate the stairs. I knew I could safely care for him at home. I had done it before. The social worker agreed to consider it. I feared that if Duane had to go to a nursing home now, even for rehab, he would give up. I knew my Duane. He was not ready. Neither was I.

"They might not let me go home." The pleading, terrified deer-in-the-headlights look on Duane's face when I entered his room stiffened my backbone and my resolve. He had called me "Olga the Hun" when I took on the nurses a year earlier. Olga was back, determined to take him home. Now he was terrified and confused. There was no coordinated plan; no one at the hospital seemed to know what to do with him. The weekend was at hand and there was no plan started, let alone in place, for intermediate care in a nursing home anywhere. Certainly I could do as well for him at home.

I was adamant with the social worker and the RN — Duane was coming home with me and that was that. He had done very well with home care when he was much weaker than he was now. I didn't waver. After hours of deliberation and phone calls, Duane was discharged to go home in my care on one condition — he could not be left alone, ever.

Bringing him home was the right decision. Thanks to a night in his own bed, he was stronger than he had been at the hospital and was determined to work hard with the therapists and regain his strength, whatever it took. We had been successful in September and would be again, together, at home.

Neil, the evaluator for home health care, was astonished when he met Duane Saturday morning. The weak, frightened man he had read about in the hospital report was not the same man he was evaluating. This man exhibited sheer will, doing the exercises and stairs with less trouble than expected; for no apparent reason, the rib pain was gone.

Monday morning we met the new physical therapist aptly named Faith. An aura of joy and peace surrounded her, and I felt we were in the presence of an angel. She was a tiny woman with a child-like voice; her otherwise pretty face was scarred and disfigured on one side, the result of a birth defect and many subsequent surgeries. She was also an excellent therapist, compassionately working with Duane, gently encouraging him as she evaluated his abilities. She, too, was pleasantly surprised at how much better Duane performed than was indicated by the hospital report. She was also surprised that he was doing the treadmill (six minutes on Monday). That first day everything seemed to be going well. Unfortunately, Duane's newfound strength did not continue.

The Funnel

*There is no greater calling in life than to be
needed by the one you truly love.*
– Robby Smith

<hr>

"Mary! Where are you? Are you coming home?"
Duane's frantic message was left on my cell phone while I was
at a funeral. Over the weekend, Eric's friend Sara had lost her
twenty-one-year-old brother in a car accident and I had
wanted to be at the service to offer my support. My sister
stayed with Duane the short time I was away. Even though he
was not alone, he had called three times, frustrated that my
phone was turned off while I was in church. To my knowledge
he had never been as anxious when I was away before. It was
clear all he wanted was me. Something was wrong.

Journal entry
April 3, 2003

*We had to go out today for the next MRI. Thank God, Wes
offered his help last week. Today I needed his help to get
Duane down the stairs and into my Jeep. This is more
than weakness; he couldn't lift his feet. Duane admitted, "I
couldn't have done it without Wes."*

*With the help of a wheelchair, Duane and I managed okay
at the hospital. Leaving was another story. It was a nasty,
rainy/sleety day, 31 degrees with a strong wind. Here I stood
out in the elements in front of the hospital struggling to get
Duane from the wheelchair to the Jeep with no success*

whatsoever. Again he could not lift his feet. He was too unsteady for me to support him while trying to raise his leg. We were helpless and terrified he would fall again. Fortunately, two angels in the form of passers by — first a young woman and then a young man — stopped to help me get Duane into the safety of my front seat.

Wes appeared out of nowhere when I pulled into our driveway. He held on tightly as Duane struggled to climb the stairs. Once upstairs, Duane had trouble controlling his walker. His arms were weak, and again he has pain in his ribs.

Later in the bathroom, I had to help him drop his pants. He tried to do it himself, but couldn't stand without supporting himself by holding on to his walker. Once again he had trouble with balance; this time, however, he was going to fall to his right. We were thinking things we didn't want to share with each other — not yet. Something was different. In the past the weakness has always been on the left side, opposite the tumor. Now for the first time the weakness is on the right. He blankly said, "My legs won't do what I tell them."

Was it just last Tuesday I found him on the floor? Where is this headed? Will he ever regain strength again? Or is he going to continue to deteriorate? How long am I going to be able to help him? I am afraid of the answers. He is so much bigger than I am, and now he has no physical strength. When he falls, he is dead weight. I am afraid the time is coming soon when I'll have to keep him downstairs again, or worse. And then what? Dr Fowler's words about a nursing home are haunting me. I don't want that to happen. I will hate it. He will hate it. He'll give up. He will die.

Yesterday Dr. Phil did a show on newlyweds with sexual problems. Duane had tears in his eyes saying, "Honey, I'm so sorry I'm not taking better care of you." We have not had sex

186

in over a year. I lied, telling him that it doesn't matter to me at all. Of course it does! I miss how it used to be. He was passionate, loving, generous, and tender. He truly "made love" to me. " Anyone can do what we're doing, but with us it is so special." I miss feeling "special." I miss lying in his arms having pillow talk. I miss needing him. I miss feeling like a woman.

I also miss time alone, then feel like a brat. A friend reminded me that Jesus also needed time away to be alone, and understands my need and my frustration. Lately, I literally have been feeling the walls closing in on me.

I have been more discouraged in the last few weeks than I have been in the past year. The anniversary, the fall, the unanswered questions. Why did the pain start four days before the fall? What is causing this? Weak muscles, weakening bones, all from the Decadron? Could be. What else? His feet are swelling and he has developed purple spots on his skin, all more side effects of the drug. Who knows? All I know is that this relapse has deflated us both. It is hard for me to do anything these days. I have no energy, no ambition. I snack all day long, and relax with brandy and peanut butter in the evening, trying to fill the chasm within me. I realize that, and I know it isn't working, and that one of these days I'll need to get in control again. Today I just don't have the energy.

The gigantic interactive yellow funnel at the Science Museum fascinated my grandsons and me on a February visit. We playfully tossed coins into a slot at the wide top of the giant funnel then watched in fascination as they slowly circled the perimeter, then gradually gained momentum as they descended, moving faster and faster in tighter circles until they eventually reached the tiny hole at the bottom and disappeared from sight. Now Duane and I were like two coins tossed into some huge, horrible funnel on our way to an unstoppable outcome.

Somehow I had to accept the fact that Duane would need additional care in a nursing facility before long. Perhaps it would be temporary, perhaps not. The daily changes indicated something would need to be done soon. After he went to bed each night, all I could do was cry. How could I be at peace with this?

God answered this time through Duane's old friend Dick. His wisdom and empathy helped ease my fear and I began to at least entertain the notion of a nursing home with slightly less anxiety.

―――・―――

No one — certainly not I — can possibly understand what you are going through. God obviously has given you a lot of extra strength and I'm sure he has a special place for you in his heart. Please understand that he wants you to cry. Crying is a release. It is necessary. It is good.

You have a special place in the hearts of many, including mine and please know that you can use me to "vent" or, for anything else, any time you want. I wish there was more I could do.

Dick related his fears, doubts, and frustrations when his mother had recently been placed in a nursing facility and the surprisingly positive effect it had had on her and his entire family.

I'm not suggesting that Duane won't do things for you or that you are not doing everything humanly possible for him. I'm suggesting that there might be another path that could be good for both of you. As hard as it will be for you to read this, especially from an outsider — as hard as it will be to think about — as hard as it will be for you and Duane to discuss and to make a decision, a rehabilitation/nursing home could be a good thing. It is not a permanent move. It is a move that will allow skilled people to care, encourage, bolster, and treat Duane while allowing you to take a break and rest and reclaim some sort of better personal, more healthy, less tiring lifestyle.

You will still want to be there every day. Probably for many hours every day. Especially to see that critical medicines are administered properly and on time. But — after arguing with yourself, you will go home each night and crash. Crashing is good in this instance.

Forgive me if I am way out of bounds. This is not a thing to "discuss" via email. It is probably not a thing you want to hear from me at all, let alone "discuss." But now that I've inserted my nose where it shouldn't be, if you want to hear more of my limited experience, or questionable opinions — or if you just want to yell at me — let me know and I will call you at your convenience.

While I will never argue your submission that Duane is a "class act," he is no classier than you. You are wonderful. Beyond belief. I thank God that Duane has you. No one could be better for him than you. Thank you for who you are.

Love, Dick

Faith was astonished at the extent of Duane's decline when she returned on Friday. By the end of the second week, we discussed our needing additional help at home and she showed me how to use a transfer belt when moving Duane. She said she would instruct us on how to transfer him to and from the wheelchair when she returned on Monday. Before she left, she helped Duane get into bed where he collapsed and immediately fell asleep.

"I was just thinking about our dads," Duane explained later that afternoon when I found him in tears, sitting on our bed looking at my parents' portrait. "I think they would have liked each other, don't you?" We talked about how much we missed our dads. My father had been a vital force in my life for fifty-three years and profoundly influenced my children into their adulthood. He had lived to enjoy not only his grandchildren but also his great-grandchildren. Duane was only twenty-eight when his father died, shortly before David was born. Duane had missed his dad throughout most of his adult life; he especially missed him now and spoke of him often. He didn't say so, but I believe he was also thinking about David and Will and the years he would not be spending with them.

"Dad, I think you should sell your truck. If you need one again, this won't be the right vehicle for you." Thus David found the words to approach this long-avoided subject as he came to help his father shower for the first time on Saturday morning. It was no longer possible for me to handle Duane safely in the shower. Agreeing to have his son bathe him had been a major concession for Duane. Now he was faced with the prospect of selling his beloved truck and link to his lost independence.

As I helped Duane undress in preparation for his Saturday shower, I was horrified to see blisters where I had applied the thermo wraps to his chest the night before. This was another astonishing change. For months the wraps had soothed the pain from his so-called broken ribs, and now they had burned him. I was mortified, staring in disbelief as I covered them with ointment and gauze bandages after his shower. Following our normal routine, I moisturized his now dry skin, applying specially formulated oil to his scaly feet, and helped him dress. Then, grasping his walker, he headed out of the bedroom to finish his taxes with David.

"David! Help us!" I screamed as I grabbed Duane, whose legs gave out at the bedroom doorway. Instantly David was there holding his father to keep him from collapsing to the floor. Was this what had happened two weeks before? Did Duane's legs quit working, causing him to fall? I will never forget the look on David's face, a combination of fear and heartbreak. Realization of the inevitable set in as we looked into each other's eyes while trying to get Duane to safety. David had never witnessed his father become so instantly helpless before. I had several times, but this time something was different. I knew something was changing in Duane's traumatized brain.

"Dad, have you thought at all about what will happen when Mary can no longer care for you?" The question was no longer "if" but "when." We had come to the point alluded to by Dr. Fowler over a year before. As painful as this was to accept, I found comfort knowing we had done all we could for the past thirteen months. I couldn't do any more. The three of us discussed intermediate care. David, a Fairview employee, would contact friends on Monday to start the process. He brought up the once-dreaded wheelchair from the garage and removed the footrests, making it possible to maneuver the chair in our townhouse. If nothing else, at least for now Duane was safe and we were working on a plan to keep him that way.

The coins tossed into the funnel gained momentum as they continued the spiral down.

Agonizing changes were at hand. For the first time Duane

had needed his son to bathe him. He also faced the loss of his truck, his mobility, and soon his home. The catastrophic losses Duane faced that morning as the victim of a grade IV brain tumor rivaled those of victims of a grade IV hurricane. Entering the living room after David left, I found Duane sobbing with his head in his hands, his body heaving in anguish. Never had I witnessed him in such despair. I dropped to my knees and held him, my gut-wrenching sobs matching his. We cried together until there were no more tears, then we simply clung to each other as abandoned shipwreck victims clinging to debris in a churning sea, finding comfort in each other's embrace.

When we were finally able to speak, he said, "You write your book and I hope you make a million dollars. You deserve it." Others had been encouraging me to write this story — our story — for months. Others had been helped and encouraged by it. If Duane had not encouraged me or given me his permission to share our story, I would never have done it.

Duane's son was not the only child affected by what was happening in our house. My children were frantic with worry, not only for Duane but also for their mother. Whenever I saw them or spoke to them on the phone now, all I could do was cry. They urged me to get more help for Duane, knowing I could not continue to care for him alone.

The next day Ann's family was visiting Eric and his boys. David stayed with Duane so I could join my kids for a day at Eric's. Little Nadia, age three, grabbed my knees as I got out of my car. Eric, Ann, and Tom cried with me as I related the events at our house. Simply said, they loved him. They respected him not only for how happy he had made me, but also because of who he was, the quality of his character, and the positive impact he had made on each of their lives. Like everyone else, they believed that he could beat this thing. He seemed larger than life itself. For them, like for me, the prospect of his loss was devastating. They grieved along with me for the agony he was in now.

The recent death of Sara's brother had profoundly affected my little clan, making our time together even sweeter. This day we truly celebrated our being together. This time spent with my family was affirming and healing, assuring me that regardless of what lay ahead, I was blessed; my children and my grandchildren would be with me no matter what. I returned home later that afternoon more relaxed and refreshed than I had been in a long time, more prepared for the week ahead.

On Monday Faith came for her last scheduled visit, giving us suggestions on how to keep us both safe. There was nothing more PT could do for Duane. Then she asked to hear our story — how we met, how long we had been together, and what our lives had been like. She told us how much she had enjoyed working with us; "You guys are such a healthy couple. Duane, you are always so pleasant, and Mary, you give him such loving care. I don't often find that with my patients. The way some people talk to each other, you wouldn't want to hear." She said she found us to be both realistic and hopeful. Duane and I would miss seeing this delightful little woman who offered us peace and comfort along with her caring therapy. Faith had the aura of an angel.

Our health care professionals had been reporting to Dr. Trusheim regarding Duane's deteriorating condition at home. I also called his nurse, Kathy. Duane and I wanted to be prepared for his appointment on Thursday. "What did the radiologist's written report of the latest MRI say?" I asked. After consulting with Dr. Trusheim, Kathy conveyed the radiologist's findings. Then I slowly hung up the phone, dazed in disbelief at what she had told me.

My hunch had been correct. There was more swelling, creating pressure in his brain; Kathy said it was "pressing on things." I didn't want to ask, "What things?" I had a pretty good idea. A build-up of fluid was causing pressure around dead tumor tissue. Wanting to provide Duane with some "quality," Dr. Trusheim was leaning toward surgery to remove it. He would arrange an appointment with Dr. Rodman to schedule the surgery within the month. We were to increase the Decadron and continue with Thalidomide but discontinue his chemo until he had healed from the surgery.

I wrote an update to our team, the first in two weeks, giving a quick recap of all that had transpired since Duane's discharge from the hospital.

Guys, these have been the hardest days in the past year. I have briefly summarized the past few days. There is much more. Duane said tonight he is getting sick of all this. His exact words were "Why bother?" We both have been more discouraged, frightened, depressed — shed more tears — than we have at any time during this journey. The time is coming soon when I can't care for him at home. Maybe this is so hard because things were going so well. We always knew someday things would change, yet we still weren't ready. We were enjoying this false sense of security. We hit a mogul and just didn't see it coming. It really threw us.

In the light of all the pain in the world today, our pain seems minor. Correspondent David Bloom, the same age as my son-in-law, died of a pulmonary embolism in Iraq. Duane also suffered from blood clots in his lungs in August. As agonizing as the ordeal was for him, his life was saved. The pain that Duane and I feel pales in comparison to anguish of Sara and her parents at Tony's tragic death — or that of our friends Ron and Ruth Tryon from Duluth whose son Rex died unexpectedly in January — or that of the spouses and parents of our servicemen and women in Iraq — I can't imagine. All I know tonight is our pain. We are in agony. How can I be his cheerleader when I am so scared? All Duane wants to know is that I'll be here. I will. If any of you have any encouraging words, great advice, etc., please share. And of course, keep us in your prayers!

I'll check in again after we see the doc on Thursday.

Love, Mary

We all see angels; if we never recognize them its because they come in ways we don't expect.

– Eileen Elias Freeman

If I had been asked years ago who would provide the most support in a crisis, I would have never have imagined who it would be. The beauty of this journey was found in truly unexpected places — in people who I hadn't known well, or at all until recently, and in people with whom I had lost contact until God called them forward to comfort and strengthen Duane and me. The first response to my latest Update came from my classmate Paul, who had been a quiet kid when we were in junior high, and whom I had teased relentlessly. Why he was even nice to me now one can only imagine.

It's always easier to give advice than to follow it, but since you asked, here's my 2 cents worth. Don't give up and don't let Duane give up! He's come a long way. He's beaten the tumor. Compared to that, the scar tissue is just a nuisance — just one more thing to deal with and, after all you two have been through, it's hard not to ask yourselves, "OK, what's the next thing to go wrong?" I'm not a doctor, but I'd guess that, unlike a tumor, scar tissue won't regenerate. That being the case, it should be the last time they have to go inside his head. Then it's just a matter of medicating to control any swelling from the surgery for a while, and you should be "home free."

Confucius say, "When one is swimming up from the bottom of lake, not seeing light above water may only mean it is nighttime. No take breath until head above water!"

Hang in there. – Paul

———————

Bob Callahan understood. This quiet man in his mid sixties sat down in the chair next to me the first day at the Coaches Training Institute a few years earlier. We became good friends. Since the onset of Duane's illness, Bob had been a steadfast supporter and source of strength. He himself had walked this walk with his first wife, who had died of cancer several years before.

———————

Mary, I just read your update and I'm sooooo sorry — it truly is a roller coaster, and with each downward dip it seems to get harder to come back up. But if anyone can fight it, "Sunny" can. You have been so valiant in your support, energy, and devotion throughout this process. There isn't anything more that you could have or can do than you have been doing. But I know it's so very difficult to be in the midst of it and see the pain and related depression that can come with it and at the same time to stay strong for him.

Has anyone from Prince of Peace stopped by to see you and Duane lately? If not, would you like me to contact them for you?

I am with you in prayers and in spirit.

With the love of Christ, Bob

———

Robby was a classmate but we were never close friends. We occasionally saw each other at reunions, but that was all. Now her message wrapped around me like the invisible cloak I had felt all those months ago. This cloak would remain with me for the days and weeks ahead.

———

You said, "All Duane wants to know is that I'll be there." He wants you. The look of you, the touch of you, the sound of you, and the smell of you. Whatever comes, he wants you. There is no greater calling in this life than to be needed by the one you truly love. I can't imagine your pain. The images you create are outstanding. I see the two of you together and I weep. But what if you had missed Duane along the path of life? If the cross we are given to bear is no more than we can handle, does this mean you will be able to transcend grief and pain and be his light? I don't know. But God does and that is why Duane has Mary. You have traveled a path I hope to not follow, but the person you have become, or the one I have been given the honor of seeing after all these years, is a model of true humanity and love.

Love, Robby

———

Thank you for this, Robby!

Not having Duane in my life these last eight years would have been an even greater loss than the one I am facing now. A psychic had told me we had chosen this path for ourselves. We knew we were right for each other the day we met. I am loved more passionately than most women I know. This year has been our love story. How blessed I am to be loved by this man! I walked over hot coals to find him. He is my mate, my love, and my true spouse. He completes me. And now, I catch Duane just staring at me — those huge brown eyes fixed on me like he is trying to take in everything about me. At first it made me uncomfortable, and I asked if there was something wrong — did I have a smudge on my nose or something? He would reply, "No, I just want to look at you. Isn't that okay?" Of course it is, and I started looking back — deep into his eyes, even as I type the words, I can see into his eyes and feel the connection of our souls.

How would I ever have endured this painful ordeal without supportive friends lifting us and holding us close? Without them, for sure I was a "weak little nothing." With their strength, I knew we could go on.

Duane was stronger on Wednesday; maybe since there were no nurses or therapists coming, he could just "be." We spent the day at home alone, just the two of us. His spirits were boosted by a long phone call from Dave Nystrom; it was good to hear Duane laugh again.

Willy came over after work, telling Duane horror stories about the new remodeling project at the dealership. We were saddened to hear that Larry was also not doing well. Duane kept saying that one of these days he'd have to call Larry. And Willy, everybody's caretaker — including mine — had lost weight, had a sallow complexion, and had that "look" in his eyes. He had lung cancer now, which probably had spread to his lymph nodes. After his bout with his brain tumor, he had refused all treatment. All he would take now was pain medication. He calmly told us, "Well, whatever happens, happens." He was at peace. His face lit up as he showed off pictures of his baby granddaughter. He was working six days a week and was getting his boat out to go fishing on Sunday. He offered to come over someday soon to help me with the aquarium. No matter how hard I tried to keep it going with regular cleanings and the proper amounts of salt and drops, the fish kept dying. It was more trouble than it was worth, but Duane loved it. "You take care of yourself too, Dear," Willy instructed me. "Call me anytime, day or night."

Wednesday, April 9, we had enjoyed a good day at home together, a day to which we would sign our names. I thought of Robby's comments, "He wants you! The look of you, the touch of you, the sound of you, and the smell of you. Whatever comes he wants you." All I wanted was him, too. We held hands as we went to sleep together for what was to be the last time in our own bed.

The Decision

Before dawn the next day, I made coffee and spent time alone in prayer, preparing for the day at hand. It was Thursday, April 10, the day of Duane's appointment with Dr. Trusheim. I was apprehensive, yet relieved to have been warned about the MRI.

I gave Duane his Decadron at six o'clock. "Would you sit with me for while?" he asked. I pulled a chair up next to his bedside and wrote in my journal while he slept another hour or two. All he wanted was to have me by his side, and there was nowhere else I wanted to be.

Journal entry:
Thursday April 10, 2003

Strange thing, what bothers me the most is looking at Duane's hands. Big, strong tough hands — a fisherman's weathered hands, tanned from the sun and the wind, sensitive enough to detect structure on the bottom of a lake or a river, able to detect the slightest tug on a lure, with fingers able to tie delicate line into perfect knots — strong fisherman's hands. Strong, yet sensitive hands and fingers that could rouse me to the sweetest passion with a touch. Duane's strong hands.

Duane's hands look smaller now. They are thin and bony. When I hold them I can feel the slight "tic" of a seizure deep within his brain. They are no longer tanned, but pale and waxy, with purplish bruises, like Christ's imprints of nails.

Funny, they remind me of my grandfather's hands. I don't remember much about him except that he was sick; he died in his eighties when I was eight. When I look at Duane's hands, I see my grandfather's old hands, but I remember the strong, tanned fisherman's hands of my lover.

It took all morning and much of his strength to get Duane washed and dressed for his appointment. Looking handsome in a new red plaid shirt and khaki pants, he descended the stairs. Wes held him tightly as he trembled with each step. Exhausted, he needed to sit on the landing to rest before taking the next four steps to the foyer. His energy was renewed by a call from his Aunt Dorothy and his two "girl cousins," Patty and Janet, before resuming his journey. With a broad smile on his face, he took the last four steps to the foyer, then a few more steps to the garage and the awaiting wheelchair. I wheeled him past the Warrior — his beloved walleye boat, past rows of fishing rods and shelves filled with tackle, then out of his home into the driveway.

It was a beautiful spring day. The sun was shining brightly, birds were singing, and the smell of spring filled the air. One year ago we had such hope at the beginning of April—the beginning of treatment and the onset of spring. What would this one hold for us? We would know soon enough as we headed across the river on our way to Dr. Trusheim's office in Edina. "The weekend is supposed to be beautiful. Should we open the deck for a barbecue? You could get a little sun." "Yeah, I'd like that. Maybe the kids could come over." He chatted about his cousins all the way to Edina, telling stories of childhood adventures on the farm.

His mood was upbeat and positive; we were prepared for the appointment to discuss the MRI films which Duane now held in his lap.

"How safe do you feel with Duane at home?" Dr. Trusheim's pale blue eyes focused directly on mine as he asked this question. After checking Duane's strength, he showed us the new films, pointing out the swelling and the changes in the left side. Now his gaze was riveted on me, like that of a prosecutor at a murder trial. I knew the weight my answer held.

"Some days are okay, but right now they aren't. I am afraid for his safety and for mine. I never want him to fall again, and I don't want to hurt myself either. I can't guarantee I can keep us safe." My voice was shaking, as were my knees and my hands clasped tightly in my lap.

He gave us a choice; Duane could either be admitted directly to the hospital right now, or if we had something special going on, we could spend the weekend together at home and come back to the hospital on Monday. As much as I wanted more time with him at home, I couldn't do it. "We really don't have anything . . . ." Dr. Trusheim stopped me in mid-sentence, "Fine. I'll arrange his admission." It had been decided. It was out of our hands. Dr. Rodman would see us on Friday after he reviewed the films to discuss surgery. Social workers would start the process for intermediate care. Duane's journey down his stairs and through his garage had been his last.

As David wheeled Duane out to the lobby, Dr. Trusheim gave me the large envelope containing the MRI films to hold as he made arrangements for Duane's admission. I placed them back in his hands as his secretary, Lori, wheeled Duane across the street to the entrance of Fairview Southdale Hospital. That was it.

Waiting in the hospital lobby for Lori to complete the admission and a transport to bring Duane to the eighth floor, I knelt in front of him and held him in my arms as we wept. I kept telling him how sorry I was. He wasn't coming home. My head was telling me this was the right thing — the only thing. But oh my heart — that was a different story all together. At this time Duane believed he would be treated, get stronger again, and come home, just like he had before. I knew that was no longer probable.

After he was settled into his room, I went back home to get his Thalidomide and the CPAP machine necessary for his sleep apnea. I also packed his favorite things — the quilt I had made with my Oneida Street sewing club in Duluth; Olga, the teddy bear I bought him on an early hospitalization; some favorite photographs; and Chase's and Payton's recent artwork to decorate his walls — then headed back to the hospital to stay with Duane until he was ready for bed. Driving home later that night, I was surprisingly at peace. Duane was safe. I knew I done my best for thirteen months and had no regrets. I could sign my name to them.

Early Friday morning I discussed Duane's placement in a nursing home with an oncology social worker. When we were looking for rehab placement the previous summer, we had been told that Ebenezer Ridges Care Center in Burnsville (just two miles from our house) was not an option. Insurance would pay for Ebenezer in downtown Minneapolis, but not in Burnsville. Why not? The only nursing homes on the preferred list were across town, far from our home. Now I pleaded for placement in Burnsville, asking the social worker to grovel if necessary on our behalf. We deserved a break — whatever it took. She said she would try her best. At least that door was left ajar.

Our future hinged on Dr. Rodman's words. Late morning his nurse, Gina, told us he would be in to see Duane after surgery that afternoon. We waited. I didn't leave the room for fear I would miss him. Shortly after four o'clock I saw Dr. Rodman at the nurses' station just outside Duane's door. It wouldn't be long now, or so I thought.

David arrived at five, just as a nurse came in to tell us that Dr. Rodman had read the chart and the written report and just needed to look at the actual films. At seven there was still no word. What was taking so long? A nurse then told us that Dr. Rodman couldn't locate the films (the one's I had placed in Dr. Trusheim's hands when we left his office the day before) and had gone home. We had waited anxiously for him all day and no one had told us he was no longer in the hospital. After a frustrating and tedious day, I too went home, leaving Duane and David to have some time alone.

The night before I had sent an Update. Now the answering machine was filled with messages from worried friends. Carol Streitz, one of the Loose Ladies, implored "Mar, remember you have enjoyed your mother for fifty-six years now. Give your children the same opportunity to have you." Her concern made me a little more comfortable with giving others the responsibility for Duane.

The messages on my email reinforced this feeling. I had done all I could for Duane and it was time to take better care of me.

———————

Oh Mary,

I am glad you feel a sense of peace.
I am in awe of the wonderful job you have done with Duane. Just think if something were to now happen at home

and the ambulance / doctor etc couldn't get there in time. That would be devastating too.

Yes, you are correct —- everything is in God's hands now. That is exactly why you feel peace. And the two of you have had a very rich blessing for the short time you have been together. Each of you has had the opportunity to feel truly loved. Many people never get to know that.

Bless you both. Kay and Rich

God's hands are gentle, yet strong, and especially caring. Duane is in the best of care. Take time for Mary; it is a must, not a luxury.

With my prayers, Suzanne

Somehow we endured the exasperating weekend. As if we were not worried enough, David was told that the MRI films were missing. David knew exactly where he had seen them last—in Dr. Trusheim's hands when we left his office Thursday afternoon. I vowed that they would be found on Monday if I had to find them myself.

Monday morning Duane was still sleeping as I slipped into the chair beside his bed and quietly watched the sunrise from his eighth floor window. It was bright and golden in the cloudless sky, the beginning of what appeared to be another beautiful spring day.

I was determined to be there when Dr. Trusheim arrived. He usually made rounds early; at least he had done so every other time he had seen Duane in the hospital. Today, of course, he did not. More waiting.

Around noon Duane was sitting on the commode in his

hospital gown, his exposed backside facing the foot of his bed. The door was closed, and the curtain round his bed had been drawn to assure him some privacy. Dr. Trusheim stood behind Duane, telling us that the tumor was growing. If we opted for more aggressive chemo without surgery, he said, Duane could either die or be severely impaired. If we continued on our current course, Duane would continue to gradually decline. "If . . . if . . . if"—words defining our future were told to us with Duane seated on the commode.

I was incensed at the disrespect Duane was shown. Couldn't the doctor have waited a few minutes, or at least faced him? Was his schedule so tight he could not afford Duane some dignity? Yet Dr. Trusheim was the best doctor, and now we needed expertise more than diplomacy.

We were being dealt another "really bad hand" and we desperately needed something — anything — to go right. As I had requested, the social worker was doing her best to get Duane into Ebenezer Ridges. His insurance company agreed to consider it if we could get a referral from Apple Valley Medical Center. I immediately called Dr. Loken from Duane's bedside, only to be told that she was out of the clinic until after two o'clock Tuesday. I explained our plight to the phone nurse on duty, who suggested I call back the next day. My hope dimmed. We needed a miracle and we needed one now. "Oh please, God . . . ." I could not even finish my prayer. Ten minutes later, Duane's bedside phone rang; it was Dr. Loken calling on her day off to tell us everything had been taken care of. We had our referral. Thank God for Dr. Loken. We had a chance.

The good news was the MRI films had finally been located. Gina told us she would personally hand carry them to Dr. Rodman's office across the street. The bad news was that Dr.

207

Rodman was in surgery at another hospital all day and may not be in. There was no way of knowing; it all depended on how long surgery lasted. Early in the evening, we were told that he would not be in to see us until the next day.

You have to live for today and not even think about the next appointment.
Holding your breath means it is taking up too much of your thinking.   *– Mary Del Euretig*

For days I had held my breath as we anxiously waited for answers. When the answers came, I wanted to turn back the clock to the "not knowing" of the weekend. I had wasted precious time being frustrated and fretful instead of enjoying the reprieve we had been given. Now Dr. Rodman was standing before us leaning back against the wall which was covered with the grandchildren's artwork. His arms were folded across his chest, and his legs were crossed at the ankles—his closed body posture spoke volumes. He did not recommend further surgery. The problem was not the tumor itself, but the feelers that were now long and widespread. Another complication was Coumadin, the blood thinner Duane needed to prevent more clots. He would have to discontinue it to have any type of surgery. Without it, he would be at high risk for more blood clots. The risk far outweighed any possible benefit.

"Do you have any questions?" Duane immediately asked, "Doc, what about my son? What can he do not to get this?" There was no answer. No one knows what caused this insidious tumor. Dr. Rodman shrugged his shoulders, then pointed to the window and the skyline of Minneapolis in the distance. "See that haze of pollution over the city? The world we live in contributes as much as anything. If there is anything else I can do for you, just call." And with that he was gone.

What would happen next? We had been preparing for more surgery, never considering that it would be too dangerous. This time we didn't have to wonder very long. Dr. Trushiem arrived shortly thereafter to discuss our options.

Inter-arterial chemo would most aggressively attack the tumor; the best case scenario was that Duane would be in a nursing home, "badly beaten up by the treatment." It would buy him "maybe a year," but his quality of life would be gone. There was also a minimum twenty percent chance of severe damage, either leaving him in a vegetative state or killing him.

We could also continue the present treatment and see a gradual decline in Duane's condition. Duane asked, "What are we looking at, Doc?"

"Three to six months."

The third choice was to stop the present treatment, in which case we would see a rapid decline. "Do you understand what I am telling you, Duane?" We were to take the day to discuss it and give him our decision in the morning.

Caregiving means letting your loved one decide.
– Jessica Schaver

We sat in stunned silence for a few minutes. Then Duane said, "Wow. That doesn't sound very good, does it?" I held his hands and, choking back the tears, told him I would support whatever decision he made. "I don't see why we don't just keep on with what we are doing. It's worked so far." I was relieved. It gave us a little time with a chance for quality. Discussing the options with David later that afternoon, we all agreed to continue with the present course. The coin tossed in the funnel gained momentum.

In the quiet of the family lounge, David and I sobbed in each other's arms as we faced the end of Duane's journey. We would make every one of Duane's days count. If possible, we would take a family day trip to Two Harbors so he could sit by Lake Superior or maybe just drive along the river. For sure we would be with him every day.

David said he had been trying to write me a letter telling me how much I meant to his family — that I was "amazing." It was nice to hear. I knew they loved me and appreciated everything I had done for his dad.

Late that night I shared the events of the last several days with our team ending with,

I know some of you have not met Duane, and some of you have not met me (or either one of us, I hear). I want you to know why I love him to the core of my being. Every person who has been in his room to work with him — doctors, nurses, therapists, visitors, even the cleaning lady — has commented on his character, his attitude, his warmth, his smile, his appreciation, and his willingness. His physical therapist said today, "I just love coming into this room." Today as we faced facts that no one wants to face, he made it easier for David and me. This strong man — my knight in shining armor — used to having his own way, his time alone, who until March 2002 had never been sick, who loves his life, his home, his family, his friends, and me (he still makes me weak in the knees the way he looks at me), made his choice for quality. He accepts that he can't come home. The Kennedys have their "Profiles in Courage" award. This is courage. This is character. I am so proud of him, and that he loves me.

210

Today I read, "He who does not know prayer does not know power." Your prayers have gotten us through all of this. We thank you for your power. It has given us comfort and strength these last thirteen months. Our most challenging days lie ahead. Please continue to pray for us and never, never doubt the impact of your prayers. Now we need Duane to be at Ebenezer in Burnsville. The rest will take care of itself.

We are all cried out. The worst is not knowing. Get the facts, make a choice, live with it, and don't look back — trust. Faith is taking a step when you can't see where you are going. We have faith. We are at peace. Please pray for us.

Our team shared our pain as they read this last update and forwarded it to others. Amazingly, the most poignant responses I received were from people I didn't know were reading these — people I hadn't heard from before. One was from a former supervisor:

Dear Mary,

Deb forwarded me your last email regarding Duane's condition. I cried because I felt the pain. I then realized that you are about to set sail on one of the most loving journeys of your lifetime. You have been called by God to participate in Duane's journey home. It will be one of the most beautiful experiences you will have.

My mom was diagnosed with terminal cancer last July. I was soooo devastated. She died last November. I spent every weekend with her and moved in with her during her last 30 days. I prayed all the time. We prayed and talked about her ascent from this life. We laughed and cried. We opened our hearts knowing the time was limited. We cherished every minute. I gained a relationship with God and was given the grace in return to realize that this journey was a blessing beyond belief. It was a gift. I was able to say everything I wanted to say. I was able to love like I had never loved. I was able to reverse roles and take care of her. Hospice allowed me to keep her home. She died in my arms. I miss her terribly but am still warmed by her love. She is not gone. She has simply gone on.

You will find strength you never knew you had. It is clear from your emails how much you love this gentle man. I have a suggestion. Buy the book "Embraced by the Light," by Betty Edie. Read it yourself, then read it to Duane. It will comfort you.

I have always loved you, Mary. You are in my prayers.
Mary M.
P.S. I pray a lot.

Another unexpected and moving message came from a woman I had met only once, a friend's sister-in-law:

Dear Mary,

Hello! I don't know if you remember me or not. Kay has been forwarding your updates to me. Mary, my heart goes out to you and your family. Granted, I have not gone through this with my husband, but I have gone through it with my mom. As a matter of fact, she just passed away Sept. 19th. Got a moment for her story?"

She recounted the beautiful story of her mother's ten-year battle with cancer and her last nine days, which she described as the "most fulfilling days of my life." She continued:

I know in my heart God was with my mom every step of

the way. He guided her, eased her pain. He helped us with her. No matter if Duane is at home or at Ebenezer, as long as you hold on to your deep faith (as you eluded to in your last email) and have that enormous prayer chain going for you that you have—you will have peace. All of you.

I know you said you were all cried out. You will find from here on out your tears will come in waves. Some will be because you miss your knight in shining armor and perhaps feel robbed of the twilight years you were supposed to have together. Some will be because you have the most beautiful memories God allowed you to have. You'll cry out of happiness; you'll cry out of sadness — the hole in you heart will never go away. Take these remaining days you have with Duane and cherish them. No matter how hard or seemingly easy they might be, these are memories that will be locked in your heart forever. For you see, we, unlike many who have lost their loved ones, have one advantage. God has given us the opportunity to say every day until our loved ones' last day, "I love you." "Thank you for a wonderful life." "You are the world to me."

Sorry if this got a little long. I just wanted you to know that you and your family are not alone in this battle. There are those, like myself, who have been through it and can comfort you with our experience — we feel your pain. There are those who have not been through it, but because of their love for you and Duane, can offer an abundance of support and understanding. And even though you feel you have cried yourself out, remember, God said: 'Blessed are they that mourn for they shall be comforted.'

I will continue to say my prayers for you, Duane and your family because I am a firm believer that the grace of God is the only chance any of us has to get through the hurdles life throws in our paths. Please know that we are here for you, if not in the physical sense, definitely in spirit and thoughts. Hang on to your peace of mind, Mary. Your

days may become harder before they become easier, but
you have the good fortune to realize you have God's peace,
and that inner peace you will carry you through Duane's last
days and every day following his passing until you are
together again. I know because it is that same peace that
gets me through every single day since Sept. 19th, 2002.
Keep walking the path of faith and you will always be in the
right direction.
  God bless you and your family.
  Karen

⸺✦⸺

I sat in awe and disbelief as I read through these messages. "Out of the depths" I cried, frightened and grief-stricken. I couldn't bear the thought that Duane was dying. How strange that for this entire time, for all these months, I did not concern myself with his death. Oh, it was always there, and he had come close a couple times, but it had been a remote possibility. I had my eyes fixed at where we were now, at present, not at the unseen end of the road. Duane always focused on living, not on dying.

In March of 2002 I had knelt by his bedside in the ICU, asking God, "How can I help him prepare to die?" I was so unprepared. "I am this weak little nothing." He had answered, "You can do this." "Okay, but you've got to help me." And he did.

Within that "really bad hand," everything had indeed gone right. "Out of the depths" I cried out to God, and he always answered. He never, never left us alone. He held us up. He gave us his strength when we were fresh out, his hope in our despair, and his healing touch in our pain. Without God I was a weak little nothing, but he had spoken to me through his

214

angels on earth, often through email — just as he was doing now through unexpected sources. These women had taken the time to share their stories, their pain, and their hope with me. No matter what, there was hope.

We had been given an incredible gift, a gift that had been unfolding step by step, day by day, as Duane and I embarked on this awesome journey together. My daughter, Ann, had said it best a few nights before, "You two taught each other how to 'be.' "

Ebenezer

It's not the load that breaks you down –
it's the way you carry it.
– Lena Horne

A prayer was answered; late Wednesday afternoon, Ebenezer Ridges in Burnsville agreed to admit Duane into their Temporary Care Unit. He would be admitted before noon the next day.

Maundy Thursday, April 17, 2003

David and I assured Duane we would be with him every step of the way, then drove him to Ebenezer ourselves rather than sending him by hospital transport. Even in the "bad hand" of moving Duane to a nursing home, everything went right. The friendly staff welcomed us as David pushed the wheelchair into the beautifully furnished front lobby that could have been in a fine hotel rather than a nursing facility. Light streamed through the stained glass windows of the adjacent chapel, adding a sense of peace and serenity to the surroundings. We were then taken by elevator to the rehab wing on the third floor. Even the elevators were wallpapered and had beautiful framed prints hanging on the walls. My first impression was, "Maybe this won't be so bad."

Then the elevator door opened on the third floor. It too was tastefully decorated, bright, clean, and fresh smelling, but everything else resembled any nursing home anywhere in the country. The residents with white unkempt hair were sitting like rag dolls in their wheelchairs, blank expressions on their faces. Someone was moaning. Others were sleeping in their chairs, drooling, with their heads hanging on their chests. A voice in my head was screaming, "Noooooooooooo!" I had hated putting my father in a nursing home when he was ninety, now here I was admitting my Duane, thirty years younger. I wanted to turn his wheelchair around and run out of there as fast as I could. I couldn't see his face and was thankful he couldn't see mine as tears welled up in my eyes.

Fortunately, this was not the Temporary Care Unit. I pushed Duane's chair past the aviary filled with brightly colored birds and down the corridor to the TCU. Just past the nurses' station was a door with Duane's name on the nameplate. He was home.

The TCU was unlike any nursing facility or hospital room we had ever seen. Duane's lovely private room again reminded me of a nice hotel. A restful print of a farmhouse with a big white porch hung on the papered wall by his bed. At the foot of the bed, a large credenza housed the TV. Only the lift bar hanging from the ceiling and the call button on the bed suggested the real purpose of the room. We personalized it by putting favorite photos on the windowsill, taping the children's artwork to the closet doors, and putting the Oneida Street quilt on his bed. With a five-minute drive home, I was able to bring in everything else he needed to make his stay comfortable.

We enjoyed a quiet dinner together in his room that evening rather than join the other patients in the cozy TCU dining room. Duane was exhausted, physically and emotionally, from the move. Originally, I had planned to be with Christi and her parents at the Elton John / Billy Joel concert that evening, but now I only wanted to be with Duane this first night at Ebenezer. I was thankful Christi had been able to sell the ticket Duane had given me for Valentine's Day. After the nurse administered his nightly doses of medication, I kissed him goodnight and left for home with no regrets about having missed Elton John and Billy Joel.

I marveled how my Duane spent this first evening in the nursing home without a complaint. He never pleaded, "Get me out of here" or questioned, "Why can't you take me home?" He was gracious and appreciative of the excellent staff who welcomed him and tended to his every need. Duane made what could have been a very difficult day much easier for David and me.

The next day, he told me about his first night at Ebenezer. "Last night I was thanking God for my many blessings, especially for Mary. Not only because she is so beautiful, but . . . I forgot the word, but you really would have liked it." How I loved Duane! On his first night in a nursing home he was thanking God for his many blessings, just as he had that night thirteen months before, when gliobastoma multiforme became part of our lives.

Good Friday April 18, 2003

Right after breakfast, occupational, physical, and speech therapists evaluated Duane to determine a starting point for measuring his balance, strength, endurance, and cognitive abilities. He could remain in TCU for a maximum of sixty days, as long as he continued to show progress; the therapists assured me they could measure progress in many small ways, so we were not to worry. It wouldn't have taken much for Duane to show any improvement, as he was exhausted from the move to Ebenezer and from his current round of chemo, The schedule would be demanding — two and a half hours a day — having speech therapy each morning, and OT and PT each morning and again in the afternoon. David put his dad's name on the waiting list for the Long Term Care Unit at Ebenezer, and we started looking at other facilities in the area, just in case.

When Duane went to lunch in the TCU dining room, I crossed the parking lot to attend the noon services at Prince of Peace. How different this Good Friday was from the one we expected just a few weeks ago. Duane was not joining his old cronies from his ad agency days at the Officer's Club at Fort Snelling for their annual lunch. In Duluth, my daughter was at her church ready to sing *The Seven Last Words* with her choir. At one time I had hoped I could sing it with her, then hoped at least to be in attendance to hear it. Eric, Tom, and the kids were now there without me.

I did not know many people in the huge Prince of Peace congregation and usually sat alone. Good Friday, as I entered the church, I encountered Woody and Linda, a couple whom I had met in a discussion group at church. I hadn't seen them in over a year; now here we met inside the doors of the sanctuary as if our getting together had been choreographed.

Woody asked, "Are you okay? You seem to be in pain." For the first time I actually said the words out loud, "My Duane is dying." These simple words sounded like dialogue spoken by an actor in a play, words that still did not seem real. Somehow by saying the words, the impact of that truth penetrated my heart like a dagger. Linda comforted me, saying she understood how I felt because she had recently lost a close friend to a brain tumor. Linda held my hand throughout the entire service, consoling me as the tears streamed down my cheeks. The words I had spoken had opened a tiny crack in my self-imposed protective wall for my pain to leak out. We left the darkened sanctuary together in silence, but lost sight of each other amid the exiting crowd of worshipers as we went our separate ways. Walking back across the parking lot to Ebenezer, I knew Duane and I were not alone. Through this "chance" meeting, God had reminded me once again that ministering angels were with us at Ebenezer, just as they had been with us throughout this journey.

Easter Sunday, April 20, 2003

———•◦•———

Oh Mary! You were on my mind all weekend. I tried to picture you with your family on Easter, but sensed you were "on duty"—running back and forth, being there for Duane.

What was Easter like for you? Probably not a bright new beginning. You and Duane are lucky to have each other, to experience real love and commitment. I can't imagine how awful it is for you right now — or for Duane — to face losing this wonderful love.

One day at a time, Mary, maybe one hour. You will get through this. You know how many people love you both and are praying for you. Just breathe that in whenever things get tough. Breathe in our love and God's love. Just breathe.

Love, Dee

———•◦•———

What was Easter like? Painful. Frustrating. Heartbreaking.

I planned to have dinner with Duane at noon and go with him to a church service in the beautiful first floor chapel at

2:30. Then I would go to Barb's to see my family, including Eric, Chase, and Payton. I was desperate to spend some time with my grandsons. David, Christi, and Will would come over later after having had dinner with Meg, so Duane would not be alone on Easter. We had it covered.

When I arrived at Ebenezer early Easter morning, Duane was in a deep sleep. Saturday had not gone well. The stress of the move and the current round of chemo had exhausted him. The mystery pain in his chest had suddenly returned. The two Percocet needed to control his agony all but rendered him unconscious. I was devastated to learn he was now incontinent and was wearing Depends. Duane wearing diapers. How must he feel?

Sitting by Duane's bed, I was troubled by how frail he looked. There was a quite rap on the door. "How ya' doing, Dear?" It was Willy. Out in the corridor I cried in Willy's arms. He didn't look good either; his color was ashen and his eyes looked weak and sunken. When I asked how he was, the answer was always the same. "Don't you worry about me! I'm okay. I'm okay." Willy, choosing quality of life over treatment for lung cancer, was supporting his friend — and me. "You need to take care of yourself now. I can see what this is doing to you." What did he see? New wrinkles, a few more gray hairs, and dark circles under my eyes? The stress surely was taking its toll on my body. I was sad and exhausted. Having always been a "stress eater," I had gained ten pounds. I remembered Duane's words to me the previous Easter when I returned from church, "Did everyone stand up when you walked in? You look so beautiful." I hoped he still thought I looked beautiful. We went back in the room; Willy stayed for a while and told Duane to "hang in there" when he left, but Duane didn't wake up until much later.

Duane was too tired to go to Easter dinner in the dining room, so I fed him while he remained in bed. He couldn't work his fork and was having trouble staying awake. We found the movie *Jesus of Nazareth* on TV and decided to watch it rather than get him ready for church. Duane fell back into a deep sleep.

So here I was on Easter Sunday, wanting to be with Duane but missing my own family. I wanted and needed to see my son and his little boys. I had been with Duane for hours and he had been asleep most of the time. He had always encouraged me to spend more time with my family, and I knew David would come and be with Duane after dinner. So I gave Duane a kiss, told him to have a good nap, and said that I would be back later. I wanted to see my grandsons. Duane did not stir when I left.

As soon as I arrived at my sister's, Duane was calling my cell phone wondering where I was. "Are you taking me to church or what?" I was too far away; the service started in ten minutes. The staff took him to Easter services in the chapel while I dined on my second Easter dinner with my family, feeling guilty for not being able to be in two places at once. Barb gave me a small gift with the instructions, "Do not open this until you are home."

To my surprise, Duane was alert and laughing with David when I returned to Ebenezer later that afternoon. It was hard to believe this was the same man who had been unable to hold his own fork earlier that day. I apologized for not taking him to church and promised that we would go together the next week. Duane replied, "That's okay, Honey. We'll go to church together next Easter."

Later at home, I opened my gift from Barb, a beautiful ornately decorated little bottle —a tear bottle. Barely two inches high, it was hardly large enough to contain my tears. I thought I was all cried out. I was wrong. Later that night I went into the bathroom, closed the doors, and screamed until my throat was raw. I cried so hard that I threw up. There was no one here to be strong for anymore. It was no longer necessary to mask my unrelenting pain. I had been hanging on trying to be brave, to hold everything together—including myself. I couldn't do it anymore. I called my big sister. Barb could not offer any advice or sisterly words of wisdom — she could only listen to me as I screamed and cried from the depths of my soul. I was losing my Duane. Even then, though, I knew his beautiful love would not die. I knew that it would be with me for the rest of my life.

Monday morning Duane was in terrible pain once again. Tuesday it was unbearable. I realized that this was happening on a monthly cycle, that it was getting progressively worse, and that it had nothing to do with broken ribs. The common denominator was not falling — it was the Temodar. That had to be it. Nothing else made sense. I discussed my theory with Kathy at Dr. Trusheim's office.

My theory was correct. One out of a hundred patients on Temodar develops severe chest pain; the reason is unclear. By now Dr. Trusheim had about a hundred patients on Temodar, and Duane was the unlucky first one to suffer from this particular side effect. Kathy said she would request additional information from the Temodar rep as to what, if anything else could be done to alleviate the pain, but for now Duane was given Percocet. Unfortunately, it turned him into a Zombie and threatened his sporadic progress in therapy and the likelihood of his remaining in the TCU.

"Hi Mary. This is Amy from Ebenezer. We have an opening in our Long Term Care Unit. Do you want it for

Duane?" The call from the social worker came on Thursday afternoon while I was walking my dog during Duane's naptime. I was shocked. Already? Duane had only been there for a week and David had just put his name on the long waiting list. Yet they had an immediate opening for Duane.

The staff had quickly assessed that Duane would need permanent placement and moved his name to the top of the waiting list. The care would remain the same; he would still have therapy with the long-term goal of going home. It was terribly important to David and me that we did not take away his hope of returning home. In Long Term Care, there would be no time limit on his stay — no pressure to improve. He would have a quiet, private room by a small lounge on the second floor. David and I immediately agreed this was a godsend and took the room. We were spared the hassle of finding alternative care, and Duane was spared the trauma of yet another move.

As with every other phase of the past year's developments, we were in God's hands. A vacancy had occurred within the week. Every challenge, no matter how simple or complex, was met with a positive solution — including the long-dreaded move to a nursing home. Duane would be moved right after breakfast on Monday morning. As with every other phase during the past year, we were embraced by the love of our family and friends.

"Mary, how do you want to handle this?"

Meg and I stood in the hall outside Duane's room. "Handle what?" I asked.

"My coming to visit Duane."

"My God, Meg! Come any time you want, as often as you want. Duane needs all the love and support he can get now. The more people he has to show him he is loved, the better."

"I knew you would say that," she gently replied, "but I had to ask."

Like Duane, this lady is one class act. She did not want to infringe on whatever time I had left with Duane, but she loved him too. Her pain was no less than mine. He was her son's father, they shared a grandchild, and they had been lifelong friends. They should have been the poster couple for divorced parents. She and I supported, respected, and liked each other. I was more than willing to share Duane's remaining time with her. She came often, bringing flowers, fresh-baked bread, and most important, their grandson.

Duane enjoyed the weekend before the move to the second floor visiting with family and friends. Outdoors on the patio enjoying the sun and fresh air, he delighted in watching Will dart to and fro, climbing on the garden rocks and dancing atop the picnic tables. He laughed at Will's diligent attempts to say "umbrella." Duane's cousin Janet and her husband drove an hour to visit, bringing chocolates and fresh flowers from her garden. As much as Duane enjoyed his time on the patio, he soon tired and asked to return to his room.

Saturday afternoon Dick stopped in on his way back to Chicago, spending hours at Duane's bedside reminiscing about past misadventures they had shared in over thirty-five years of friendship. Two years before I had been their "designated driver" as these guys spent an evening with old cronies at Mayslack's, an infamous Northeast Minneapolis eating and drinking establishment. It had an ambience all its own, from the 1900's decor tin ceiling, straight-back wood booths, and massive wood bar and back bar. When I retrieved Dick and Duane, the air had been filled with sounds of loud laughter and the aroma of beer, garlic, and Mayslack's famous roast beef sandwiches. On the table in front of Duane were the labels carefully peeled off his empty bottles of Budweiser, a habit developed and perfected over time. Now Duane, lying in his bed in a nursing home, was telling Dick, "I still think I can beat this thing, but if not . . . ." His voice trailed off, as he shrugged his shoulders, indicating that he hoped he would recover, but realized the odds were against it. Even so, Duane was not ready to give up. As I walked Dick to the elevator, he knew he had visited with his old friend for the last time. There would be no more visits to Mayslack's. "If there is anything you need, anything I can do, call me any time." There was nothing anyone could do now; just knowing they were there was enough.

Journal entry:
Sunday, April 27, 2003

So much — fear, loneliness, having to find joy in new places. So much pride in Duane. Chemo is less effective now. Duane not only cannot walk he can barely stand or lift his feet. He will be in a wheelchair for the rest of his life. I know he won't be home.

What was it Ann said? We taught/learned from/inspired each other. Everyone tells me how "great" I am. Not so! Yes, I have risen to the occasion of a lifetime here, but Duane is truly the wind beneath my wings. I am in awe of him.

He is walking this path with the same class he has exhibited throughout his life. He is teaching me, not only how to die, but how to live. He struggles in therapy but has affirmed to his therapists he is not giving up. He regrets when he can't remember to say his prayers — not for himself but for the troops in Iraq.

Strong? A while ago I wrote about his hands. Today he

227

held my hand so tight the pattern of my wedding ring is still imbedded in my fingers. Oh how he looks at me! That look penetrates my very soul.

Last week he asked me about the past year. " This past year we've had our ups and downs, but it hasn't been so bad, has it?" Bad? Absolutely not! It has been the most incredible gift. I have learned everything about love—real love, from him. How he fights! This is strength. This is courage.

*Devotion. Love. Compassion. Strength. Humility. Faith. Annie said it all — we have taught each other how to **be**.*

Long Term Care

Easy? No. Life? Yes.
– Mark Dslyn

———

Two and a half weeks after leaving our home for the last time, Duane settled into his new home in the Long Term Care Unit at Ebenezer. He was only five minutes from our house but an eternity away from our former life.

Over the weekend, David, Christi, and I prepared Duane's new room by decorating the walls with his trophy largemouth bass, familiar artwork, and Will's calendars. We covered the bulletin board by his bed with memorable photographs of happier days. His new, smaller recliner and a reading lamp stood in a corner by the window. By the time we were finished, the room looked cozy and familiar, furnished with some of his favorite things.

I placed a vase of red roses on the windowsill to welcome him and remind him of how much he was loved. A pot of pansies from Meg added to the cheerful ambiance of the room. When the aide wheeled him into his new abode, he felt reassured and appreciated our efforts to make it homey and comfortable. What a relief he did not need to be moved to a different facility. Just being wheeled from the third floor to the second completely exhausted him.

While he was in the TCU, we had eaten our meals in the small rehab dining room. Now Duane was among the gray-haired residents slumped in their wheelchairs waiting, always waiting, near the elevator to be taken to the main dining room on the first floor. Duane hated waiting. He had an internal clock and was never late; when it was time to go, he was ready and on his way. If he were meeting his friend Loren to go fishing and Loren was late, too bad; Duane would leave without him. Now he sat in his wheelchair, silently waiting for his turn to be placed in the elevator with the others. His downcast eyes held no spark. On the main floor, I stood with him as the wheelchairs were lined up single file for entrance to the dining room, where a staff member washed each resident's hands with a disposable cloth and placed a large striped terrycloth bib around the person's neck. Then we were taken to Duane's assigned place at his table.

As with most nursing facilities, women far outnumbered the men at Ebenezer. In the dining room, Duane was assigned to one of the only tables with other guys. Paul was a small, bent-over man with stringy white hair, a large nose, and a sour disposition. Jerry was a large pleasant man with pale blue eyes, an innocent expression, and a perpetual smile on his face. A stroke victim, he was always silent. His devoted wife, Marge, was with him during meals to help him eat. That was a relief to us, since Duane also frequently needed help at mealtime and might now feel less self-conscious. Also, it provided a means for a little conversation at the table. Duane just picked at his supper of soup and a sandwich made with an unidentifiable lunchmeat. He was terribly discouraged, as was I. One thing for sure, I wouldn't leave him alone at mealtime. We were in this together.

I tried to make every day as pleasant for Duane as possible. One beautiful spring day I took him outside for a "walk" around the grounds, pushing him in his wheelchair along the garden pathways to enjoy the fresh air and spring flowers. The wild plum trees that lined the sidewalk and patio

230

were in full bloom, the sweet fragrance of their pink and white blossoms filling the air. I pushed Duane's chair right into the trees so he could take a full deep breath as he reached up to pull a branch right up close to his face. A man raised on a farm, who had spent his entire life with agriculture, hunting, and fishing, needed to experience and enjoy the fresh scents of spring.

Another afternoon was highlighted by a surprise visit from Warren, his college roommate now living in Illinois. He and his wife, Bonnie, had faithfully come to see us when enroute to visit their son's family. As exhausted as Duane was, he greeted Warren with a welcoming smile, a firm handshake, and the reassurance that he was doing well. The two of them relived a road trip to California in their youth, compared notes on their children and grandchildren, and planned another visit for the upcoming Memorial Day weekend. When Warren hugged me good-bye at the elevator, I could feel his chest heaving as he stifled his tears.

In the spring, "a young man's fancy turns to thoughts of love." The same could be said for my man. We were no longer young but still had our thoughts of love. A former English teacher of mine had accused me once of being "an incurable romantic"; Duane could also be quite romantic himself. Under normal circumstances, we surely would have had our Friday "date night," going out to dinner to celebrate the arrival of spring. Now he was not able to get out for a date, so I brought one to him.

I canceled our "reservations" for dinner in the dining room one Friday evening and reserved the table in the lounge outside his room. The small lounge area was restful, with a lovely, soft rose-colored sofa, matching chairs, and a round table, perfect for a cozy dinner for two. A corner bookcase housed a boombox with a variety of CD's to enhance the mood.

While Duane slept that afternoon, I set our table with placemats, china plates, and stemmed goblets from home. My best cloth napkins with bright spring flowers were rolled in clear acrylic napkin rings, and I set a jar of fresh daisies in the center. Unfortunately, I was unable to dim the bright overhead lights and light candles, but the atmosphere was romantic nonetheless. To Duane's surprise, instead of being wheeled to the elevator for the usual trip downstairs, he was escorted to our own private dining room just outside the door to his room. With his eyes brimming with tears and a huge smile on his face, he kept saying, "You did all this? When did you do all this? Oh, wow, oh wow!" Soft piano music on the boombox played in the background as I poured strawberry lemonade into our stemmed goblets.

No nursing home food tonight; I brought in our favorite take-out from Leanne Chin's — Peking chicken with fried rice for Duane and lemon chicken for me. Once Duane would have adeptly maneuvered chopsticks for this meal, but tonight we were pleased he was able to use his own fork. He would normally have devoured all of his dinner and half of mine; now he enjoyed the few bites he could eat, saving the rest for "another time." We had enjoyed many wonderful date nights in the past, especially the night at Toby's on the Lake the previous March, but none were as precious as our "date night" at Ebenezer.

Duane needed special times like this to give balance to the difficult days he now faced. Although he had occasional strong days, overall he grew physically weaker. His therapy sessions were more and more demanding and depressing. In spite of Duane's determination, his stamina was waning. His therapists treated us both with kindness, respect, openness, and humor, urging him on during his sporadic decline. Yet I could tell by their faces that Duane would not be a good candidate for therapy much longer.

One morning PT had to be canceled because Duane was in such pain he was unable to participate. He was dejected as we waited for the elevator to take us back to his room. Suddenly, a cheerful woman with pretty red hair and an infectious smile greeted him, "Hi, Duane! Do you know who I am? I'm Connie. You were at my house back in the eighties." Connie, the recreational director at Ebenezer, was married to a school friend of Duane's from Winnebago. Duane was thrilled to hear that her husband, Bill, and another old chum were coming to visit him soon. His mood immediately improved, and he chatted the rest of the morning about his school days in Winnebago.

Some mornings after his therapy sessions, Duane and I would sit at a bistro table in the corridor near Nancy's Coffee Shop on the first floor, treating ourselves to gourmet coffee and hot freshly baked cookies. We would imagine ourselves at some exotic, far-away location — Paris, a cruise ship or overlooking the Grand Canyon, anywhere but in a nursing facility. Soon he was too tired for our morning escape, opting to nap instead.

The afternoon therapy sessions were dropped from his schedule after his first few days in LTC. Progress was sporadic at best. "I'm not giving up," he emphasized to his therapists. His goal was to get strong enough to return home. I knew chances of that were highly unlikely; perhaps he did too. Nonetheless, he gave it all he had. His therapists marveled at his strength, courage, and perseverance.

The family care conference on May 2 confirmed my suspicions. When admitted he needed minimal assistance 25 percent of the time. Now he needed full assistance 80 to 90 percent of the time. His cognition scores were plummeting. If he continued to deteriorate, insurance would no longer pay for therapy and it would be discontinued. We had one more week.

The days were stressful and I needed the time away to regroup. I usually left shortly after dinner, so David could have time alone with his dad. The two of them played cards and went over Duane's family tree, outlining David's and Will's lineage. Together they entertained the friends that came to visit Duane in the evening.

After David left at the end of the evening, Duane became more confused and agitated than usual. He would call me late at night terrified. "Where is the nurse? Where are my pills? Are you coming back?" He'd say he didn't have a call button, which of course he did; he had forgotten how to use it. Every day I had been with him for over twelve hours straight. He was in good hands, I kept telling myself. Nonetheless, I felt terribly guilty. Robby's words "All he wants is you" replayed in my head.

I wanted to be with him when he was afraid and needed me, but I was on the verge of collapse myself. We were back skiing moguls. Every day was different. Every day was worse. I was exhausted and didn't know what to expect. I didn't know if I wanted to know. I just knew I noticed things I didn't like, and I noticed everything. The coins in the funnel were going down faster and faster and faster.

Positive people continued to be my salvation. My dear friend Bob Callahan had contacted the Spiritual Care ministry program at Prince of Peace to find support for Duane and me. Two years before, I had enrolled in the training class for that program myself, thinking it would be a good use for my skills as a life coach. Then Duane became ill and I wasn't able to participate. Now we were in need of this ministry ourselves.

A young mother named Stephanie had just completed her training and accepted the call on our behalf. She was a tiny, perky woman with abundant enthusiasm and an unshakable faith. She too had battled cancer and recently had been blessed with a miracle cure. The tumor that had been taking her life disappeared for no apparent reason other than the prayers of many diligent people. Steph came to meet with us at Ebenezer the last Tuesday in April. She was very sweet, and did everything right, listening, encouraging, and praying with us.

Duane thought she was a nice young lady, but I could tell he didn't connect with her. Not being able to explain why, he thought the visit "could have gone better." I thought he might better relate to someone stronger, older, perhaps a man.

Journal Entry
Wednesday, May 7, 2003

I just miss him. I miss taking care of him. I miss hearing the squeak of the wheels on his walker when he gets up in the morning. I miss his appreciation when I give him his breakfast. I miss his laugh. I miss sitting in bed with him holding hands while watching TV. I miss his touch. I miss making love. I miss dreams. I miss taking him for rides. I miss hearing "Hi Babe" when I walk through our front door. I miss being the one to count out his pills, take him to the doctor, schedule his appointments, being the one to help him. I just miss his being here — in his house, in our home. I miss our life. I miss everything.

Tonight in his room at the nursing home, I pulled my chair up next to his. He put his arm around me and held me tight as I rested my head on his shoulder. I felt safe, secure, and loved. It was as intimate as making love. Suddenly an aide came in, interrupting our beautiful moment; it was time for her to get him ready for bed and time for me to leave. Back to reality. I miss uninterrupted time alone together.

In order for therapy to continue, he has to show improvement this week. This is not happening and part of me is relieved. It is just too much for him. He doesn't have it in him anymore. Speech is the worst. Duane is so intelligent, quick, well informed. He could do math in his head faster than I could turn on a calculator. Now he struggles to figure out simple exercises to measure his cognitive skills. It is pure torture for me; I can only imagine what it is like for him. He is failing so.

Now all he wants to do is sleep. He hardly eats at all, and now I join him for all three meals a day — even breakfasts — just to get him to eat. He has trouble feeding himself and increasingly needs to be fed. Since he came to Ebenezer he has lost over ten pounds. I found them.

He is having trouble breathing and is now on oxygen. Yesterday he complained of not feeling well, said his throat hurt, and was spitting up a lot of phlegm. Even though he was not running a fever, he was too hot, especially with his bib on.

Months ago the words "brain tumor" and "oncology" filled me with dread. Yesterday the staff mentioned a new word that has the same effect — "hospice." Have we considered it? Of course, we have. Am I ready? No. He also cannot be on hospice if he is on chemo. All treatment must be discontinued and we are not there yet. The staff is very concerned about his current condition, telling me more with their eyes than they say in words.

*I had "coffee" with Bob Callahan today. It was helpful —
we talked about what it was like for him when his first wife was
dying of cancer. It is nice to know I'm "normal" in this strange
New World I'm in, but oh this is tough. He told me about a
movie he had seen. Bottom line — the depth of our pain is in
direct proportion to the depth of our love. No wonder; I have
never been in so much pain.*

*We talked about the death of dreams. Now I am facing the
death of my hope. I know Duane will never come home
again. I know his decline will only continue. I now just want
him to be comfortable and at peace. In therapy today we
talked about changing our goals and expectations. I don't
think Duane realizes how bad this is. Last weekend he told
me he thinks he will get over this easier this year than last year.
I don' t want him to suffer. I don't want him to be in pain. I
also don't want to take away his hope.*

*Bob is going to see about getting a male lay minister for
Duane tomorrow. I like Stephanie, and will continue to talk
with her, but Duane needs to talk to a man.*

*Tomorrow we see Dr. Trusheim again. Nancy has arranged
a transport to take Duane and me to his office after lunch.
Round twelve of chemo is due to start next Wednesday. I am
so scared. Hope David can be there.*

*I know I will get through this. I promised my kids I would
get through this. Friday I hope to go to Duluth for
Grandparents' Day at the girls' school. Barb and Meg will
come to be with Duane so he won't be alone all day. Meg
even offered to be with Duane on Mothers' Day Sunday, so
that I can be with my mom and kids.*

I know I will be okay. But oh how I miss him!

A Day Laced With Love

Most days of our lives pass by like "sands through an hourglass" (to quote the promo from a popular soap opera). Others, like November 22, 1963, September 11, 2001, and the days our children and grandchildren were born are forever etched in memory. Thursday, May 8, 2003, is for me another one of those days — an extraordinary, unforgettable day.

I was having my morning coffee and writing at the round table outside Duane's room when Chris and Wanda, the managers from PT and OT, came to see me. They said that Duane was too weak to continue therapy. He could finish out the week, but that was all. I expected this and, seeing how frustrated and depressed Duane was becoming, prayed for this. Even so, I hated hearing it. My heart broke as I witnessed his painful decline. For months he had worked so hard, fought so hard, trying everything that was asked of him. Now his therapy sessions were torture for him, physically and emotionally. He gave everything he had, but he simply had no more to give; his poor body was worn out and failing him. At least now he could have some peace.

Chris and Wanda cried with me, then showed me ways I could exercise him during the day in his room to keep him limber. Today had been his last day of speech therapy. His last day of OT and PT would be Saturday. His struggle was ending.

Donna, the chaplain at Ebenezer, also came by to visit us that morning. We talked of practical matters and Duane's condition. "Duane, do you ever think about dying?" she

239

asked him. "No, not very much," was his reply. Then she asked to hear our story. We told her how we met, our joy, our love for one another, and about our marital status.

I told Donna about the sermon blasting "the evils of cohabitation" and my visit to the pastor afterwards in which I told him our story (as we had just told it to her), complete with our reasons for not legally marrying. I recalled that I had said to him, "If this is not a marriage, what is? If Duane and I could have our 'marriage' blessed and not involve the state, we would do so." Donna was shocked when I told her that the pastor had replied, "Of course that cannot be done."

I told her how Duane had wanted to have Pastor Paul bless us when we had gone to see him the previous spring but hadn't asked. I mentioned that he had spoken of it again after Stephanie's first visit: "I should have told that lady about Prince of Peace, why I quit going." For the first time since our meeting with Pastor Paul a year before, Duane had indicated he wanted our union blessed. I hadn't known this was still on his mind.

Right there, in Duane's room at Ebenezer, Donna asked that we all hold hands. She asked God to bless our union as she pronounced us "husband and wife in the name of the Father, and the Son, and the Holy Ghost. Amen." At 11:45 a.m., May 8, 2003, we were married in spirit by Pastor Donna Erickson, a fully ordained Lutheran minister, in room 236 at Ebenezer Ridges Care Center. Our wish was granted. Duane's entire body posture changed from sagging and forlorn to erect and positive. He was beaming, clinging to my hand and looking at me lovingly with tear-filled eyes. Donna and I both cried as the three of us hugged each other before she had to leave us.

My third wedding could not have been more beautiful.

The bride wore jeans and Duane's light blue shirt from the Cana Island lighthouse in Door County. (Duane had actually gained weight in recent months and this shirt was now too tight for him.) The groom wore elastic-waist tan pants and a red, plaid, short-sleeved shirt. There were no flowers, candles, music, attendants, or guests, just Donna, Duane, and me with God. "Whenever two or more of you are gathered in my name . . . ."

Instead of a limo whisking us off to a lovely reception, a hospital transport took us to Dr. Trusheims's office in Edina. Duane was secured in his wheelchair in the back of the small van. I rode in the front seat alongside the driver, an obese man with a mass of long stringy unkempt hair under a greasy-looking baseball cap. I couldn't have imagined any circumstance in which I would be riding alongside such an unsavory character, but here I was. Sunglasses hid his eyes. A black t-shirt barely covered his protruding belly. His arms were covered in tattoos. Despite his repulsive appearance, he was kind and respectful, easing over bumps in the road so as to not jar Duane and cause him any unnecessary pain. He even took an alternate route by a park filled with trees in full bloom and flower gardens bursting with color to show us a prettier drive.

David met us at Dr. Trusheim's office. As expected, the news was not good. Chemotherapy was being discontinued. Duane was too weak to begin his twelfth round of Temodar as scheduled for the next week, and Thalidomide would be stopped immediately. He was experiencing too many side effects with no positive results.

"Do you understand what I'm telling you, Duane?" Duane said he did. David and I certainly did. After eleven months of actively attacking the tumor with chemotherapy, it was time to

241

stop. Without treatment, the decline would be immediate. Doc gave a glimmer of hope saying that this could all be changed if Duane were to get stronger again at some point, but I knew that was highly unlikely. It was over. Without ongoing treatment to prolong Duane's life, all we could do now was bring in hospice to provide him comfort.

Be still, and know that I am God!

– Psalm 46:10

It had been a phenomenal day thus far. Duane was exhausted and welcomed a nap when we returned to Ebenezer. I too was exhausted—both physically and emotionally—and went home for a much-needed rest. In the quiet of my home, I received a phone call from a man named Dave, the new head of Spiritual Care at Prince of Peace. My friend Bob had relayed my request for a man to visit Duane. Dave said he had just the man in mind.

Once again I found myself telling our story to a complete stranger, this time a voice on the phone. Today I added not only the sad news of our visit to Dr. Trusheim, but also our good news—our blessing from Donna.

I was standing in our kitchen when this stranger on the phone uttered words I had heard my entire life — words I had never heard like I did then, spoken slowly and deliberately, with a pause between each word: "Mary, do - you - know - how - much - God - loves -you? Do - you- know - how- much - God- loves - Duane?" I literally dropped to my knees, like the wind had been knocked out of me. Yes, oh yes, I did know! I was just beginning to realize how much. God had held us both in his hands this entire journey, and I knew we were safe with him now. I had known this in my head and

242

in my heart, but emphasized by the faceless stranger on the phone, I now realized this truth in every cell of my being.

Duane was amazingly refreshed when I joined him for dinner, considering what an emotional and busy day this had been. He held my hand and looked at me with such devotion. Our blessing that morning was more important to him than learning his chemo was being discontinued. I joined him for dinner downstairs where he ate everything on his plate—stuffed veal (he hated both veal and stuffing), mashed potatoes, and gravy. He even ate an oatmeal raisin cookie, another non-favorite choice. He explained, "The doctor says I need to eat so I can get strong again. Otherwise I'll die." My darling Duane was still fighting.

David spent the rest of the evening with his dad while I went home to rest and write an update to our team regarding our incredible day. Duane was also visited by the two men from Prince of Peace.

May 8, 2003
Duane Update

Guys, sometimes we need to be hit in the head by a 2 by 4, but today I really got it. I now understand just how much God loves me, God loves Duane, and God loves you. We are getting help through all of this because we asked for it. He has remained faithful to us every day.

I know I should be screaming in pain and agony now—been there done that. Talking with my wonderful friend Dee tonight, I learned that only 6 percent of people find the quality of love that Duane and I have for each other. My parents had it. I'll never forget the way my dad looked ay my mom when he was on his deathbed. The way Duane looks at me stirs me to the

243

*depths of my soul. I have been through hell to find him.
I don't know how I can let him go now; I just know I will
have to. Our journeys will soon take different paths,
only to meet again later in another place. I also know
that Duane and I have been incredibly blessed with our
time together. Amazingly I feel at peace.*

*Heartbroken? Scared? Lonely? Frustrated?
Overwhelmed? Devastated? All of the above. But at
peace. We truly love each other, and we are truly loved.*

*Once again, thank you for being with us on our
journey. Please keep those prayers, calls, and cards
coming. He enjoys seeing the cards I have taped to the
walls of his room assuring him he is not alone. Thank
you for your response, and let's fill up those walls.*

Love, Mary

That night I did feel an incredible sense of peace, holding
in my heart "the peace of God that passes all understanding."
I had no way of knowing at that time how much God was in
control of the entire situation and how we were being cared
for. I didn't know until six months later.

The man Dave had in mind to minister to Duane had just
completed his spiritual care training at Prince of Peace. His
name was Rich Mavis. When Dave called Rich to offer him
his first assignment, Rich was naturally apprehensive and
asked for a little time to think about it — to pray about it.
Dave told him not to take too long, because the man didn't
have much time. Six months later, I learned that when Rich
got off the phone, he started to pray " God be with Duane,"
then stopped in mid-sentence, wondering why he had
called the man Duane. He had not yet been told the name of
the man he had been asked to visit. Rich accepted the
assignment, then met with Dave at Ebenezer before going to

see Duane later that evening. It was only then that Rich was given the name of his first assignment—Duane Leach. God chose Rich to be in our lives for the last leg of our journey. When Rich and Dave asked Duane what he would like them to pray for, he asked them to please pray for "My Mary. She's my angel."

Angels Among Us

If you've ever felt love, then you most
certainly have been touched by an angel.
— Kathryn Schein

———————

Friday, May 9, was a cold, gray, rainy, windy day in Burnsville, as nasty as spring could be. Conditions did not improve as I drove north to be at the Grandparents' Day program at Elina's and Nadia's nursery school. My body may have been on the way to Duluth, but my spirit was still back at Ebenezer. I knew in my head that I needed to care for myself and be with my family, but my heart longed to be with Duane. I thought of a message I had received from Robby Smith a few weeks before, "All he wants is you." Barb and Meg would be with him in my absence, and the staff would keep a close eye on him, but all he wanted was me.

During the two-and-a-half-hour drive, I reflected on the blessing of our last fourteen months. We had received our miracle. Once I prayed for a miracle like John Schuler's — that the tumor and all those tentacles would disappear and someday Dr. Trusheim would tell Duane that he did not have to see him for a year. That was not to be our miracle; our miracle had been our year and the quality time we had spent together. When faced with a relentless disease, the unimportant gets stripped away and all we are left with is what really matters — our love, our relationship. Our love had grown in ways we could never have imagined. Whatever the days ahead would bring, I knew we would be lifted up and sustained just as we had been for the past fourteen months.

"He leads me besides the still waters." I feel closest to God near the water; being on the shore of Lake Superior usually "restores my soul." Having plenty of time before I needed to be at the girls' school, I drove out to Brighton Beach near my old neighborhood. So many of my memories were here — my children throwing rocks in the water, walking along the shore with my friend Judy, sometimes enjoying a glass of wine, and lastly sitting on the rocky shore with Duane in June enjoying the waves.

This day the beach felt strange and empty. The waters of Lake Superior were anything but still as the wind roared and white-capped waves unleashed their power, crashing on the rocks. Duane would have loved it; all he had wanted in recent weeks was to come back here to look at the lake again. That was not to be. Life as we had known it was coming to an end.

Thank God for the joy of little children. At the school, Nadia ran to me squealing with delight. She hugged me hard around my knees and, wanting to stay with me, refused to go with her pre-school class to sing at her program. Never mind that she was wearing her prettiest dress and knew all the words to "My Bonnie Lies Over the Ocean"; she was staying with me. Cuddled up in my lap, she looked up at me with huge blue eyes, reminding me of a little blonde Precious Moments doll, and said, "Mummu, I like you!" I had made the right decision to be with my family that day. My family would provide the love and strength I would need to face the grueling days ahead. They were my angels.

The Grandparent's Day concert featured all Beatles' songs. The cloud of my impending loss hung over me as the children sang, "Oobla Dee, Oobla Dah, Life Goes On" and "When I'm 64." Even with little Nadia on my lap and my daughter beside me, I felt like that character with the black cloud and lightning bolt overhead in the Lil' Abner cartoons.

After the concert, the girls proudly showed me their schoolrooms and introduced me to their teachers. Elina had been the "Star the Week" in her kindergarten class. Her "bio" was posted on the bulletin board telling about her family, her dogs, and her favorite food (mac and cheese), and listing her "3 Wishes." At the top of her list was "I wish people would never die."

Duane was like a frightened child when I arrived at his room late that evening. A new medication had been prescribed for his increasing anxiety, but he did not feel safe until I came through his door. I sat by his bedside reassuring him until he finally drifted off to sleep.

"Mom, you better get over to see Duane right away." Ann and the girls had returned with me from Duluth for Mother's Day weekend. Early on Saturday morning, Ann left for Ebenezer to give Duane one of her tender, relaxing massages that he loved. She found him terrified and extremely agitated.

"I wanted to call for you and David to come right away. I couldn't breathe! I thought I was dying!" His eyes were filled with terror as he relayed to me his feelings of suffocation. By the time I arrived, his nurse had increased the amount of oxygen he was receiving. His breathing difficulty had been alleviated; his fear had not. For the first time, Duane and I talked about his dying.

"Are you afraid?"

"Darn right! When God is calling you home, you're afraid!"

I reminded him of the conversation with Dave from Prince of Peace, and how God had cared for us all these months. I pointed out how many people still had us in their prayers.

"God loves you so much, Duane. He has sustained us through all of this and won't abandon us now. When the time comes, he will put his arms around you and gently lift you up. Your parents and sister will be there waiting to welcome you. I promise I will be with you every step of the way until then, and that you will be within my heart forever. When the time comes for me to join you, you will be holding my hand, just as I am holding yours now. We are in this together now and will be forever." We held each other and cried, hanging on to everything we had left. He understood, he believed, but he was still afraid; so was I.

God sent us angels. Angels were everywhere making their presence known through the people in our lives. Kellie, one of Duane's occupational therapists, was one such angel. We had felt an instant connection with her on our first visit. She was thirty-something, with twinkling eyes and long, curly, auburn hair. Therapy with her was more like a game than hard work. Duane welcomed her delightful sessions, as she would ask him about fishing, tease him and make him laugh, and flirt with him, telling him how handsome and how well dressed he was. On days when she didn't see us, she would stop by his room to say hello, telling us she hadn't had her "Duane and Mary fix" that day.

Monday, Kellie came to see me even though Duane's therapy sessions were over. Sitting beside me outside Duane's room, she took my hand in hers and looked me straight in the eyes. "I want you to know that I know what you are going through." She leaned closer, emphasizing every word, "I mean I know *exactly* what you are going through." With tear-filled eyes, she told me how much in love she had been with her husband. Like Duane, he was her knight in shining armor; he treated her like a queen. They were newly pregnant with their first child when he was diagnosed with cancer. He died at thirty-eight when their daughter was six months old. Oh yes, she understood my anguish and shared her pain to assure me that I was not alone. No wonder she related so well to Duane and me.

Monday afternoon I returned home for about ten minutes. Just as I was leaving to go back to Ebenezer, the phone rang. It was another angel.

"Hello Mary, this is Linda Varberg. We were in church with you on Good Friday." Good Friday? Church? Was I in church on Good Friday? My memory was blank. Then I remembered the synchronized meeting with the nice couple from my discussion group in the church aisle. She and Woody had been trying to contact me ever since. She didn't even know my last name. She had contacted Pastor Paul, who remembered praying with us just before Duane's second surgery a year before. Somehow he located our unlisted phone number for her. "I just wanted you and Duane to know that Woody and I are praying for you and holding you close."

Back at Ebenezer I related this story to Duane, who just shook his head in amazement. I told him, "A person has to be deaf, dumb, blind, and incredibly stupid not to see God's hand in all this." He agreed. There were angels. They were showing up everywhere.

Duane's new Spiritual Care minister, Rich Mavis, was another one of those angels. I first met Rich late Monday afternoon. I sensed the aura of an angel as this trim balding man with short gray hair, glasses, and shy grin slowly walked down the hall towards Duane's room. A sleek silver cross hung around his neck over a green pullover sweater. He carried a Bible in his hand. I felt an immediate sense of peace as he introduced himself, looking intently at me with kind compassionate eyes. "This is how Jesus would look at me," I thought.

At first I wasn't sure how Duane would respond to Rich's visits. Duane's faith had grown the past year, but he was still not "religious." Except for the previous Saturday when he could not breathe, he did not want to talk about dying. He was too busy trying to live.

But Duane looked forward to Rich's visits. Every conversation revealed more things they had in common. They were about the same age, both loved to fish, and both had been raised on farms in Minnesota, where each had helped give birth to baby pigs. They had both lived close to Washington, D.C., and talked about all the mutual places they had enjoyed visiting. Rich's two adult children were named David and Christi. The similarities were astonishing.

They didn't read the Bible or talk about dying; they talked about fishing. One day Rich asked, "Duane, do you think there is fishing in heaven?" Duane gave him a look like, "Duh! Of course there is. Otherwise, why would anyone want to go?" Every day before he left, Rich would ask Duane if he could pray with him; Duane always said yes. The three of us would hold hands, and Rich in his quiet unassuming way would pray for Duane and for me. Then Duane would anxiously ask, "You are coming back, aren't you?" "Yes, I'll see you tomorrow." "Good."

Every day we sought out whatever ways we could to find beauty, joy, or simple pleasures to enhance his life. Duane enjoyed visits with friends and family. Meg would sit Will on Papa's lap so they could look at books together. He loved getting out in the sun and smelling the fresh air. He delighted in small tastes of a DQ Blizzard or a cup of good coffee at the bistro table by the coffee shop. Simple things enriched his life.

It was Tuesday night, May 13, when a simple thing enriched mine. We were in the wheelchair line awaiting supper in the first floor dining room. I was standing behind Duane's chair embracing him, my arms wrapped around his shoulders, crossed on his chest, a posture frequently repeated as I tried to hold him close. Very gently, he picked up my hand in his, slowly moved it to his lips, and began to softly kiss each of my fingertips, then gradually, tenderly, moved his lips up my ring finger, stopping on my wedding band, then continued across the top of my hand, ending at the cuff on my shirt at my wrist. The touch of his lips and the softness of his whiskers felt like butterflies gently caressing my skin. Every nerve in my body tingled with the softness of his sensuous kiss on my hand. He was making love to me, sitting in his wheelchair waiting to have his hands washed and getting his bib before going to his assigned seat for dinner.

"I feel like a little kid whenever you walk into my room." When he told me this, I felt terrible at first. Did he think I was not treating him like a man anymore? In spite of the fact that he was increasingly dependent on me as his body failed him, he was still and always would be the epitome of strength and courage—a man's man in every sense. I would never want him to feel otherwise. He told me that was not the reason. His feeling like "a little kid" was only because he loved me and was excited to see me. I knew exactly how he felt, as my heart skipped a beat whenever he would look deep into my eyes.

A few weeks earlier, I had written in my journal about his hands, his once huge, strong yet tender hands, now weak, fragile-looking and bruised. Now he held my hand so tightly in his, it left the leaf pattern of my Black Hills gold wedding band imprinted in my skin. He was holding on to me and to our love with every ounce of strength he had left in his body. Simple things, loving things, forever things.

Wednesday morning, May 14, when I arrived at Ebenezer, I was greeted in the lobby by two women who lived on Duane's floor. One was a little lady who always wore a skirt and nylon stockings, reminding me of my aunt. "He was calling out for you again last night," she complained. "I'm sorry, did he disturb you?" I replied. "Yes," she snapped, "and I didn't sleep all night." Her companion jabbed her in the ribs scolding, "That's enough. He can't help it." A short time later, the skirted lady walked down to Duane's room offering me a treat carried in the basket of her walker. "Would you like a brownie?" she asked apologetically "My daughter made them. She just brought them yesterday." This was to be another challenging day, yet through this act of kindness another angel offered more than a brownie — she offered comfort and strength for the day ahead. Once again, God reminded me we were not alone.

When I arrived in his room, Duane was highly agitated; he didn't want me out of his sight. He pleaded with me, "Don't go!" when I left to get him the ice water he had just requested. The pain was intensifying, his skin was beginning to break down, and he was developing bedsores.

This was the morning David and I enrolled Duane in hospice. Maybe now more would be done to keep him comfortable. Because he was so helpless and needed two people to assist with transfers, I couldn't take him home to die. If coming home was not an option, I wanted to make sure that everything possible would be done to keep him comfortable and relaxed, making his dying easier — for all of us.

Ruth, the hospice nurse, assured us they would be available twenty-four hours a day. We could call anytime, day or night. Duane's was dejected after she left. The impact of the word "hospice" had overwhelmed me the first time it became part of our reality. Its impact on Duane must have been devastating. I tried to be as positive as I could possibly be, reassuring him this meant he could have more help and would be comfortable. Did he think we were giving up? I don't know. I think so.

What a difficult place to be, hovering between then — and now — and when. After the meeting with the hospice nurse, I paced in the hallway, dazed and numb. The charge nurse, Nancy, was at the medicine cart. She was very efficient, businesslike, and I thought somewhat aloof. She didn't provide the warm fuzzies that others on staff did so well.

This day she asked, "How's it going?" I told her about the sinking feeling I felt in my gut every morning when I rounded the corner to Ebenezer, wondering what was waiting for me when I opened the door. She took her eyes off the medicine cart and looked directly into mine for the first time. She knew the feeling.

"My five-year-old daughter died — I came home to it," she said. "My stomach knots every day I turn the corner onto my street." I told her that I felt like a brat. Her loss was worse than mine. Immediately she corrected me, "That is not how it is. Death is equally difficult, no matter whose it is." Her loss was no greater than mine. God had again reminded me he was here — we were not alone. He spoke through another angel.

I asked Nancy what I could expect, how Duane might die. There is no pattern with brain tumors, she said. Anything was possible. Duane could continue to gradually decline for several weeks, or he could just not wake up some morning. There was no way of knowing.

Just before dinner, David, Christi, and Will arrived with pizza. Instead of going to the dining room, we had a little party in the lounge, enjoying the pizza and Will's first attempts at the piano. Will stroked Duane's face and tried to say "beard." Now able to run, Will enjoyed the long hallways, squealing with delight at the sound of his voice echoing off the walls. Duane liked nothing better than to watch Will burning up all that toddler energy and his parents, especially his father, running after him.

I stayed with Duane until late, making sure he was calm and ready to sleep. Then I went home exhausted and spent. I had calls to return but was talked out and sad. I couldn't write. I tried to pick up around the house but couldn't. I tied Buddy out in back instead of walking him. I watched TV, not knowing what was on. I just felt small and lost. Everything was useless. I felt this huge empty place in my heart, knowing the hardest days were yet to come.

The Gathering
of the Witnesses

Thursday, May 15, 2003

The knot in my stomach tightened as I turned in to Ebenezer's parking lot. What would this day hold for us? Taking a few deep breaths, I said an extra little prayer as I crossed the lobby to the elevator. Duane's nurse, Sandi, was counting out pills at the medicine cart and stopped me as I headed down the hall towards his room shortly after eight o'clock Thursday morning.

Sandi was a beautiful, exotic-looking black woman with high cheekbones, almond-shaped hazel eyes, and a full head of blondish-colored Nubia locks. An exceptional nurse, she was strong yet compassionate, sensitive, and respectful, always referring to us as "Miss Mary" and "Mr. Duane." Looking me in the eye, she steadied me with her gaze and said, "Miss Mary, Mr. Duane has had a restless night and is not having a good morning. I have already given him his Percocet and more Ativan, and I think he has settled down some. I think it's best not to get him dressed today. His breakfast tray is being sent up to his room." Her eyes penetrated into mine and straight to my soul, telling me without words what she saw.

Duane was sleeping when I tiptoed into his room. I saw it immediately. He looked more frail than ever lying in bed still in his hospital gown, his face turned toward the wall. There was something else — something looked different, something I couldn't explain, but I knew instinctively what it was. The change was subtle, yet as evident as if he had been painted a bright pink. He was preparing to die.

Curling up in his recliner, I read the section on death in *Illuminata* by Marianne Williamson, in which she described the angel of death as being "the most gentle angel of all, coming to us in the most terrifying times." Then I picked up the handbook given us by hospice the day before and, with tear-filled eyes and a pounding heart, read about the signs of approaching death — extreme anxiety, restlessness, withdrawal, disorientation, weakness, cool clammy skin, change in breathing patterns. Duane had them all.

"Oh my God! I am so not ready for this," I screamed in silence. Never had I felt so frightened and alone. This was it; Duane was actually preparing to die. In a sense I had been preparing for this since March of 2002, but "My God! Oh help me, I am so not ready! Stop this! I can't do this. I am so alone!"

My cell phone rang. It was Stephanie calling me on the one day she had told me that she would not be available to come. She had planned to work all day at a neighborhood garage sale; yet she was on the phone now, telling me she was on her way to see me. I had been on her mind during the previous night and this morning, and she knew she needed to come. Her husband was taking her place at the garage sale until she got back.

Steph and I sat at the corner bistro table in the corridor having coffee and a hot macadamia nut cookie (my breakfast). Was it only days ago when Duane imagined the two of us sitting near the edge of the Grand Canyon? Now I was here with Steph on the edge of a great-unknown abyss. We cried together, she prayed, but mostly she was simply with me at this place and time. I kept repeating that I was not ready for this. I don't remember what she said, or if she said anything at all. She was just there and made me feel safe, cared for, and loved.

In this simple activity, having coffee with Steph "near the edge of the Grand Canyon," God told me — no — yelled at me that he was here, still in control, and that he loved Duane and me — we had not been forsaken in our darkest hour. He was the one who told Steph to come on the only day she was not available, just as he had told Duane's name to Rich Mavis a few days earlier.

This was truly the edge. I had always been terrified of heights. So had Duane; his hands and feet would even tingle watching mountain climbers on TV. I was able to look down as long as my feet were planted on "terra firma" when we were in the Badlands of South Dakota or on a North Shore cliff overlooking Lake Superior. Duane would stay far back, but I liked to see the view from the edge.

In my twenties, while skiing Aspen Highlands, my chairlift had gone over a mountain gorge on the way to top. Being suspended in mid-air, seeing mountaintops below me, I was terrified. When I got off the lift at the top of the mountain, the "edge" was all around me; my "terra firma" appeared to be about the size of a postage stamp. I was paralyzed with fear. I couldn't breathe, my heart was pounding, and I was sure the only way I would get off that mountain was to be carried off dead by the ski patrol. Never in my life had I experienced such panic. I was screaming, "Stop this! I can't do this! I am so alone!" A new friend inched me down the mountain; "Just ski over to me here," then moving a little farther, "Ski over to me here," until I felt safe again. Had I known how frightening the way down was, I would never have gone to the top.

Now we were at the edge of Duane's life, and I was as

terrified as I had been atop Aspen Highlands thirty years before. God was leading me inch by inch down the narrow mountain trail to safety.

When we walk to the edge of all the light we have and step into the darkness of the unknown, we must believe that one of two things will happen. There will be something solid for us to stand on or we will be taught to fly.
– Patrick Overton

Steph was another angel, inching me down this terrible mountain. God was using every means available to tell us that he loved us and that in our darkest hour we were not alone.

Yea, though I walk through the valley of the
shadow of death, I will fear no evil;
For You are with me;
Your rod and Your staff, they comfort me.
– Psalm 23:4

Duane slept much of the day. When awake, he was fidgeting, pulling at his gown and blankets — more signs of approaching death. He was preparing; I had to do so as well. Sitting by his bedside quietly with my thoughts, I looked back on our road together. Like going to the top of that mountain, I didn't know how terrifying the way down would be. Now I could look back on the journey from a new perspective and really see it.

During a conversation on one of Duane's first days at Ebenezer, he had said to me, "This past year, we've had our ups and downs, but it hasn't been that bad, has it?" My honest answer was that it had been amazing — a precious gift.

I wouldn't have missed the past year with him for anything. I found more love, more devotion, and more strength than I had ever known. I knew, as I sat at his deathbed now, that our love, devotion, and strength would carry us through as we were approaching the end. "I love you. Don't forget," I whispered to him. I knew even in death he would remember, and so would I.

———

Friday, May 16, 2003   6:15 am
Duane Update

Dear friends,

Just a quick note to ask you for your prayers. Duane is fast approaching the end of his journey; his condition is deteriorating rapidly. Breathing is more and more difficult, in spite of increased amounts of oxygen. He hasn't much strength left and now needs machines to lift him out of bed to use the commode. The quality of life that we were fighting for is gone. How this strong, independent man must hate this state of being!

Like everything else, he is facing this final phase with courage and grace. Yesterday a childhood friend (whose wife is on staff at Ebenezer) came to see him for a minute. "Duane, how are you?" Duane mustered up a good handshake and his welcoming smile; "I'm just fine, Bill, just fine."

Saturday we spoke of his death, and I am trying to help him not be afraid — not an easy task when I am terrified myself. The support from my church has been a great comfort to us both. God really does send angels when we need them the most. More on that later.

Please pray for us. His pain is under control, but mine is excruciating.

Thank you.

Love, Mary

Oh, Mary.

My heart aches as I read your message. This is a most difficult time and one where the meaning of love and life blares like a chorus of trumpets. And you experience how precious it is to have good Christian friends — the support of the "community" is immeasurable — but it doesn't take away the pain. Keep remembering as you said in your last message, that God loves you.

I am thinking of and praying for you and Duane. – Bob

Dear Mary,

I feel empty. There is no way I can imagine what you are going through. You and Duane have fought so hard. If it could have been beaten, you would have beaten it.

You, Mary, have taught us how to be courageous. You have shown what it means to love another person. You have done all you can do. Please remember that.

Duane taught us how to be a good person. How to live a good life. How to treat others. His life is an example all should follow.

For all of us who know him, he will leave fond memories, strong resolve, and an echo of his hearty laugh. It is that echo and the incredible smile that will carry us.

Please know, Mary, that I will always be here for you.

Love, Dick

"How was Duane's day?" This simple question asked in an email by my new friend Lisa from Iowa haunted me all the next day; the answer was, "Painful beyond belief."

Thursday I had cried, "I am so not ready!" Friday, May 16, I just wanted Duane's suffering to end. In the morning, I watched from the hallway as two male aides needed a machine to help him stand at the edge of his bed and turn to sit in his wheelchair. This once simple activity took every ounce of his strength. He was screaming. I hated to watch him struggle unnecessarily. Didn't they see he was dying? Why couldn't he just be left alone? Everyone said Duane must be moved because his skin was breaking down and he had developed a huge bedsore on his buttocks. I wanted something to be done for the bedsore but also wanted Duane to be left in peace. No one listened to me. Perhaps hospice could do something.

Nancy noticed Duane slumped in his wheelchair as he waited by the elevator to be taken to breakfast. He could no longer support himself sitting up. He was immediately transferred to a "Geri-chair" — an unsightly pale green naugahide lounge chair on small wheels. This ugly chair made me want to take back every unkind word I had ever said about Duane's blue oversized Lazy-boy recliner. It also seemed too low to the ground for Duane and looked terribly uncomfortable. Yet this chair proved to be much more comfortable for him, as he was now able to recline rather than spend energy trying to support his upper body in a wheelchair. It was a struggle to transfer him to the lower Geri-chair, but once he was situated, he said it wasn't too bad.

Only a few weeks ago, I had hated to see him confined to a wheelchair, and now this. With the Geri-chair, he could no longer have meals in the main dining room. He would have to be in the second floor sunroom with the most infirm residents. This prospect was unbearably depressing. Since either David or I was with him for every meal, I arranged to have all meals sent to his room.

Duane might have been getting more medication for pain,

but however much it was, it wasn't enough. When his aides came to reposition him in the afternoon, he was screaming in pain at the most gentle touch. He was helpless, unable to shift his weight from one cheek of his butt to the other. A new machine, called a "Hoyer," was brought in to lift him off the bed. A large sling was placed under his body as he lay on his bed. The machine would then lift him up like a side of beef suspended in mid-air and swing him over to the Geri-chair or to the commode. The device that had been used to help him stand for the last day or so was no longer effective. Duane's legs were useless.

Looking back on our entire journey, this was one of the worst experiences. Two young women came with this huge contraption, with orders to lift Duane from the comfort of his bed to the Geri-chair for supper. They maneuvered the sling underneath his body to hoist him into the chair. They turned the power on to lift Duane; now he was not only in pain, he was terrified. Helpless, suspended in mid-air, this dying man who was terrified of height was screaming and crying out for help. He was as petrified as I had been suspended on the ski lift over the open gorge in Aspen Highlands.

I was sent out of the room. I could do nothing with this door closed between me and Duane. I was listening, crying, wanting with every cell of my being to break into that room like Superwoman and swoop him up, take him home, love him, and keep him safe. Could I possibly do more harm than this? This was terrible, beyond belief. A third young woman was called in to help. In the meantime, Duane was suspended in this damn thing screaming in terror. One of the original young women was pregnant and had been hurt trying to maneuver this six-foot, one-inch, absolutely helpless, terrified man. As long as I may live, I will be hard

264

pressed to ever remember a more frightening, more frustrating, or more painful experience than this.

Finally, Duane was deposited in his chair for dinner. Loren, Willy, and David had arrived and offered to help Duane with dinner. He would be supported and cared for, and I needed to be supported and cared for too. Feeling I was on the edge of a nervous breakdown, I had to get out of there to keep my sanity.

Dee was coming over to spend Friday evening with me — we planned to order a pizza, then have a little wine and a good heart-to-heart chat. Unfortunately, I had just been diagnosed as having another bladder infection and was on antibiotics. So much for wine, I thought.

Gloria Swanson, head of end-of-life care at Prince of Peace, had stopped by to meet us on Friday afternoon. She was so genuine, open, and approachable I felt like she had been an old friend. I told her our whole story, beginning to end, and felt comfortable and understood. She asked what I was doing to take care of myself. I told her about my plans with Dee and about being on medication for a bladder infection, so I couldn't have a brandy or glass of wine to help me relax.

Taking both of my hands in hers, she prayed; among other things she asked God to make it possible for me to have some brandy or some wine while taking care of my bladder infection. I was astounded. Praying for me to be able to have a brandy?! This was foreign to my conservative Lutheran upbringing. I expressed my thanks to her as she checked in on sleeping Duane and said she would be back early the next week.

At home after the dreadful Hoyer incident, I called our pharmacist. I was assured a glass of brandy or wine would not cause me any harm; in fact, I was encouraged to have "at least one." Gloria's prayer for me had been answered. I was able to enjoy a glass of wine or two with my dear friend Dee on one of the most frustrating days of my life, in spite of the antibiotics. Even in this little thing, God let me know he was still there.

Sunday morning I was told that Duane had had another bad night. I instructed the staff to call me anytime if he needed me. His agitation was worse as he picked at his clothes and blankets, presenting more signs of impending death. Complaining of being too hot in his cool room, he kept taking off his shirt. Even with the maximum pressure on his oxygen tank, he struggled to breathe. He had developed a slight cough, and secretions were building up in his throat. When I sat down next to him on his bed, he gently pushed me away saying it was "too crowded with all those people in here."

"What people?" I asked.

He motioned to the foot of his bed and told me there were a lot of people there and all around his bed; "I can't see them but I know they are there." I believed him. I believed his mom and dad were there, along with his sister, maybe my dad and countless others who were waiting for him. I assured him that they would remain with him and he would not be left alone. Ever.

Gloria referred to this phenomenon as the "gathering of the witnesses," those who would be with him as he passed into the next life. How comforting! I thought about the "gentle" angel of death coming to us in the most terrifying of times. Now his family was there to welcome him home too.

I had experienced these witnesses before. The night my uncle Ivar died, I was sitting with my aunt Holly and my cousin Louise near his bed when I sensed the room fill up with unseen people. I felt the presence of my grandmother, a woman I had never known, yet I was certain she was by my side. Louise had the same sensation. She felt her two deceased brothers-in-law, Mike and Rolf, standing by her side as she let go of her father. When Ivar took his last breath, the witnesses vanished.

The witnesses were gathering for Duane. When I left for home that night, I knew I would be returning soon.

The Valley of the Shadow of Death

Thank you, god, for what has been.
Thank you, God, for what shall be . . .
    – Marianne Williamson

Monday, May 19

Sleep was impossible. Tossing and turning in bed, I heard Duane calling my name. When the phone rang at half past two Monday morning, I was awake, answering on the first ring. "Mary, this is Bill at Ebenezer. Duane is terribly agitated and we can't calm him. Would you mind . . . ." I stopped him in mid-sentence. "I'm on my way."

As I raced to the nursing home, Robby's words echoed in my mind, " He wants you — the look of you, the touch of you, the sound of you, the smell of you. Whatever comes, he wants you. There is no greater calling in this life than to be needed by the one you truly love." Within ten minutes I was at his bedside.

Never had I seen Duane as upset and restless, quivering like the ground at the onset of an earthquake. I pleaded with the staff to call hospice to increase his dosage of Ativan and Roxinal. They said it was better to wait till morning. "Better for whom? Duane is suffering!" I pleaded. We had been told to call hospice anytime day or night — that they available twenty-four hours a day. It was no use. My powers of persuasion, along with my patience, were wearing thin. I stayed with Duane throughout the night, embracing him, stroking his brow, holding his hand, until hours later when the long-awaited medication helped to calm him and he was able to sleep.

When I tried to feed Duane his breakfast in bed the next morning, he refused to eat. When nurse Sandi offered to help, Duane ate everything on his tray, including his oatmeal, which he had never eaten before. Though it was obvious he wanted me with him that morning, it seemed I couldn't do anything right for him. His anxiety intensified; he didn't know what he wanted or needed. He was cold, yet didn't want the blanket; I couldn't get his pillows right; it was too dark/bright in the room; sit by me/no you're too close; hold me/don't touch me; water/no water. He yelled at me. Exhausted from a sleepless night, I scolded him back. "My God, Duane! What do you want? Tell me! I don't walk on water! If I upset you so much, I'm going to have to go home."

He pleaded with me "No! Stay, please, please don't leave me! I'll be good. I'm sorry."

Heartbroken, I was at a loss. I wanted to help him, not irritate him, but I couldn't. I didn't know what to do. I felt frustrated, helpless, and alone.

Eric arrived, greeting Duane with his usual, "How ya' doing, Big Guy?" For the first time, Duane answered, "Not very good." Payton had drawn him a new picture of a Viking in a ship, but even this didn't interest Duane. His agitation and pain escalated. He was thirsty, so I went a few steps down the hall for fresh ice water. Eric told me that in the two minutes I was gone, Duane had a look of sheer terror in his eyes and kept asking when, or if, I was coming back.

Lisa, the nurse's aide who had cared for Duane since his arrival in the unit, came to bathe him. Afterwards she agreed to just let him rest without dressing him. I wanted to protect him and keep him comfortable, fussing with him as little as possible. I asked, could he please have more Ativan for his increasing anxiety and something for the pain?

Eric took me downstairs for coffee. My son was with me giving me comfort and strength the night of March 7, 2002, when this all began, and he was with me giving me comfort and strength now as it was coming to an end. He was shocked to see how gravely ill was: "We wouldn't let a dog suffer like this." He told me he didn't think Duane was very glad to see him, adding, "I don't think he wants to be seen."

When I came back to his room, Duane was trying to "call me" with the TV remote up to his ear, slurring his words. "Mary, where are you? I'm sorry. Are you coming back? Please come back!" He apologized for being upset with me, and I told him that I was sorry for my impatience, that I loved him, and that all I wanted to do was help him.

"How much longer do I have to stay here?" he wondered. Did he mean at Ebenezer? Or in this life? I knew he wanted to come home, but that was not an option. Holding his hand and stroking his forehead, I told him that he was still too sick to come home, but that I hoped he would be home soon.

Lisa fed him his lunch. As with Sandi, Duane ate everything on his plate — roast turkey, mashed potatoes with gravy, even sweet potatoes. He drank all his milk, his coffee, and his water. We teased him that the staff would feed him from now on, since he ate better for them than he did for me. After lunch he turned his head towards the wall and went into a deep, deep sleep. The last words we had said to each other were my "I love you. Don't forget," and his "I won't."

While he slept, I began writing his eulogy, knowing in my heart he would be leaving me soon. He was so miserable, I prayed it would be soon. My once strong, independent Duane, who had been so vigorous — this was hell for him. I couldn't bear to see him suffering. "Dear God, please don't let him linger like this."

I was terribly upset with myself for having been impatient with him earlier that morning. Guilt set in. That was something I had rarely experienced in the past months, but it encompassed me now. How could I have been impatient with him?

Kellie rapped softly on the door, then poked her head in to see how things were going. I went out in the lounge and cried in her arms, telling her about our troubling morning. She listened with such empathy because of her own past experience. Her husband would not let her out of his sight either, and would call out for her if she even went to the bathroom. She couldn't do enough and couldn't do it right. Everything I had experienced, she had too. Whatever I was feeling, she had felt exactly the same way.

Kellie had been a bright spot in our days of therapy. Her care — her joy, love and compassion — were beyond our expectations. By sharing her personal story with me, she made me feel "normal" in a situation that was anything but. She was another of the angels God sent when we needed them the most. She helped me see that my behavior that morning had been normal and understandable. I forgave my impatience, just as I knew Duane had. Making sure I had her home phone number, she invited me to call anytime.

As Kellie left, I saw Rich coming down the hall. Once again I felt peace and strength in his presence. He was shocked to see the drastic change in Duane.

Ruth, the hospice nurse, had been flooded with phone calls regarding Duane's condition and came to see him a day earlier than scheduled. I was glad Rich was with me; I needed another set of ears for this discussion. Finally Duane would have relief. She was increasing his dosages of Roxinal for pain, respiratory distress, agitation, and shortness of breath and Ativan for anxiety and agitation. "Thank you!" I exclaimed. She said yes, absolutely, hospice was to be called twenty-four hours a day after this—even in the middle of the night. That is why they were there. Thank you again. I told her how terrified Duane was of heights and being suspended, how he had been screaming in terror on Friday. The Hoyer would not be used again. Thank God. Duane would finally be left to die in peace.

Then she told us Duane would linger like this "for weeks." She came to this conclusion because: when she had seen him on Friday, he seemed "pretty good" to her; he ate and drank well today; and because of his size, it would take his body a while to shut down. I couldn't believe it. Weeks? No way! I didn't think he had days, let alone weeks, left in him. I expressed my opinion, relating that he had sensed the "gathering of the witnesses" on Sunday. With that she said, "Oh . . . OH! Perhaps I better go in and look at him." She had no idea he would have come to this stage so quickly.

When Ruth re-joined Rich and me, she said, "Forget everything I just said. This is not the same man I saw on Friday. He is preparing to die." She told us that there was "very important" work going on as he slept, preparing his body, mind, and spirit. His right lung was no longer working. She was writing all new orders. He wouldn't be waking up again. Oh no. Deep breath. Okay. Awake he was suffering; I didn't want that — he had suffered enough. What else was there to say? I felt a heartbreaking sense of relief.

Thank God Rich was with me. We both had tears in our eyes as we stood on either side of Duane's bed. I said, "Honey, Rich is here." Rich spoke to Duane and read the reassuring words of the Twenty-third Psalm. Stephanie had made us a booklet of relevant verses; from it I read Mathew 11:28-29. "Come to me, all you that are weary and carry heavy burdens, and I will give you rest. Take my yoke upon you, and learn from me; for I am gentle and humble in heart, and you will find rest for your souls. For my yoke is easy and my burden is light."

Stroking Duane's brow, I whispered, "Thank you for a wonderful life and for loving me. I will miss you terribly but will carry your love in my heart forever. I love you so. Don't forget. Don't worry about me. I'll be fine. When you are ready to let go, it's okay, just let go."

Rich and I turned him over to God with love, sensing that Duane was aware of our presence and heard our words. His mouth moved slightly and he seemed to be more peaceful.

Before he left, Rich reminded me of what Duane had said to me just over a week ago, "When God is calling you home, you're scared." I had missed it; I heard, "you're scared." Rich repeated the first part of Duane's statement, "When God is calling you home . . . ." Home. Duane knew where he was going. He was going home to God. He knew he would be fine, and so did I. Dear Rich. He may have been called to minister to Duane, but he was my angel as well.

I sat by Duane's side in the dimly lit room. Throughout this agonizing day, I had held up quite well for the most part. I had been strong, calmly caring for Duane the best I could, explaining his condition to others, and advocating for his comfort and peace. I comforted his Aunt Dorothy and Cousin Patty who had driven an hour in a downpour to see Duane. I had given him permission to die.

Then Dr. Loken walked through Duane's door, not as a doctor but as a caring friend. Having received numerous calls throughout the day, she said she just had to come. Looking at Duane with such tenderness and sadness, her expression spoke volumes. "How are you holding up?" she asked me. No longer needing to be strong, I erupted in heaving sobs with the woman whom we had first met in Urgent Care all those months ago. She had given us both such loving care that I had changed clinics myself to have her for my doctor. Now she held me tenderly in her arms as we faced the end of Duane's fight.

"I'm okay now — but later I'll probably be a basket case. I can't imagine 'later' — I can't go there." "That's okay." she replied. "Come see me any time and we'll put the basket back together." I learned then that her own father had just been admitted to a Rochester hospital; yet she had come to see us first. "Some patients are special, and you two are it."

Dave Nystrom came to tell Duane about his weekend fishing trip to Lake Vermillion; as Duane slept, he told me about it instead. On some level we knew Duane heard that the weather had been ideal, the conditions perfect, the walleyes were biting, but that something wasn't right. Dave was hurting. How he missed fishing with his dear friend and partner, Duane.

Exhausted, I left Dave alone to say good-bye to his friend. David would also be there soon, so I kissed Duane goodnight and told him I would return a little later. Somehow I knew Duane would not die without me at his side.

At home I had an email saying, "You must be angry with God for all this." Angry with God? Absolutely not. How could I be? He had held us in his hands, giving us an amazing, beautiful year together. Even now he was sending "ministering angels" to our aid daily. In the midst of our agony, we were receiving love from many, many people —

from family, old friends, and people we hadn't known a month earlier. I was eternally grateful, not angry.

Tuesday, May 20

The phone rang at three o'clock Tuesday morning. Again I was awake, already sitting on the edge of our bed preparing to leave for Ebenezer. Bill, Duane's nurse, reported that there were "significant changes" in Duane's condition and thought I should be notified. I asked him to call David, and left immediately.

The night charge nurse, a compassionate blonde woman I had not met before, met me at the elevator door, hugged me, and walked me down the hall to Duane's room. She told me what a fine man Duane was and how much she had cherished the time she cared for him. She would do all she could for us that night.

Duane's color was now gravely ashen, and he struggled for every breath. He was freezing cold, and the nurse tenderly pulled my cozy, double-fleece blanket up under his chin as she checked his pulse. His heart was pounding so hard I could see it beating through his layers of blankets.

Kissing his forehead, I told him I was there and thanked him again for our wonderful life, for loving me. I told him again how much I loved him — "Don't forget" — and reaffirmed that I would be fine. I told him how much God loves him, then read to him the section on death in *Illuminata*, about how the Angel of Death is "the most tender and understanding of all coming at the most significant and frightening moment." I read/prayed Marianne Williamson's Prayer for a Peaceful Death on his behalf:

Our love is larger than death.
  Our bond is eternal. . . .

David arrived shortly. We held each other and cried as he whispered, "I'm so glad we had this year." I asked David if he had given his dad permission to die. He said no, so I left them alone for a while so David could say whatever he needed to say in private. A short time later, we both resumed our vigil as we sat on either side of the bed and watched Duane struggle for every breath.

Bill gave Duane more Roxinal at four o' clock — no relief. Again at five o'clock — no relief. At six o'clock the dosage was increased. "What a strong guy!" Bill exclaimed. "It shouldn't be this hard." For years we had been concerned about Duane's heart, and now it kept pounding, struggling to stay alive. David called Christi, telling her it looked like it would be a long day. Then he held his father and said, "I love you, Dad."

About half past six, I put my head next to his and whispered in his ear, "Honey, remember what Jesus said to the thief on the cross. 'Today you will be with me in Paradise.' Just think, Honey, today. No more struggle. No more pain. No more disease. You will not only walk, you'll soar! Your dad, your mother, and Everell are here waiting to take you home. Whenever you've had enough, it's okay, just go. It's beautiful there — it is paradise. I promise I'll be okay. I'll carry your love with me forever. I love you. Don't forget."

Meg came in about a quarter of seven. She told me that she had felt the spirit of her late mother come to her on her drive over and said, "Mom, it's time for you to come get him." Her mother was one of the witnesses gathered to welcome Duane home. Meg and David held each other as they stood near the foot of the bed.

Just before seven o'clock, Duane turned his head toward me, opened his eyes and once again looked deeply into mine. His eyes, like mine, were filled with tears. Looking into my eyes, he let out a last gasp and was gone. With his last ounce of strength, he had told me good-bye.

> *And ever has it been*
>> *that love knows not its own depth*
>>> *until the hour of separation.*
>>>> *– Kahil Gibran*

How does one prepare for this? In 1999, I stood by my father's side with my family as he slipped peacefully away during "The Lord's Prayer." It was beautiful. I thought I was ready for Duane to leave too. Praying for the end of his suffering, I told him it was okay. I would be fine. I thought I was ready.

I was wrong. There are no words to describe the pain that ripped through my body and soul when he died. Sobbing, I held him in my arms, kissed him good-bye, and closed his eyes — his warm, dancing brown eyes that had stared so deeply into mine to the depths of my soul — eyes that had looked into mine as he took his last breath. He had taken something of me with him, just as he left part of himself within me.

I turned on Duane's call light to notify the nurse; first came Lisa, then Sandi and Nancy. All of my favorites were there, grieving with us. Duane had endeared himself to them in the short time they had cared for him. At 7:00 a.m. on Tuesday, May 20, 2003, Nancy pronounced Duane dead. Fourteen months and thirteen days after this journey had begun, twelve days after our tender blessing ceremony, it was over. Duane's pain had ended; mine was just beginning.

Christi appeared in the doorway with Will in her arms. How Duane had loved this little boy! "Ahhh, Sunshine!" "I always knew I was going to love being a grandfather, I just didn't know how much." "I'll pick you up from school, and we'll go catch us some crappies. Then we'll go to the Dairy Queen. They're really going to know us at the Dairy Queen."

Rich came immediately, and I took him in to Duane, "Honey, Rich is here." The staff joined us as we gathered around Duane's bed and held hands. Donna conducted a lovely service of farewell, giving closure to our time together. These compassionate people — the nurses, the aides, the therapists — had become part of our family in these last weeks and had walked these last steps of our long journey with us. Now it was time to go.

Alone in Duane's room, I held him one last time. He was already cold. I kissed him good-bye, telling him again how much I loved him — "Don't forget" — and that he would be with me forever. I couldn't imagine life without him. "Thank you God for what has been. Thank you God for what shall be." With a heavy heart and lead feet, I left his room to go home alone.

The ominous gray clouds of the past days of suffering had finally disappeared. Duane's pain, along with the wind-driven rain, had ended. The morning sun was shining brightly in a brilliant blue sky. It was a beautiful day to die.

Saying Good-bye

Don't cry because it's over! Rejoice because it happened.
– Ted Geisel (Dr. Seuss)

Saturday, May 24, 03 9:12 p.m.
Final Update

Hi guys,
This long journey has finally come to an end. Thank you for the outpouring of love, prayers, and support over the past year, and especially over the past few days. How people can get through life's toughest times without friends and faith is beyond me. I have received such strength from all of you, from the first days of March 2002 through the funeral and burial yesterday. Please remember me now as I have to reinvent myself and begin my life without him. Considering his care has consumed my life for the past 14-1/2 months, I'm going to need a little help.

My darling Duane is finally at rest. He was in such agony when he died; it was a relief to see him at the mortuary on Thursday. He looked peaceful — handsome in his suit — free of pain and disability. I took great comfort in that.

We celebrated his life at his funeral service at Prince of Peace yesterday. Many said the service was not only the best funeral they had attended, but that is was also the best church service they had attended. My pastor, Paul Gauche, spoke as if he and Duane had been lifelong friends, even though they had met only once.

Dave Nystrom, Duane's fishing partner, choked back tears telling how Duane was now "pre-fishing new waters and was waiting for the rest of us to show up." Somehow I had the strength to speak as well, wanting everyone to know how courageous Duane had been, and how he ended his journey as he lived his life — with class and dignity. I was so proud of him, and proud that he loved me.

We returned him to Winnebago, a small farming community in southern Minnesota, where he will rest next to his parents in one of the most beautiful little cemeteries I've ever seen. Just inside the gate is a large granite sculpture of an open Bible with the Lord's Prayer carved into its pages. Majestic spruce and oaks are interspersed amongst the headstones.

There are times in our lives when the unexpected happens, events that we will laugh at in days to come but at the time are painful and agonizing to endure. The trip to Duane's burial was one of those times. After passing through Mankato, Annie and I were deep in conversation when I noticed signs for towns I didn't recognize, and the highway signs no longer said 169. Thank God for cell phones! I called David and to my horror discovered we had missed the turn 169 took south toward Winnebago and we were headed straight for South Dakota. "Oh my God, David!" I pleaded. "Don't bury your dad without me!" The angels must have been surrounding us as Ann drove 90 miles per hour on the now two-lane country highway, on the Friday of Memorial Day weekend, trying to get me to the cemetery on time. We avoided both an accident and the highway patrol.

One thing that Duane and I had in common was, as some would say, we were both punctual to a fault. If a friend was late meeting Duane to go fishing, Duane would leave without him. Neither of us was ever late. In 14-1/2 months we were always early for doctors' and therapy appointments. After priding myself on doing everything right on this journey, I caused Duane to be 20 minutes late for his own burial! The gracious local pastor waited for me to arrive and reassured me this turn had been missed many times by others.

My last vision, looking back on the gravesite, was one of peace — his beautiful hard maple casket covered in red roses, lay under the shelter of tall, beautiful evergreen trees on a hillside. Bridal veil framed the road by his grave. The air was fragrant with the scent of flowering shrubs in full bloom. Birds were singing. The late afternoon sun filtered through the trees and was shining on his casket like a spotlight. His body was home, and he is with God.

Love, Mary

P.S. My little granddaughter, Nadia, (who will be 4 tomorrow) saw a clipping of Duane's obituary today. (It has a wonderful smiling photo of him taken in Nov. of 2001.) She said to Ann, "Mamma, there's Duane. He sure looks happy in heaven." I know he is just that.

And now what? The services were over, boxes of his personal effects were piled up in our garage, and for the first time in months there was nothing I needed to do, nowhere I needed to be. After months of being totally focused on caring for Duane, it was beginning to sink in; Duane was really gone and now I was alone. He may have been gone, but I still felt his love surround me.

Messages of consolation revealed how the events in our lives had impacted others. I was not alone in my grief.

I search for words that can convey how much your sharing your chronicle of your and Duane's journey has meant to me. It has renewed my faith, prompted me to ask for forgiveness, and let me see my love in a different light. Thank you.

Praying for you, Mary S

Bless you. There are no words I can offer up in consolation. The airwaves were full of Duane for the last few days; he was constantly on my mind. I do believe the angels were busy and actively spread throughout the universe. For Duane I am happy. For Mary I am sad. Remember when I told you all he wanted was you — the smell, the sound, the touch, the smile? That 's what it's all about. You are loved and respected by so many in the world. I am so sorry. – Robby

---

Thank you for sharing with me. Your last email allows me to finish my relationship with Duane, even though I never met him. You are in my thoughts and prayers. May Duane look down on you with God by his side. He is now embraced by God's love.

Please continue to share our thoughts and feelings with me. We will stay with you now as you continue to need us. Grief is work and we will not leave you alone as you embark on yet another journey.   – Elizabeth

---

Yesterday I stopped for a few minutes by your lake "for you." The air was cool but the rocks were warm from the sun. The water was clear. It was the perfect day to offer up prayers for comfort, healing, and peace.

Today the lake was gray and sad. Light raindrops fell like slow, gentle tears and I thought of you. I am thankful I had the opportunity to meet Duane and see you together. When you tell of him looking at you with such love in his eyes, I know because that love was in his eyes the night you introduced me to him. The aura of gentleness that surrounded him is rare. I thanked God for bringing you and Duane together, even for such a brief time. Your great love for Duane helped him usher him into the next life and you will carry his great love for you in your heart forever.

Love, Jan B.

———

Dr. Trusheim sent a personal letter telling me that it had been a privilege to care for Duane during his battle and how impressed he had been by our devotion to one another.

Dr. Loken wrote that losing Duane was like losing a family member, and also commented on the importance of our devotion.

I also received a card signed by all the staff members of the front office at the medical center, another signed by all the lab technicians, and another signed by all the pharmacists. Our devotion to one another affected their lives, and for that I was grateful. Something good had come from our pain.

Lost in Oz

The presence of that absence is everywhere.
– Edna St. Vincent Millay

———

The dreaded time when I had to face life without Duane had arrived. The worst had hapened; he had died and I was alone. I thought I was ready — I wasn't. I promised him I would be okay and believed it. I was wrong. I had told someone I would be alone but not lonely. Wrong again. Nothing could have prepared me for this — nothing.

My life lay shattered around me like broken glass; angry, jagged shards threatened in every direction. there was no safe place for solace. Without Duane I had no purpose, no direction. I was lost.

The shores of Lake superior had alwys restored me, until now. Early in June I returned to Two Harbors seeking comfort, but I found none. My family home was now unwelcoming; the once familiar lakeshore seemed foreign and foreboding. Where did I belong? I felt like I had been thrust into the middle of Lake Superior and did not know where to look for shore, nor did I care. All I knew was I could not stay in Two Harbors.

Where would I go? I was scheduled to visit my daughter's new home in Ely, but I wanted to go home instead. Or did I? Like a leaf in a windstorm, I didn't know where to land or where I belonged. I visited my friend Seija in Esko on my way home. the morning after a sauna and a lengthy conversation, I heard Duane's voice in my mind telling me, "No brainer. Go see your daughter." After being with Ann in Ely for a few days,

I felt the beginning of peace. Then I grew restless and needed to be home again.

Home. The townhouse I had shared with Duane was my refuge, the only place I felt safe. Every inch of this place was "his home." Eventually I would need to make it more mine, but not now. Now I was paralyzed with grief.

I forced myself out of bed in the mornings only to sit for hours playing solitaire on the computer. It required that I concentrate on something — that was the best I could do. I could no longer read, I could not write, I could not even complete the most simple crossword puzzles. Many days I thought I was going insane.

I was lonely. I had been alone before, but that was by choice. This was different. Duane was the only one I wanted, the only one who could ease my pain, and he had been ripped away. Oddly, I was less lonely in my empty house that we had shared than I was when I was with other people. The people I expected to support me the most vanished. They didn't get me. They didn't understand.

"At least you had . . . ." Yes, but I don't have it now and I want it back. The void is unbearable.

"Do you know how lucky you were to be loved like that?" Yes! That's why this is so awful.

"Life goes on . . . ." Shut up.

"How ya' feeling now? Good?" No! I am just getting over feeling numb. The pain is excruciating.

"Are you ready to go back to work?" Work? Doing what? I don't know who I am, let alone what I want to do.

When having these conversations, I felt like an alien from another planet or from Oz . We spoke the same language but something was lost in translation. I no longer fit in, and retreated to the shelter of my home.

Grief looked like the tangled leafless branches of a winter forest — cold, barren, gray, and unending. They were covered with sharp, ugly thorns. In meditation I looked inward and saw overwhelming emptiness — black, void, and without form.

I mourned not only for Duane, but also many other losses — our life together, our dreams, our aborted trip to Alaska, our future. I mourned caregiving, having a purpose. I grieved for my father, my aunts and uncles, my cairn terrier, my failed marriages, my lake property. I even grieved for my job. Grief was overwhelming, all-encompassing. Would it ever end?

Grief would rear its ugly head in unexpected situations. Whenever I went to the supermarket after Duane's death, images of my loss stood out in every aisle. All of those familiar things were there — strawberries and bananas for his smoothies, mineral oil and his favorite brand of orange juice, Coffee-mate, Ensure, the plain white bread I had always teased him about eating, Velveeta cheese slices, Squirt, buttermilk and eggs for his pancakes, blended yogurt, Ben & Jerry's Phish Food ice cream, chunky peanut butter cookies. Wherever I turned there was something that I bought for him on a regular basis — something I would never buy for him again. I could not get out of there fast enough. Back in the sanctuary of my car, I would break down sobbing, gut-wrenching sobs from the depths of my heart and soul. Even simple items lined up on the shelves in the grocery store were a haunting reminder of all I had lost.

The pain in my heart manifested itself in my body. My back, hips, and legs ached, making it difficult for me to get out of bed in the morning. What did I need to get up for? I had no purpose; no one needed me. The worst pain, however, was in my feet, which throbbed with every step I took. I could barely walk. My feet had grounded me; my feet had propelled me. Now I was anything but grounded, and was unable to move both physically and emotionally. The pain intensified along with my grief.

I had to heal. I chose to heal. Somehow I had to survive this pain. Maybe the Grief and Loss Support Group at Prince of Peace would help, I thought at last. The sessions were held in the Christian Life Center across the parking lot from Ebenezer. Sitting in my car that first night, all I wanted to do was go home. How could I face that parking lot?

I promised Duane on his deathbed that I would be fine. He had always believed in me, often more than I had believed in myself. Together we had faced catastrophic illness and death with faith and courage. I felt his presence, his strength, and his love surround me as I made the first tentative steps to creating a life without him. I avoided looking at the building where Duane had died as I shuffled into the meeting. The pain in my feet shot through my entire body.

The speaker that night said that for each of us there, our pain was the worst. Could anyone possibly hurt more than I did? I doubted it. She referred to our homes as a cocoon. I felt normal. Yes, my home was my cocoon — a safe place where I could just "be." It was then I realized it was there I would heal. It was there I would become a new person — a butterfly. I wanted to fly.

How does one become a butterfly? You must want to fly so much that you are willing to give up being a caterpillar.
–Trina Paulus

Going to this group was the first step. I discovered I was normal. I was not going insane, I was only grieving. I felt safe

290

here with others who shared and understood this agony. One woman had also played solitaire all day. Another could no longer fill in the words in a crossword puzzle. Everything I was experiencing was normal — the heartache, the inability to concentrate, not fitting in with my friends and family members, the sobbing, the overeating, the physical pain, even the trouble in the grocery store.. I was not the only one. I learned that all my emotions were appropriate. By sharing my grief, I would learn to heal. New friendships were born as we treaded on unfamiliar but common ground. Together we would find the way out.

The only way to get through grief, I discovered, is to experience it, be with it. I learned from others that this must be done or we cannot get beyond it. It cannot be avoided or rushed. A pamphlet called a CareNote likened grief to driving on ice. When we start to skid, we have to drive into it. "The way in is the way out."

There is no right way to grieve. There is just your way. It will take as long as it takes.

— Rusty Berkus

I knew I would heal. I knew I would be led through this new phase of my life if I were open and receptive to whatever means were presented. Kellie told me I would experience "unexpected coincidences." As with Duane's journey, my journey of healing took me on unexpected pathways as I was led to wholeness once again.

"Ditto"

*It is this belief in a power larger than myself and
other than myself which allows me to venture
into the unknown and even the unknowable.*
– Maya Angelou

I do not understand how a computer works — how my
keyboard and screen in front of me can connect me with
friends, loved ones, and the World Wide Web. I don't understand how it works, but it does. I trust that it will and I use it.

The same could be said for my TV, radio, telephone, and
car engine. I don't understand how they work either, but I
know they do because I use these mechanisms every day to
receive information, communicate with others, and easily
travel outside the boundaries of my own neighborhood.

I believe some people have the ability to communicate with
others in another world as well. I don't know how it works, or
understand why — I just know that it does because I have
experienced it myself.

I need to say I have always been a rather traditional,
conservative person. I was not a flower child in the sixties.
I did not do drugs nor burn my bra. Speaking of
communicating outside of normal means does not come
readily for me. What I tell you about next is real. Some
people blow me off, unable to understand, unwilling to accept
what cannot be explained. If the situation were different,
Duane would have humored me in listening to this, but would
not have believed or understood a single word of it.
Nonetheless, what I tell you actually happened. It is true and

is as important to my story and my healing as anything written so far — perhaps more so.

In the months preceding Duane's death, I told him repeatedly, "I love you. Don't forget." I spoke these words to him as he was taken to surgery on March 8, 2002; I slipped a note with these words on it into the drawer of his casket. In the days, weeks, and months since his death, Duane has communicated this message to me — sometimes in the exact words, sometimes in the form of sensations that bring the words to mind. The night he died I felt the warmth of his energy embrace me as I crawled into our bed alone. Heat radiated into my back as I felt held by an unseen presence. I felt the energy that we exchanged staring into each other's eyes when he died had gone with us.

The day of Duane's funeral, the actual words were sent to me through an unexpected messenger. My friend Lillian has the special gift of being able to receive messages from a different dimension. Lillian and I worked for the same company. We were not on the same team, so it was unlikely that we would get to know each other, let alone become friends—but we did. She also had ties to both Ely and Two Harbors, even though she had been born and raised in Iowa.

I knew of her special interest in other-world communication but didn't quite buy it. We sometimes talked about it before work in the morning, but I thought some of what she said was a little far-fetched. Lillian had never been to my home, met Duane, or seen photographs of his family. Yet, at the lunch immediately following his funeral service, she sought me out, telling me to call her as soon as I had a chance because she had something important to tell me.

"No way! You tell me now."

"He was here, and he loved it."

"Who was here?"

"Duane. He was here and he loved it. He was right by you. He was with a man and a lady." Probably his parents, I thought, not being particularly impressed. That seemed obvious. "The man had a hooked nose." Hooked nose? Now she had my attention. She had just described Duane's father.

"He kept telling me, 'Tell Mary ... tell Mary ... tell Mary ...' I couldn't get what he was trying to say. Finally, he held up a sign that simply said 'I LOVE YOU!' and printed his name."

With that I almost dropped my plate. He didn't say, "Tell Mary I love her." He held up a printed sign that Lillian described, printed as if from a computer. She described the font used for the message written in all capital letters, and the bold print used for his name. I have that sign. A few years before, when he had left for his trip to Canada on my birthday, he left behind that sign on my pillow. He had printed it on his computer just as Lillian had described seeing — "I LOVE YOU" in capital letters, and then his name in bold type.

Whenever Duane had something important to say, and he wanted to make sure he was understood, he would write it down. For such a strong "man's man," he was a real softie. When he asked me to move in with him, he gave me a letter printed on his computer and cried while I read it. When we participated in a chemical dependency intervention for a good friend, he had everything he wanted to say written down but was too emotional to read it himself. Holding up this sign for Lillian to see — for me — was pure Duane.

In the movie *Ghost*, Sam instructs a medium to tell the grieving Molly, "I love you." Molly doesn't believe the message is from Sam until he says, "Ditto! Tell her, 'Ditto'." Duane's sign shown to Lillian was my "Ditto." He was there.

He wanted me to know he loved his service and that he loves me. He didn't say "I loved her"; it was in the present tense. He still loves me. Love doesn't die.

Soon after the funeral I tore the house apart until I found that note tucked away in a desk drawer. It was a bit wrinkled, but still there. It is now framed and hanging in the center of my house — a constant reminder that Duane still loves me — "Don't forget."

"Don't Forget"

Early in July my plate was more than full. The pain of grief was unbearable as the full impact of my loss was settling in. In addition, my mother was in a rehab hospital after recent emergency surgery for blood clots in both legs. She had pulled through, her legs had been saved, but her future was in doubt.

Coming home late one afternoon, I had a message from Larry Pedersen's widow, Jan. Larry had died on June 12, three weeks after Duane. Now three weeks later, Willy was dying. I was devastated. Willy and I had talked just over a week before, and now I was losing him too. His last words to me had been, "Is there anything you need, Dear?"

What did I need? I needed someone to hold me and let me scream my guts out, someone to make sense out of all this pain and loss. I felt so terribly alone. I needed to talk to Dee.

"I had a dream about your sweetheart last night," she told me. She usually didn't remember dreams, but this one was crystal clear.

She was riding on a train looking out the window. Suddenly she saw Duane standing alongside the tracks, smiling at her and waving. She waved back. Suddenly he turned into a wild animal — a cougar — leaping, bounding, and playing. Then he was a deer, then a lynx, a tiger, an otter — about seven different wild animals in all, each one leaping, bounding, and playing as if to say, "Look! I can be this, and I can do this, and I can do this." Then he was himself again, smiling broadly and waving goodbye. She waved and mouthed the words, "See ya.' "

The dream had been vivid and real. We discussed it at length, and both of us immediately realized its meaning; Duane was telling us — telling me — he was fine. He was free, no longer trapped in that body that didn't work. And he was still here.

Why did she have the dream and not me? Concerned for my mother and grieving for Duane, Larry, and now Willy, I was not open to receive it. I had too much going on. He knew Dee would tell me. He was still telling me he loved me, "Don't forget."

The most cherished gift I received from Duane was the pendant he gave me on our last Christmas together — a chain holding a little silver heart with my name engraved on one side and the words "Lord knows she tries" on the other. He said at the time he thought I would either love it or think it was the "stupidist thing" he had ever done. I loved it and told him I would never take it off. The pendant fell off the chain in our driveway later that same day. No matter how I tried to fix it, it would still come off.

One day I was very upset thinking I had lost it, but Duane reassured me it was "easily replaced." I soon found it had a new, tighter ring put on it. Still, on occasion, it would slip off, most often in my bed at night.

In the wee small hours of one Sunday morning in July, I got up to use the bathroom and noticed that once again my pendant had slipped off the chain. This time I didn't find it in my bed, or on the floor, or in the garbage, recycling, the car, garage, driveway, anywhere. I searched for it all night, going through every inch of my house, but this time it was gone. I felt Duane telling me, "Don't be upset. It's easily replaced." In the grand scheme of things, it was just a small pendant, but still . . . .

I spent most of the day with my mother at the rehab hospital, walking her outside on the beautiful park-like grounds. Later I went to Eric's apartment for a swim. About half past five that afternoon, while playing with my grandsons in the swimming pool, I felt something poke me on my derrière. Reaching my hand inside my swimming suit, I felt it. There, stuck to my skin, was my pendant. I started crying, holding my little heart in my hand, thinking of how many times during the day it could have been lost — restrooms at the rehab hospital, which I used many times during the day, walking on the grounds, changing into my swimsuit — and there it was stuck to my butt.

The very next day I took my necklace to the jewelers and had the pendant soldered. It hasn't come off since.

When I related this story to Pastor Paul at coffee a few weeks later, he laughed and said, " Duane, what a rascal. He just kept his hand on your butt all day."

Once again Duane had told me, "I love you. Don't forget

The Angel Lady

Our love is larger than death. Our bond is eternal.
– Marianne Williamson

————•————

Many things happened to me in the days, weeks, and months following Duane's death that I do not understand and for which there are no adequate words of explanation. Lillian's experience at his funeral was one of many such occurrences that defy reason. I do not understand them, I only know they happened and I was profoundly blessed because of them. We cannot understand, explain, or put limits on God, saying, "It can't be this way. This cannot have happened." Faith is believing what can't be seen. I have faith in God, faith in my Lord Jesus, faith in the power of prayer, and faith in the power of the angels.

Angels had sustained Duane and me throughout this arduous journey, most often speaking to us through mere mortals. Angels on Earth comforted and encouraged us with their strength when we were at a loss. They sent email messages, cards, and letters. They visited us at home, in the hospital, and at the nursing home. They prayed for us and eased our pain. They were at my side at the cemetery.

I had always believed in angels but never really understood the impact of their active role in my life until after Duane died. That was when I met Kay Seliskar, a certified angel therapist who has the gift of speaking to angels.

I met Kay through our mutual friend Dee late in June when the numbness of the first weeks had dissipated and I was now

301

experiencing the raw pain of acute grief. How lucky I was to have Dee, a grief counselor, as my friend and mentor. She invited me to her home for lunch with Kay, a tiny woman who radiated peace and joy.

"How did you start talking to angels?" I innocently asked. She told how she had been asking for signs. I began telling her my story about asking for a sign that morning on my dock when the loons came into the bay, the sign I had received days before meeting Duane. Then I noticed she was no longer looking at me, but over my left shoulder, a smile of delight on her face. Suddenly a peaceful shiver went through my body, like a wave of shock. I had never experienced anything like it before.

"He just gave you a hug," she said. "Duane is standing right behind you." She added, "You are never left alone." Then she asked, "You've never met Duane's father, have you." I replied, "No. He died long before Duane and I met." She told me that Duane's father was with him, describing the man with the hooked nose just as Lillian had done.

"Duane has the ability to touch you, which he does often. Do you ever feel a sensation here?" She was standing behind me to the left; one hand was on my left shoulder, the other on my back just to the right of my neck. I told her that I often would catch myself putting my hand on my left shoulder and felt comforted. She encouraged me to continue doing that, for it connected me to Duane. How reassuring it was to know that he was with me, that he was fine, with his dad, and still looking out for me. The words "I love you. Don't forget," blared in my mind. How often I had told him that. Now again he was telling me.

Several weeks later, Dee and I spent a weekend with Kay and her husband, Tom, at their cabin on Shagawa Lake near

Ely. Ever since I was a child, I had felt a special connection to the divine near the water, the granite rocks, and the white pine at my own lake property in this enchanted area. Angels had spoken to me here. One particular night, I was awakened from a sound sleep around three o'clock in the morning. I walked to our sauna in the dark to discover the ceiling in the steam room was on fire. What prompted me go into the sauna alone in the middle of a moonless night I didn't know. This was something I had never done before. Yet something had led me to the sauna to encounter the fire that would have burned our sauna to the ground, along with countless trees and possibly our cabin. The weekend at Kay's and Tom's cabin proved that the mystical powers of this land were not reserved to the property I no longer owned on Burntside Lake.

The first evening there, we sat around a blazing bonfire meditating to the sound of drums. Kay had placed a smooth glass heart in my hand and asked me to hold it during the meditation. It was a beautiful, crystal-clear glass with flecks of gold suspended within it. Closing my fingers around it, I could feel its weight as it lay centered in my palm. During the meditation it seemed to disappear. I no longer could feel it and wondered how I could have dropped it when I hadn't moved my fingers. When the drumming stopped and I was able to open my eyes, the glass heart was still in my hand.

Where had it been? I was confused about what had just happened as I had never participated in a drum circle before and was a novice at meditation. All I knew was that I felt a sense of peace and contentment that had been long missing from my life. No drugs or alcohol were involved; this was a purely spiritual experience.

Kay smiled as she explained how she had once held this glass heart to her breast as she meditated on Jesus. The peace of Jesus had filled the heart. While I held it during the meditation, the energy of that peace had been absorbed into my body, into my broken heart. How it happened, I don't know; I just know I felt that peace.

I hesitate to tell of the experience of the next night. It was one of the most profound experiences of my life, yet it does not fit inside any "box" of beliefs I typically considered normal at the time. I also need to emphasize that no alcohol, and certainly no drugs were involved. What took place was purely a happenstance of the spirit.

There were only three of us in the tiny cabin — Kay, Dee, and me. Kay and I sat on the floor, facing each other. Dee was on a nearby couch. Kay called on the angels on my behalf; how many did I need? 100? 1000? 10,000? 100,000? I thought I would need at least 100,000 angels to take away the pain in my heart. As we talked, Dee picked up a notebook to record what was happening.

Kay said the Archangel Michael was there directing her. She asked if she could put her hand on my heart. When she touched me, a single tear ran down her cheek. This woman, the epitome of peace and joy, felt my pain and shed a tear.

I began to sob, heaving sobs from the depths of my soul. Kay's hand remained on my heart as tears streamed down her face. I began to feel arms embracing me in a vice-grip as I cried. Who was holding me? It was not Kay. She was seated on the floor in front of me. Dee remained on the couch. There was no one else in the room. "Let it out. Get it out," said an unfamiliar voice coming from Kay's mouth as I wailed in anguish. The invisible arms held me tighter.

An astonished expression came over Kay's tear-stained face as she uttered, "Who is this?" At that moment I felt like I had been hit by lightning on the back of my neck. My entire body flinched at the impact of this energy. Kay told me it was the Angel of Hope. The strong arms continued to hold me in their vice-like grip. The Angel of Hope would mend my broken heart. To heal I needed to put my hand on my heart and ask, " Hope be with me now. Be in me now. Be one with me now. And so it is."

When the encounter was over, I felt a wave of peace wash over me. I could feel Duane touch me, and knew he was always near. When Kay, Dee, and I were dancing in the living room, I could actually feel him hold me, dance with me. He also encouraged me to take steps to move on. Through Kay he said, "Ask her if she remembers, 'Catch and release,'" a practice used by fishermen.

I can't explain what happened on the shores of Shagawa Lake near Ely that weekend. It does not fit with conventional thinking. But I believe messages from angels sometimes have to take unconventional methods to get our attention — like burning bushes. They are all around us but cannot interfere with our lives unless we ask them for their help.

Kay told me that Jesus used her hand to touch my heart, and he had used her tears to take away my pain. In the months that followed, whenever I felt the pain of grief was too much to bear, I asked Jesus to put his hand on my heart and take away the pain. I asked the 100,000 angels to hold me close and let me heal. The pain in my feet that had burdened me since Duane's death, disappeared. The pain in my heart eased when I asked for their help. Angels had comforted and sustained Duane and me during his final journey. They continued to comfort and sustain me as I embarked on my new journey without him.

I Hope You Dance

"The firsts" had been awful. The memory of happier times on our anniversary, Duane's birthday, and the Fourth of July was surpassed by the sorrow I felt realizing that we would never celebrate them together again. For some reason the hardest "first" for me was my birthday in September. My anguish surprised me because, during most of our relationship, Duane was not at home for my birthday. He was fishing in Canada — except for the last year.

My mother was staying with me this year. The night before my birthday I was crying, missing Duane, dreading my birthday and the year ahead.

"You shouldn't cry," my mother instructed.

"What? Why not? If this isn't a good time to cry, Mother, please tell me when is!" I was angry, frustrated with having to justify my agony once again.

Why did so many people expect me to be "over it" now? After all, it had been four months. Was that too long to grieve? Even close friends, unable to comprehend my anguish, would greet me with, "How you doing now? Fine?" Hell no! I was grieving! I was in torment, anguish, and unbearable pain. No one seemed to be able to shoulder that pain with me. They had gone on and assumed I should be able to do so as well. My mother's remarks were just one more of many.

I wanted to go out for lunch on my birthday. It was too taxing for my mother, at almost ninety-three, to navigate my stairs and get to a restaurant, so I called Applebee's To Go. Instead of driving directly to the restaurant to pick up the order, I went to the bank, then the post office, and then decided to buy myself some roses. Duane had always given me roses, and I knew he would want me to have some now. I dilly-dallied around for a half-hour. Only after running these errands, all of which were unnecessary, did I turn onto Cedar Avenue, heading towards the restaurant.

Just then, I noticed and recognized the car directly in front of me. Shock waves went through my body. It was a pea-green Aztec, the ugliest vehicle ever to come off an assembly line. This particular Aztec had a Valley Olds sticker of origin on the back bumper. It might have been the same vehicle Duane had driven as the courtesy car at Valley Olds at the time of his diagnosis. How he hated that ugly car! He would apologize to customers for having to drive them in it. I had not seen it since he was diagnosed. Now it was directly ahead of me on the street, and it turned onto the service road leading to Applebee's parking lot. It caught my attention, telling me, "Heads up!"

As I opened my car door, music from the outside speakers of Applebee's public address system greeted me in the parking lot. Like the pea-green Aztec, the music caught my attention as well. It was Lee Ann Womack singing "I Hope You Dance." Perfectly synchronized as if it were in a sound track for a movie, the song followed me throughout the restaurant as I was picking up my order. The words gave me shivers as I realized that this was Duane's birthday message to me. Whenever a door closes, another opens. He was encouraging me to look at the world again with eye of faith, hope, and wonder. He wanted me to be renewed, to embrace life again, and dance. If I had gone directly to the restaurant to pick up our order, I would have missed it. Through a serendipitous chain of events, Duane reminded me, "Don't forget."

El Día de los Muertos

"Sign me up!"

Days before Duane's death, Dee told me about a week-long grief retreat she and a colleague were putting together for the "Day of the Dead" (El Día de los Muertos) in Acapulco. It was scheduled for the last days of October and the first days of November. I readily agreed to attend.

El Día de los Muertos is a Mexican celebration of remembrance for those who have passed on. Unlike somber days of remembrance in my culture, Mexicans celebrate with fiestas, mocking death, laughing in its face. They believe that the spirits of the dead return to visit their families on October 31 when the veil between the worlds of the living and the dead is thinnest, and leave again on November 2. It is not a morbid time but a time of joy and celebration.

Families hold all-night vigils at the cemeteries to welcome the spirits of their loved ones. Entire families, from babies to the elderly, gather at the graves, give them a thorough weeding and white-washing, then cover them with special marigolds which bloom at this time of the year. Then they celebrate all day at the graves, eating, drinking, and singing to live music played by family bands. The Mexican people confront their grief and honor their dead by inviting them to participate in their fiestas.

For those of us on the grief retreat, the week offered a unique opportunity for healing. Dee, her co-facilitator, Lynn, along with three other participants, and I arrived at a private villa overlooking the Pacific on October 29. My roommate, Arlyce, had recently lost her twenty-one-year-old son in an automobile accident. Three years before, Lynn's daughter, a pilot, had been killed in a plane crash. Dee had lost her beloved mother, and recently her son-in-law had committed suicide. Sandy had suffered many losses, most recently her ex-husband and a life-long friend.

Rachel's loss affected me the most. At fifty-three, she was finally grieving the mother she lost when she was twenty-seven years old. Twenty-six years later, her grief was a raw as mine after only five months. Because she had not dealt with her grief when her mother died, she had suffered chronic illness and emotional trauma for most of her adult life. Her life gave credence to words I had heard in my support group, "Pay now, or pay later. Whenever if is, you have to pay." I vowed that no matter how painful the grieving process was, I was going to pay now. I could not imagine being in this acute pain for years. I wanted to heal.

As we relaxed on the verandah of the villa the first evening, Lynn asked each of us why we were there. The words "I am afraid to go where Duane isn't" spilled from my mouth. I had never expressed or realized that before. He continued to be an integral part of my life, part of every conversation I had, part of my very existence. After five months, I still could not imagine life without him.

We were also asked what activities we might like to do during our free time that week. I heard myself saying, "I'd like to go deep-sea fishing." Did I say that? I'd rather shop. Rachel immediately said, "Great! I'd love to go with you." On the flight from Minneapolis, I had found her to be somewhat irritating, so the prospect of the fishing trip — with her — was less attractive than ever. Oh well, chances of this happening seemed highly unlikely that first night.

The next day, while our group was walking on a city street,

310

we needed an interpreter for Diane to purchase bandages. Suddenly a mangy-looking local man appeared out of nowhere and helped her with her purchase. Then he asked, "Would any of you ladies like to go fishing?" He introduced himself as "Popeye the Sailor Man."

I had no intentions of going anywhere with this character. The next thing I knew we were all on a city bus heading for the marina with him. I was repulsed not only by "Popeye," but also by the gagging odor of over-heated bodies crammed together on the crowded bus this sweltering October day. What was I getting myself into? Popeye showed us the boat, introduced us to the captain, and negotiated the fee. Even though the price was cheap by U.S. standards, everything within me screamed, "No!" This was not the way to hire a fishing charter on Lake Superior, let alone the Pacific Ocean, a trip schmoozed by a con-man calling himself Popeye the Sailorman. Rachel pleaded, "Please, please, please, I'll even pay!" Against my better judgment, I heard myself agreeing to this outrageous proposition. We scheduled our fishing trip for the next morning.

I didn't sleep all night, listening to the roar of the ocean and the crashing of the waves, imagining all the terrible things that could happen on that fishing boat in the morning. Had I entirely lost my mind? My wise friend Dee told me that if I was afraid I could ask the angels to protect me. That I did — all 100,000 of them. Besides, what was the worst-case scenario? The boat would sink and I would be with Duane again. I just dreaded the process.

It was Halloween, the day the Mexicans believed the veil between the worlds of the living and the dead was the thinnest. Early in the morning Rachel and I left Acapulco harbor on our fishing trip. Popeye was already making moves on a receptive Rachael, but I told him in no uncertain terms to leave me alone. I was grieving my husband.

The sky was azure blue. The sea was calm with the hot tropical sun shimmering on the water. Sitting alone on the back of the boat gazing out on the ocean, I felt the breeze caress my face. Then I felt Duane — not only beside me but also within me. He was seeing the ocean through my eyes; he felt the breeze through my skin. We were one. Adequate words to describe the sensation that I felt elude me; I simply knew he was part of me, sharing this experience. I felt him. I felt the gentle touch of his hands, one on my shoulder, one on my back. I reached my hand to my left shoulder and felt my body tingle at the slight pressure of his touch.

Popeye said, "Your husband. He is standing by you."

"How do you know that?" I asked.

Popeye stood behind me, put one hand on my left shoulder, the other on my back just below my right shoulder and said, "I saw him, like what do you say? In the desert? Yes, a mirage. I saw him as a mirage."

His hands were exactly on the places where I had always felt Duane's touch, where Kay had placed her hands that day in Dee's kitchen. There was no way Popeye could have known this. He saw Duane; this repulsive character had the vision of angels, and had tenderly and respectfully told me what he saw.

Kay had taught me a prayer that began, "Open my eyes that I may truly see." I was amazed at the lengths God would go to answer that prayer. Somehow I was on the Pacific Ocean with an irritating, promiscuous woman on Halloween, experiencing an intimate, sensuous encounter with my lost love. This extraordinary experience had been witnessed and validated by an unsavory character who called himself

Popeye the Sailor Man. Writers of soap operas could not have invented a more unbelievable scenario. As strange as it seemed to me, this astonishing occurrence opened my eyes and my spirit to the renewal of my life. I felt a peace within me I never would have dreamed possible, a peace beyond understanding. Duane showed me through this fishing trip, which I had resisted, that he was with me, helping me through the valley of grief. Holding me close, he told me, "I'm here. I love you. Don't forget."

His presence remained with me throughout the retreat. Each night while I was in Acapulco, I felt his touch as the ocean breezes caressed my body. I could feel his eyes and his smile encouraging me as I took baby-steps towards healing. By participating in the ancient ritual of a foreign culture, I welcomed the return of his spirit.

Mexican families make special marigold-covered altars in their homes to welcome the spirits of their departed loved ones. The altars are adorned with candles, incense, breads baked in shapes of skulls, and photographs of their dead. The staff at the villa helped us create our own altar on the verandah to welcome our loved ones. It too was covered with marigolds, candles, and incense. The small skull-shaped breads hung from the flower-covered arch. Skulls made of sugar and glue adorned with sequins represented each of our loved ones; fresh fruit, a bottle of beer, and a glass of water welcomed their spirits after their long journey.

The evening of November 1, we honored the spirits of our dead at a candlelight memorial service on the verandah. One by one, we shared our stories of our love and pain as we placed photographs and mementos on our marigold-covered altar. I played Josh Grobin's song, "To Where You Are" on the boombox as I placed a framed photo of Duane's smiling face on the altar along with his favorite lure — a blue shad rap — and a well-worn fishing hat. Fireworks soared in the sky across the gulf. As we filed out of our sanctuary on the verandah in silence, I felt a sense of relief, peace, and joy I had not felt in a very long time.

Acapulco is famous for the fearless young divers who defy the cliffs and plunge into the ocean. As part of our healing experience, we watched as these young men dove from the "safe side," swam across the twelve-foot channel of ocean, then climbed 120 feet to the top of the opposite cliff. They knelt in prayer at colorful altars surrounded with flowers and candles, flexed their muscles, then dove gracefully into the roiling channel below.

What did we learn witnessing this event? The cliff divers struggled to get to the top of the cliff. They were prepared, they had trained, and they had faith. They prayed. They faced their fear and did it anyway. They not only believed, they knew they would succeed as they dove off the cliffs into the dangerous waters below.

On our last day at the villa, we participated in a related exercise. We gathered fallen leaves, then wrote on each one the fears or obstacles in our own lives that we wanted to leave behind when we left the sanctuary of our secluded retreat. Gathered on a platform overlooking the ocean, we faced our fears as we read to one another the words we had written on our leaves. Thinking small. Self doubt. Fear of death. Settling. Isolation. Bad habits. Expectations of others. Playing it safe. Not trusting. One by one we threw our leaves into the ocean. Then one by one we climbed down a ladder, steep and slimy with algae and moss, into our own little channel of the ocean. Our footing on the ladder was perilous; the pull of the ocean tide was strong. We were all terrified as we descended the cliff by ladder into the ocean. But we all did it. We faced our fears and plunged in. We climbed out exhilarated.

During the week at the villa I stayed open to my pain and shared it with five unique women, all grieving important losses in their lives. Together we faced and explored our grief, our healing, and our hopes for the future. We cried together, but also laughed, shopped, and went skinny-dipping in the moonlight. Returning home, I felt renewed. I heard Duane telling my soul, "I'm with you. I love you. Don't forget."

The only problem I had with the flight home was being seated next to Rachael. She kept harping at me, "Now you have to take a cruise." No matter how many times I told her my story and how painful this memory of my lost dream was, she just would not give up. "No. I will not ever take a cruise, certainly never to Alaska, or anywhere else." By the time we arrived home, I wanted to strangle her.

A few days after my return home I was leaving Marshall Fields. A woman best described as a "bag lady" approached me. She certainly was not the type of person one would expect to see outside the door of an upscale store like Marshall Fields. Her beautiful smile and gleaming blue eyes captivated me as she approached. "You look so happy. Stay that way," she said. I looked around to see if she was talking to someone else. Looking happy? Certainly that could not be me. No one had accused me of looking happy in a very long time. How could they? I wasn't. I didn't remember what being happy was. Looking around, there was no one else there. She was speaking to me. When I turned around she was gone. Perhaps she was an angel, reinforcing my tenuous new state of peace. "Don't forget."

The Cemetery

Journal entry
December 1, 2003.

My grief journey had been incomplete, as I had not yet returned to Duane's final resting-place in the beautiful little cemetery on the outskirts of Winnebago. My new friends in my support group spoke of visiting their loved ones' graves often, but after almost seven months I had not made the two-hour drive to visit Duane's grave. I felt something missing in my own grief work. Every time I saw a road sign for highway 169 south, I felt an urge to make the turn and visit Duane's grave. Now it was time — I needed to go before Christmas. I had visited my father's grave in Two Harbors often enough, and had recently experienced moving celebrations at the cemetery in Acapulco, so I felt it was time. I was ready.

It was an idyllic winter day, perfect for my long-awaited trip to Winnebago. The sun shown brightly in the clear blue sky and glistened on the blanket of fresh white snow. Bright sun, fresh snowfall — it was a beautiful day for the drive.

My mind replayed other drives down this same highway. The last time Duane and I had driven this way together was in October of 2002. We stopped at an orchard to buy apples, a favorite ritual of Duane's for years. This last trip he maneuvered his walker through the aisles of tables loaded with bags of apples, selecting his favorites along with apple butter and syrup. The last time I had been on this road was another beautiful day. Ann was driving me to Duane's burial. This time I did not miss the turn on 169 that I had in May, and was surprised at how well it really was marked.

Just inside the gate of the cemetery, the sculpture of the open Bible with the Lord's Prayer carved into its pages was a welcoming sight, especially today. The road had not been plowed leaving the landscape pristine and white. Fortunately, a truck had just driven through, so I was able to tell where the road went and would not drive over anyone's gravesite. Even with a path to follow, I was thankful for my Jeep and 4-wheel drive. It was so peaceful, so white and still. The only tracks on the snow were those of deer and a squirrel. The black monument engraved with the name "Leach" stood in stark contrast to the snow, and tugged at my heart.

I carried the wreath made of evergreen boughs to the grave. I thanked Duane's parents, Eva and Bill, for raising such a wonderful son, and told them how much I love him and miss him. I drew "I (heart) U" and DGL in the snow over Duane's grave. I placed a note with the same message, adding my usual "Don't forget," in the snow and stuck a bouquet of red silk poinsettias on top. As the temperature was only one degree above zero, a real one wouldn't have lasted long. The setting was beautiful, peaceful, and still.

The quite was broken by uncontrollable sobbing that came from deep within my heart. I completely fell apart — and wasn't expecting it. I couldn't bear to think of Duane there! Under this blanket of snow his body was lying still and cold in the frozen ground. I thought of his hands, those strong hands that had held mine, the arms that embraced me, his "dancing eyes," his silver hair — my Duane, gone forever. I just poured out my heart, sobbing harder than I had in months. I had to leave.

Just past the cemetery gate, I was compelled to turn around and went back to the grave. I noticed my footprints in the snow, leading from the road to the grave and back. They *made an almost perfect heart. Josh Grobin's CD was in the car, so I rolled down the windows and played "To Where You Are" for us. There was not a breath of air, not a branch moving, yet when the words "You are my forever love" were sung, a single tuft of snow fell from the branch of a large evergreen near Duane's grave. I felt he was there with me, and he was crying too. Once again I felt him near me.*

This whole experience really shook me. I don't know what I expected to happen, or how I expected to react, but this wasn't it. In Mexico I saw families celebrating on the graves of their loved ones. I felt Duane's spirit close to me, in me. I said I would never feel mournful visiting a cemetery again. I was at peace on the way to Winnebago. But then I was there. Duane's grave. Those other graves were for other people, another time, a far-away place. Now I was in Winnebago where Duane lay entombed beneath the snow in the frozen ground.

I've never felt this way at my father's grave, maybe because he was cremated and his grave contains only some of his ashes. I didn't feel this way holding his ashes in my hands as Barb and I scattered them at Burntside Lake. But as I stood at Duane's grave in the stillness of that winter day, my grief was as raw and deep as it had been the first days of June.

With an empty heart, I headed home. I cried all the way to St. Peter, where I stopped at a Scandinavian gift shop to buy myself a Christmas present from Duane. This is what he would want me to do. I saw them immediately, a pair of Kosta Boda crystal candleholders placed together in the shape of a heart. This was more expensive than anything I would ever buy for myself, but it was perfect. Duane would have selected it for me himself. The taller one is a perfect tear drop; the shorter one curves next to it forming a heart. It is called

"2 Sweet Hearts, perfect together." I always called Duane "my little sweetheart"; little — no, a sweetheart — absolutely. We were perfect together. The glow of these lighted candles will always remind me of our forever love that did not end at the grave in the beautiful country cemetery in Winnebago.

Christmas Without Duane – 2003

You don't want to miss it!.
– Pastor Mike Foss

———————

Remembering the joy Duane and I had felt the previous Thanksgiving, I had found this year's to be especially painful and empty. Then, shortly thereafter, my first visit to Duane's grave had produced the unexpected wailing and renewed agony. How I dreaded the coming Christmas — the first without him.

Pastor Mike's words of wisdom spoke directly to me the Sunday before Christmas. Since Duane's death, it had been difficult for me to attend church. When I did go, I'd sit in the back because I wasn't able to stay through the entire service. Spiritually, I felt extremely close to God — very loved, cared for — but for some reason being in church was difficult for me.

It was difficult until Advent. I've always loved Advent services, with the lighting of the candles, the music — "Oh Come, Oh Come, Emmanuel," the anticipation of Christmas. Pastor Mike urged, "You don't want to miss it!" The miracle, the beauty, the Child! No, even though I was grieving — especially because I was grieving — I didn't want to miss it. According to Pastor Mike, when we are willing to see unexpected miracles, we are more able to receive them. My grief journey thus far had been filled with unexpected miracles.

This particular Sunday I sat in my former spot in the second row for the first time in well over a year. Pastor Paul Gauche, who had officiated at Duane's funeral, came down from the altar area before the service started to give me a hug. Then I heard a voice saying, "Hello, Mary." It was Rich Mavis, Duane's Spiritual Care minister. I hadn't seen or spoken to him since the funeral. He and his wife usually attend another service, but now he was here sitting in the second row, giving me a welcoming, comforting hug. I would have missed him, sitting in my comfortable spot in the back.

My first miracle of the Christmas season had come through Rich. When he had been asked to write an article about the Spiritual Care Ministry for the December issue of our church's magazine, he wrote a heartfelt account about his visits with Duane. Needing to honor the confidentiality of the visits, the church asked for my permission to use Duane's name in the article. I was humbled and honored at the same time. I not only gave permission but also photographs. Thousands of people were now reading our story in Rich's touching article, "Fishing In Heaven."

God put Rich and me together that Sunday morning, another unexpected miracle. I was not in church alone. I made a promise to myself that I would not let the cloud of grief block the view of the Child. I would be open to the miracle and enjoy Christmas.

The beginning of my Christmas celebration was Saturday, December 20, the seven-month anniversary of Duane's death. All the cards had been sent, the gifts had been purchased and wrapped, and my Jeep was loaded for the trip to Annie's new home in Ely. Loading the car, I could hear Duane laughing at me, reminding me that I had to actually be able to get all this stuff, plus my dog, and my two grandsons, to Ely.

My first stop on my way out of town was for a gift exchange at David's. Although we hadn't seen each other very often in recent months, staying close to this family was terribly important to me. Someone in my support group had mentioned that "step-relationships" such as ours gradually dissolve over time. Could that possibly happen to us? I hoped not! As far as I was concerned, David, Christi, and Will were part of my family.

I asked David if he had read Rich's article. He said some of his friends had seen it and called to tell him about it. His voice choked as he said he hadn't been able to get through it yet. It was then I realized that I had been guilty of the very thing I had found irritating about others — having expectations of how someone else should grieve. I had thought David was too busy for me now, that he had gone on with his life. Seeing him this morning, I saw how much he missed his father. I felt his pain this first Christmas without his dad. He and Christi were anticipating the birth of a new baby, a child he couldn't share with his dad.

The most important gift that David gave me that morning was something he wasn't aware of — insight and acceptance. If I wanted his family to remain an important part of my life, which I did, it was up to me. They kept me close to Duane; perhaps I could do that for them too. I hoped that I wouldn't just remind David of the painful days. I had written "Expectations of others" on a leaf and thrown it in the Pacific Ocean while in Acapulco. I hadn't realized until that morning that I still needed to let this one go.

I was celebrating Christmas in a new place, not only in life without Duane, but also in a new location. This was the first time my family had ever been in Ely for Christmas. Unlike my first visit to Ely in June, when I felt disconnected and lost, I felt a warm glow as I looked at the festive shop windows while walking Buddy. Big cities can't compare with the coziness of small towns at Christmas. I remembered all those wonderful years of my childhood in Two Harbors — the store windows and the people happily greeting one another while shopping on those rare occasions when the stores were open at night. The whole town would be out. It felt right to be in Ely. In spite of the dread I had anticipated during my first Christmas without Duane, I felt peaceful and content.

Duane's nephew, Joe Murphy, and his wife, Joselyn, also lived in Ely. I didn't know them before Duane died, but now we he had become good friends. They joined me for coffee at The Northern Grounds, Tom's and Ann's restaurant, every time I was in town. This time Joselyn gave me the book *Traveling Light* by Max Lucado and insisted I read in immediately these busy days before Christmas. This book based on Psalm 23 was all about letting go of our worries and our grief. "Your rod and Your staff, they comfort me." This reassuring book now has a permanent home on my bedside table.

Joe and Joselyn told me an interesting story. The weekend after Duane's funeral, they were fishing with friends in front of their home on White Iron Lake. This day they caught their limit of walleyes, something they had not done before — or since — in front of their own dock. They claim Duane was with them that day; I know that he was. He was also with me in Ely that Christmas.

This first Christmas without Duane was not the painful experience I had long dreaded. In my grief I found comfort, love, stability, and continuity. The wonder and excitement of my four grandchildren was contagious. I had heard my daughter sing a Christmas cantata in the church once attended by my grandparents—the church my grandmother had helped build and where my grandfather had sung a solo when he was in his seventies. On Christmas Eve the antique red and green candelabra once again illuminated our table as our traditions continued. My entire family, including Eric's beautiful fiancé, Kris, gathered around me in Ely for one of the most special Christmases I ever had.

I had been willing to see the miracle. I had not missed it.

Alaska

A chance encounter in a restaurant changed the course of my life and the process of healing in ways I never would have believed possible.

Arlyce and I had been reminiscing over lunch as we exchanged photos of Acapulco shortly after returning from our trip. Living on opposite ends of the extended Twin Cities area, we met at a pub in Maple Grove, a suburb forty-five minutes away from each of our homes. We were discussing how irritated I was with Rachael's relentless insistence that I take a cruise. I had just said, "Why doesn't she see how painful this is for me? I will never go on a cruise, certainly never to Alaska. That dream is over."

A tall woman with dark hair and a warm smile approached our table. "I thought that was you. How was your trip?" Carol, whom I had recently met at my grief support group at Prince of Peace, happened to be having an early lunch with her son at this pub across town and stopped to say hello.

During our brief conversation she said, "I just heard about this cruise and tour of Alaska next August for a group of widows. I'd like to go but I really don't know anybody . . . ."

The words "Oh, I'll go with you, Carol" spurted out of my mouth. What? Who said that? I recognized my voice, but the words were not mine. I had just agreed to go on a cruise and tour of Alaska. What happened to "I'll never go?" Arlyce's astonished expression mirrored my own as we stared at each other in disbelief.

Thanks to an unlikely encounter far from each of our homes, I was going to Alaska with a woman I barely knew. Duane's words from a year before replayed in my mind, "Honey, if I don't make it, you go! You go to Alaska without me." I could see his playful smile and the twinkle in his eyes as Carol and I made our reservations and paid our deposit the next week.

August 2004

I didn't want to go. What had I gotten myself into? Excuses filled my head as I reluctantly packed. "I don't want to go on this trip! I can't afford this. I'm not even working. What if something happens to my mother while I'm away? I have all this work to do on my book. I don't know these women." I missed Duane and regretted going without him. I was afraid but it was too late to cancel.

As Carol and I boarded a plane headed for Anchorage with a group of twenty other widows, I finally was excited. Within my limited field of vision, I observed a woman tending to her invalid husband; his well-being consumed her entire six-hour flight from the Twin Cities to Anchorage. Had I attempted this trip with Duane, this would have been me.

In 2002 Duane had mentioned the possibility of his getting on a small plane to fly around Mt. McKinley. "You have a good time, Dear. I'll meet you in the hot tub," I replied. I couldn't imagine any circumstances where I would fly in a small plane. If I didn't see Mt. McKinley while in Alaska, fine.

In 2004 smoke from forest fires hid the mountains from view as our tour bus headed to Denali Park. It was unlikely that our park tour scheduled for the next day would include Mt. McKinley, now veiled in clouds and smoke. Then our bus driver and tour guide announced that the air around the mountain had cleared and the airfield was scheduling flights around the mountain that afternoon. Was there any interest? My hand shot up, "Yes! I'm going."

To my amazement, as I boarded the eight-seater, plane, I was not afraid, only excited. I felt Duane was orchestrating this, just as he had orchestrated the fishing trip in Acapulco. What was there to fear? The small plane soared above snow-capped mountains on the way to Mt. McKinley, the mountain the natives call Denali, "The Great One." I thought I would feel a shared experience with Duane, just as I had on the Halloween fishing trip; then I understood. Suspended on angels wings above the mountaintops I understood what Duane's spirit was trying to tell me. He did not need me to experience Mt. McKinley. I was not in that small plane for him; he had me in it for me. I got it. I really got it. This is my time. It is time for me to live — to embrace life for me. It was time to let go. Tears were streaming down my cheeks as I felt reborn, more alive than I had been in years.

The snow-capped peaks of Denali towered high above the clouds glistening in the sunlight against a clear blue sky. It was an epiphany. My spirit soared as high as the mountain before me. Had I listened to my fear and stayed on the ground, I would have missed experiencing the majesty of this beautiful mountain. Had I listened to my pain for my lost dream and not gone on this trip, I would have missed overcoming the most important barrier to my healing.

The death of our dream had hurt me more than I realized. I had kept it hidden; the thought of it had been more than I could bear. One word expressed the totality of my loss; that one word was "Alaska." This word expressed my loss in concrete terms. It represented something tangible — an actual

329

place I could imagine seeing, walking and traveling in. I could even get mad about it, as I had when Rachael kept nagging me about a cruise. Losing this dream was the pain I had still been harboring, the pain that had been a roadblock to my healing. It felt bigger than Mt. McKinley, bigger than all of Alaska. By taking this trip, I faced my pain and conquered it.

I realized that in 2002 Duane would never have been able to tolerate the rigorous schedule of a tour, even on his best days. His window of opportunity had been the year before when I first suggested it. No, he wanted to fish several tournaments that summer. The next year was too late for him. I found peace knowing it had been his choice. It was not his time; it was not to be.

It was my time. Duane had embraced his life, truly living it as he wanted. Now honoring him, I was free to do the same. I didn't just see Alaska, I experienced it. Even when we were on the trains that wove through the mountains on high trestles over gorges and canyons, I didn't sit in the car looking out the windows. No, I was on the platform with the wind in my hair looking down and taking pictures, embracing life. This was a total transformation for a woman who avoids ladders and the Ferris wheel.

When I called Eric to tell him my experiences, he proudly replied, "Is this my mother?" "It is now. 'The Bitch Is Back,'" I affirmed quoting the title from a favorite Elton John song. (B.I.T.C.H.=an acronym for Babe In Total Control of Herself.) "Mom, you've always been a bitch — I mean in a nice way," he teased.

Nature reflected healing after my tremendous loss as we traveled on the Top of the World Highway from Fairbanks through the Yukon. Blackened trees of burned forest spread before us as far as the eye could see. Plumes of smoke from still-burning fires rose in the distance. The landscape was a picture of grief — black, barren, angry, desolate, and lifeless. In sharp contrast to the charred trees was the forest floor, alive with bright pink flowers. Fireweed, the state flower of Alaska, blooms after a forest has been ravaged by fire. New life, brilliant and beautiful, flourished in the scarred forest after death, devastation, and loss.

This cruise/tour I vowed never to take was actually my path to a new life. The first night of our cruise, Carol and I stood on our verandah as our ship moved silently through the dark ocean water. The sign on the wall read, "Please do not throw anything overboard." We said our good-byes to our lost mates and then, ignoring the sign, we each tossed a favorite baseball hat of theirs into the ocean. We blessed them and ourselves. We set them and ourselves free. We let go of the pain.

The Cloak

"God! Why do you keep thinking I am so strong? I'm just this weak little nothing!"

The woman who cried out those words in despair is not the woman I am today. Looking back on my life since March 8, 2002, I am amazed at the transformation. I know where my strength lies and where the power is. I am no longer afraid. The journey was arduous, grueling, and heartbreaking but not to be missed. I am happy again.

Walking into my home alone for the first time after Duane's diagnosis and first surgery in March of 2002, I felt an invisible cloak wrap around me shielding me from the terror I was facing. I couldn't see it then. Now I can; in my mind's eye I see it as a tapestry.

My tapestry has varied textures. Some threads in are silky and smooth. Others are rough and coarse. Some are light and fluffy, as delicate as an eyelash. Others are jagged, ripped and torn. Woven together they create a texture that is beautiful and strong.

My tapestry contains a full palate of colors. There are the deepest shades of ebony. Coal black. As black as the darkest night. As black as death, grief, and despair. There are also shades of gray for loneliness, hopelessness, and isolation. There are angry reds and oranges, calming blues and peaceful greens, grounding browns, and passionate purples. There are shades of gold and yellow, the colors of hope and joy. There are also whites of peace and forgiveness. And there was now the brilliant pink of fireweed, the color of hope and renewal.

Woven together the colors and fibers blend into a work of art, beauty, and strength. This is not a cloak to be worn by a weak little nothing. This is the cloak of a thankful survivor.

Alone I was weak. I was nothing. I realize now how not alone I am. "Mary, do you know how much God loves you?" Yes, I do. God was there, always. Jesus held his hand on my heart to absorb my pain. One hundred thousand angels uplifted and protected me. My support system encouraged me, prayed for me, comforted me, and believed in me. My family stood steadfastly by my side. And Duane, my knight in shining armor, has shown me love — from both sides of the grave.

We faced his battle together discovering a depth of love neither of us imagined. Helping him die, I was privileged to be a midwife aiding his birth into a new life. I was honored to sign my name at the end of our journey.

After his death I was lost, without direction or purpose. But surely I did not endure the trials of the last year to settle for the status quo of my former life. My life's purpose became clear to me — helping others navigate this arduous journey so they too could know they were not alone. I realized I needed to tell our story.

Again, God verified its importance. In writing "Fishing In Heaven" for *Journeys*, our church magazine, Rich Mavis chronicled his experience with Duane and me. Our story of an untraditional couple once blasted from the pulpit, the story of a dying man who was not a member of Prince of Peace was sent to thousands of people to tell them about Spiritual Care. God thought our story was important.

Before Duane's diagnosis I had signed up for training to become a Spiritual Care provider myself, more because it fit with my training as a life coach than because it was a calling.

The time was not right. After his death, because of the extraordinary care we had received from both Rich and Stephanie, I re-enrolled in the program. Once I thought I could do this in my head. Now I knew I could do this in my soul.

The first evening of training, eight other trainees and I sat in a candlelit room telling our stories and why we came. I was overcome with emotion to learn that three out of the other eight new trainees were there because of the article about Duane in the church magazine.

At our commissioning service, Eric told me, "You know, Mom, this thing is so much bigger than just you and Duane. If you two hadn't met, he still would have gotten this thing and he still would have died, but it wouldn't have had the impact. But because you did, just think of all the people that will be helped."

My life's purpose now is using our experience for the greater good. Everyone will experience trauma. Everyone will experience the devastation of loss through death. So many others helped me survive; I want to help others. This has been the source of my own healing.

My life is completely different from the one I envisioned a few years ago. I am different. Like Dolly Parton's character in the movie Steel Magnolias says, "That what doesn't kill ya' just makes ya' stronger."

I am now a commissioned Spiritual Care minister, a trained grief counselor, and the lead facilitator of Grief and Loss Support at Prince of Peace. By diving off my own version of the cliffs of Acapulco, by circling Denali in a small plane, I faced my fear, embraced my grief, and separated from its pain.

Life goes on. How I once detested hearing those words!

Yet, in fact, it does. When grieving people are ready, we go on as well. In the meantime, life for others goes on. My son remarried, blessing me with not only a beautiful new daughter-in-law, Kris, but recently a cherished new grandson, Dylan, as well. David and Christi gave Will a baby brother, Max (who looks like his Grandpa Duane).

One year ago on my birthday, I stood transfixed in Applebee's parking lot, listening to the words of Lee Ann Womack's song "I Hope You Dance." On the eve of my birthday this year, I felt healed and ready to move forward. Shortly before midnight, I played that song in my candlelit living room. Gently I slipped my wedding ring off my finger and placed it in the silver dish I once used for Duane's pills. I unhooked my "Lord knows she tries" necklace and placed it in the dish. I replaced it with a little diamond pendant I had bought with money Duane had given me for Christmas to buy "something special you would like." The diamonds represented "Yesterday, Today, and Tomorrow." I placed the silver dish next to Duane's picture on my dresser. It was now just after midnight, my fifty-eighth birthday. With a renewed spirit I turned up the volume and danced to "The Bitch Is Back," wrapped in my invisible tapestry cloak.

Epilogue

The only feelings that do not heal are the ones you hide.
– Henri Nouwen

———

Each of us has stories to tell, stories of personal heartbreak, pain, and loss. We experience loss of homes, jobs, pets, and loved ones. We experience loss through layoffs, moves, divorce, and death. Loss is painful, yet it molds us into who we are and who we will become.

Sharing the stories of our losses helps us heal. We verbalize and define our feelings, fears and hopes. Hearing another's experience makes us feel more normal and less alone. This is why support groups are so beneficial.

Since I began sharing my experience, I discovered how eager others were to share their stories with me. My friend Carol, one of the Loose Ladies, regularly brought copies of my email updates home for her husband to read, at his request. He would read them over and over. Now he spoke with me, giving voice to the fears, pain, and regrets he had experienced as he watched his mother's long and agonizing battle with lung cancer. In the years since her death, he had never been able to discuss these feelings with anyone.

The burley young man who delivered my mattress cried as he told me about his father's death from a brain tumor — GBM. He spoke of how alone he had felt when his father was ill. He talked about the pain of not having his father around to be a grandpa to his children. His delivery partner would call from the door, "Bill, are you ready?" He'd say, "Just a minute!" and keep on with his story. He would have talked to me all afternoon if time had allowed.

One spring afternoon my dog befriended a young man while we were walking in the park. I had just finished the painful writing about Duane's death and was feeling euphoric and free. As he watched his daughter play on the swings, he told me about how beautiful his mother's death from Alzheimer's disease had been. "It could have been in a movie," he said. "I almost expected to hear the musical score playing in the background." I had never seen this young man in the park before.

The man who pumped my gas, the clerk at the pet store, and the teller at my bank all willingly shared their stories with me as I began to tell mine. Our stories need to be shared. Telling them lessens our pain. It allows us to heal.

This has been my story, one to which I gladly, boldly sign my name. Thank you for letting me share it with you.

Mary Christopherson

Additional Resources

Kay Seliskar   Webpage www.QuestForLight.com

Max Steingart   Author of Your Daily Motivation
www.maxsteingart.com

Michael Chioti   Speaker, Trainer, Business Coach
www.GetYourBookOut.com
www.InfinityCoaching.com
Speaker, Trainer, Business Coach
Author of *The Art of Building People*
36 Coaching Tools of Get More Out
of Work and Life

Pat Samples   Webpage: www.agingandcaregiving.com

Daily Comforts for Caregivers,
1999, Fairview Press, Minneapolis

Comfort and Care for the Caregiver,
ACTA Publications, Chicago, 2001

Self-Care for the Caregiver:
A Twelve Step Approach,
1991, Hazelden, Center City, MN

Order Form

Winning With A Bad Hand:
A Story of Love, Loss and Healing

Your Name: _____

Address: _____

City: _____

State:_____Zip Code: _____

Phone: _____

Email address: _____

Quantity:_____ X $14.95   _____

Applicable Tax:
   (MN Residents add 6.5%)   _____

Add shipping & handling: $3.50 first book
   Plus $2.00 for each additional book   _____

                 Total: _____

Prices subject to change without notice.

Enclose a check or money order to:
         Mary Christopherson
         Hope After Loss
         15050 Cedar Ave. #116-142
         Apple Valley, MN 55124-7047

Printed in the United States
31049LVS00001B/43-102